AN
ECONOMIC RECORD OF
PRESIDENTIAL PERFORMANCE

AN
ECONOMIC RECORD OF
PRESIDENTIAL PERFORMANCE

From Truman to Bush

Richard J. Carroll

 PRAEGER

Westport, Connecticut
London

Library of Congress Cataloging-in-Publication Data

Carroll, Richard J.
    An economic record of presidential performance : from Truman to
Bush / Richard J. Carroll.
      p.   cm.
    Includes bibliographical references and index.
    ISBN 0–275–94836–6
    1. United States—Economic conditions—1945– 2. Budget—United
States—History—20th century. 3. Government spending policy—
United States—History—20th century. I. Title.
HC106.5.C29   1995
330.973'092—dc20   95–3334

British Library Cataloguing in Publication Data is available.

Library of Congress Catalog Card Number: 95–3334
ISBN: 0–275–94836–6

First published in 1995

Praeger Publishers, 88 Post Road West, Westport, CT 06881
An imprint of Greenwood Publishing Group, Inc.

Printed in the United States of America

The paper used in this book complies with the
Permanent Paper Standard issued by the National
Information Standards Organization (Z39.48–1984).

10 9 8 7 6 5 4 3 2

For Lois Gustin Carroll

Contents

Illustrations

FIGURES

TABLES

Preface

Almost every day, Americans are exposed to newspaper and television reports on the economy. Sometimes, it may be that they simply cannot avoid the economics report because it is embedded in other, more entertaining news, but more likely it is because they are genuinely concerned about the economy, how it is performing now, and what the outlook is. Unfortunately, economic reporting in the popular media seldom conveys much perspective or context by which to judge the economic news. Long-term exposure to these media naturally leads to an inaccurate or misleading understanding of what has happened economically over time. In the end, although Americans spend a great deal of time thinking about the economy, usually, their understanding is rather diffuse and lacking in awareness of even the most basic economic historical facts. Without these facts, it is impossible to know how the economy has performed during various periods in the past and renders current and prospective evaluations of the U.S. economy much more difficult. Yet, it is very difficult to find the time to assemble the supplementary economic information needed to put news reports into perspective or to develop a systematic approach to verify their historical accuracy and create a picture that better represents the economy. The purpose of this book is to assist in these tasks.

The hard work of putting together the key indicators in a consistent and straightforward way is done here, but the potential for analyzing the indicators is far from realized. The goal of this book is not a thorough analysis of economic events but, rather, a resource with which to assess economic news. Deeper analysis ultimately can be done, but what is needed, especially in the current political-economic environment, is not another highly opinionated or ideological treatise that sets out to prove some preconceived hypothesis. Recent economic literature and journalism are already replete with efforts of this genre. The biases in such work undermine the reliability of the data and analysis and compromise the public's opportunity to examine issues critically on its own. Slanted and politicized discussions of economic issues, often presented in the various popular media, also do little to remedy the lack of understanding of the basic facts about economic performance that the same media apparently have failed to convey.

Rather, what is needed is a clearer and more objective presentation that concentrates on the facts of the economy, which, at the risk of sounding trite, seeks to empower individuals to process economic information from news reports more critically and, therefore, effectively. Thus, the intention here is not so much to interpret recent economic history nor to lay out a detailed argument on any particular point as it is to provide basic, reliable information in a comprehensible way, a kind of sourcebook or primer. Explanations in the use of the data and in relating economic and noneconomic events to the behavior of economic indicators under the presidents of the United States since World War II are also provided.

A sourcebook, by nature, tends to be simplistic. Simplicity is the price of objectivity, which is the essential quality of a sourcebook. Yet, sourcebooks have to be, first and foremost, objective if they are to be reliable. If they are not reliable, then they are not useful. The safest way to ensure objectivity is to use the most carefully measured official data and to tamper with it as little as possible. Each time data are altered, however well-intentioned and objectively minded, a choice is made by the statistician or economist, reflecting his or her own idea of what is important.

Simplicity, however, often sacrifices a fuller portrayal of economic reality that links cause to effect, and therein lies the trade-off: objectivity versus conclusiveness. The conclusive portrayal is sacrificed because simplicity, by definition, does not consider all of the complexities of reality at once. However, as more and more complexity is incorporated into the data, such as when indicators are "adjusted," aggregated, consolidated, indexed, or "massaged" and the portrayal becomes less simplistic, the data also become less objective. With each complication, the meaning of the data becomes less transparent, more elusive, and more suspect to those who either do not understand or do not agree with alterations to the data. A sourcebook tends to leave data alterations to the reader, thus, controlling for unknown biases or motives.

This sourcebook, however, contains not only raw data but also averages and trends. Even averages and trends, the simplest of calculations, involve making choices as to the type of average and the type of trend. These choices are fully and repeatedly explained in the text in the interest of limiting the very murkiness that a sourcebook should avoid.

With objectivity and clarity as the paramount concerns for a sourcebook, only a minimum of assumptions are also made in computing the averages and trends of the indicators. The main assumption imposed here is that economic policies tend to have delayed rather than contemporaneous effects on most general indicators. Therefore, a lag of one year is introduced for those indicators. For example, the behavior of most indicators for 1981, the first year of the Reagan administration, is attributed to Carter, just as the first year of Bush, 1989, is attributed to Reagan. Beyond this assumption, the data alterations were confined to two cases, employment and the money supply, where it was necessary to connect, or splice, the data series so that the time series were not interrupted, thus, improving comparability of administrations. All calculations are explained in the text and technical notes.

Another danger of a simplistic portrayal is that misleading conclusions will be drawn. Individuals may make inferences from the data that conform to their own preconceived ideas. However, this prejudging is part of human nature and is, therefore, always a danger. To limit this tendency, the text attempts to impose discipline on the reader's eagerness to make conclusions by presenting qualifications and additional considerations to the apparent messages given by the data. Thus, with the necessary set of basic economic measurements laid out in a consistent and straightforward way, tempered with text that reminds of the complexities involved in drawing economic conclusions, an honest and productive inquiry into economic issues can proceed. With this approach, the responsibility for errant conclusions will correctly lie with the analyst and not with the underlying data.

Hopefully, this presentation will bring important information to light, which is new to the public, and its usefulness will not rely on whether it can fuel a particular ideology or preconceived set of views of economic performance. Rather, this information should help the reader gain an appreciation of the characteristics of the various economic periods in the United States since World War II, develop a standard by which to view each economic indicator, acquire a sense of the spending priorities of the government as they have changed over time, and develop a firmer understanding of some recent controversies.

Acknowledgments

Many individuals contributed to this book. I thank Timothy Kiefer for data and editorial support and Tiffin B. Shewmake for extensive editing and the noneconomist perspective. George J. Viksnins made editorial suggestions and comments on the book's concept, and David G. Davies also provided comments on the approach to the book. Randall Lutter of the Office of Management and Budget reviewed Part II and provided insightful comments. Finally, Marcy Weiner provided helpful consultations during the development of the manuscript and Ellen Dorosh deserves credit for her splendid production services on this book.

I also express my appreciation to those in the U.S. government who work to produce the data by which we monitor our economy and our budget. These people faithfully provided any data that I requested, answered any questions, and even reviewed drafts of the chapters of the book. In particular, I thank those at the Department of Commerce — Bureau of Economic Analysis, National Income and Wealth Division, the Office of Prices and Living Conditions and the Bureau of the Census, Poverty and Wealth Division; at the Department of Labor, Bureau of Labor Statistics — the Division of Labor Force Statistics and the Division of Productivity Research; from the Federal Reserve Board, Board of Governors — the Money and Reserves Projections Section; the Office of Management and Budget; the Internal Revenue Service; and the Department of Health and Human Services — Social Security Administration. Their reviews of chapter drafts gave valuable reassurance against inaccuracies and misleading statements. Comments from other readers, Dennis Whittle and Karen Hartnett, are gratefully acknowledged.

Introduction

RATIONALE AND SCOPE

The phrase "presidential performance" in the title of the book refers to the "performance of the economy during the tenure of each president." It means neither an evaluation of a president's policy decisions nor an assessment of the degree to which a president's decisions can actually affect economic indicators. This book does not investigate the decision-making process and resists explicitly apportioning credit or blame to the presidents for economic trends. Furthermore, the performance is strictly an economic performance and does not make any assessment of a president's foreign or social policy. In this regard, the book cannot be considered an overall evaluation of the greatness or mediocrity of any president. Rather, *An Economic Record of Presidential Performance* is a starting point for such an evaluation. Although the presidents' respective performances are compared through rankings by each economic indicator, there are often repeated caveats about these rankings, a major one being that, for some indicators, a president's averages and trends may be more a function of the time period in which he was president than of true performance.

The primary goal of *An Economic Record of Presidential Performance* is to meet the need for a comprehensive and accessible resource documenting post–World War II era U.S. economic performance that allows individuals to pursue their own analysis of economic events supported by a basis in fact and historical context. The most important criteria for such a resource are objectivity, clarity, and coverage. Objectivity allows the information to be used for one's own analysis and allows one to form opinions without fear of incorporating some prior bias. Clarity is to present the language of economics and the behavior of economic variables in a way accessible to economists and noneconomists alike. Finally, coverage refers to the broad range of indicators necessary to create a picture of the overall economy during a time period sufficient to encompass a variety of economic conditions, business cycles, and other events and, thus, to provide historical context.

Four specific objectives were pursued in producing this sourcebook: to help evaluate and compare U.S. economic performance during historically recent presidential administrations, to enhance the newsreader/newswatcher's efforts to evaluate today's economic news by offering a longer-term perspective, to develop a tool and/or a starting point for further investigation into economic issues, and to confirm or refute some popularly held ideas about economic performance in recent years.

These objectives are pursued by first identifying the economic indicators most prominent in the public debate and descriptive of economic performance. Because some of these indicators have shortcomings, they are supplemented with other, readily available indicators that compensate for the shortcomings. To the extent available, official data for the indicators are collected for the time frame of post–World War II to the present (1946–93). This time frame is selected to provide a substantial historical period and allow the comparison of as many presidents as possible while, at the same time, ensuring that the concept of the indicators remains fairly consistent throughout the time period.

Averages and trends for these indicators are calculated for each presidential administration. Delineation by presidential administration addresses several issues: the presentation of the economic record takes on greater political relevance because discussions of economic issues often revolve around which president's policy ostensibly performed better, much of the misinformation on economic issues derives from the selfish motivations of presidents and candidates for president who have the greatest access to the media, and presidential administrations usually do represent a distinct set of economic policies that are tested during each administration.

The presidents are ranked for each indicator, based on averages and trends. Thus, each president receives a ranking for each indicator (data permitting). Chapter 15 devises and discusses a composite, or overall, ranking of the presidents. In addition, graphical illustrations depict how each indicator behaved during the entire time period, with each president's administration designated on the graph. Hence, long-term trends that extend beyond or end during a given administration also can be viewed.

Two controversies concerning this approach arise immediately: the validity of comparing presidents' economic performances and the degree of presidential responsibility for what happens economically.

Certainly, the changing economic world in which presidents govern makes comparisons of their respective economic performances difficult. The U.S. economy since the post-war period has been characterized by conditions ranging from high growth and low inflation to low growth and high inflation, with varying degrees of unemployment and wide fluctuations in other economic indicators. These significantly different characteristics, which often are part of longer-term trends, greatly complicate comparisons. This difficulty is dealt with by bringing out the important economic events that affected the indicators (addressed in Chapter 1). In any case, direct comparisons can be informative of not only relative performance but also the changing economic world itself. Responsible critiques of such comparisons may be equally informative and elevate the level of economic discussion. The illustrations and the accompanying text show where presidential administrations cut across these economic periods and how economic indicators performed on the presidents' own watches.

Because the U.S. economy is primarily a market economy governed by the actions of millions of economic participants and by economic cycles and world events, many, if not most, of the forces behind these periods are beyond the control of policy makers. Therefore, the president, indeed, may not be responsible for much of what happens economically. The real question of presidential economic performance is not simply what was achieved but what was achieved compared with what was possible to achieve, given a largely uncontrollable set of conditions (e.g., wars, business cycles, and even congressional regulatory, expenditure, and taxation policies). The inclusion of indicators that underlie economic growth and equity, such as stock market growth, productivity, investment, and percent below the poverty line, will only partially capture this conditional economic performance. Conclusions drawn directly from the data must take these caveats into account.

It is important, however, for understanding today's economic news, for making political choices, and for the historical record to examine the relative economic performance during the tenures of the top policy makers, the presidents, in some cases qualified by the role of the Congress. While the focus here is on the president as chief economic policy maker, the parties in control in the houses of Congress during the presidential administrations are also identified (see Figure 1.1).

Of course, the analysis presented here cannot be considered a complete assessment or true report card of the president's and Congress's economic policies. A full economic assessment is a complex undertaking indeed. Such an assessment would have to ascertain whether the right policies were chosen under prevailing circumstances and how close the president came to the best possible result. However, it is shown what was the economic picture coinciding with their terms of office. This step alone serves as a critical supplement to the daily newspaper accounts and broadcasts of what is happening on the economic front. Such news is usually devoid of historical context, recent or otherwise. The averages and long-term trends in the major economic variables also offer a more reliable starting point than daily economic news for any deeper investigation into economic performance.

The issue of reliance on economic news broadcasts provides an important impetus to this book. Because of the lack of context in media reporting of economic events, it is difficult to know whether the news is good or bad and to what degree. The question arises, then, of how people end up judging the president's economic performance. An excerpt from *Assessing the President* (Brody, 1991, p. 4) suggests an answer:

The American people form and revise their impressions of the quality of presidential performance on evidence contained in the reports of politics and policy outcomes — political news — in the news media. Since the public is not always certain what news implies about the success or failure of policy, it often takes its guidance on the meaning of the news from political opinion leaders. The president, other elected officials, respected members of the press, and a handful of other commentators who have earned the trust of at least a segment of the public affect opinion by interpreting events that are unclear in their political meaning. The news carries these interpretations to the public along with the details of the events themselves.

Thus, voter education is placed in the hands of these opinion leaders, who, although knowledgeable, undoubtedly reflect their own interests and biases. A coherent factual basis for these interpretations is often omitted, and the accuracy of the interpretation of the economic record is subordinated. Fortunately, a basic but comprehensive picture of the U.S. economy over a 48-year time period (1946–93) can emerge through graphical illustrations, rankings, trends, and averages. This picture serves as the needed factual basis, grounded in official figures, for the nonpractitioner of economics.

THE APPROACH IN DETAIL

This section explains the rationale for the selected time period, explicitly defines the averages and trends for the indicators, and describes the method of presentation of the indicators. The main issues debated in the approach include the relative information content of the average and trend indicators as measures of economic performance, the selection of the form of the indicator (e.g., level, growth rate) to use in graphically illustrating the indicator and as the basis on which to rank the presidents, and lagging the indicators.

Selection of Time Period, 1946–93

The year selected as the beginning of the time period is 1946. This year represents the first full year after World War II and marks the entrance to a new economic era for the United States and the world. The Great Depression of the 1930s had ended several years earlier, and the United States emerged as the preeminent power. With the return to a peacetime economy, the main lesson from the Depression, namely, how to avoid economic contractions of such large magnitudes in the future, was learned, and improved policies could be implemented. Selection of the 1946–93 time period allows for the observation of this economic era in its entirety. Details of this period and subsequent events that affected the economic indicators are presented in Figure 1.1.[1]

From a practical standpoint, the time period is selected because of improved data availability for a wide range of indicators. Hence, presidents can be compared on a broad basis. During the 48-year time period, examples of both Democratic and Republican administrations existed in each of the major economic periods, from the relatively unstable post-war period and the more stable and sustained growth of the mid-1950s through the 1960s to the first real economic slowdown of the early 1970s, the resumption of sustained growth, and the economy of today. Thus, comparison along party lines is possible to a large extent. The time period extends to the most recent data available, to be more useful in interpreting the current economic news. The economic debates of recent years, including those in presidential campaigns and the use of economic data in those debates, are also discussed. The presidents and their terms of office covered by this time period are Harry S Truman, 1945 (April 12) –53; Dwight D. Eisenhower, 1953–61; John F. Kennedy, 1961–63 (November 22); Lyndon B. Johnson, 1963 (November 22) –69; Richard M. Nixon, 1969–74 (August 9); Gerald R. Ford, 1974 (August 9) –77; James E. Carter, 1977–81; Ronald W. Reagan, 1981–89; and George H. Bush, 1989–93. For simplification, in cases of a president serving partial terms and/or partial years, the length of tenure is rounded to the nearest full year. Thus, Kennedy's indicators are measured over three years, although he served only two years and ten months; Johnson, five years; Ford, two years, although he served two years and five months; and Nixon, six years.

Selecting 1946 as the initial year of the time period does pose some statistical problems, specifically for Truman's averages and trends. In the first full year after World War II, the economy was undergoing radical economic adjustments as government spending dropped precipitously because of the ending of the war. The gross domestic product (GDP) also dropped substantially with the rapid decline in government purchases. For Part II indicators in particular, inclusion of 1946 in Truman's record dictates generally downward trends in spending. In spite of these events, which had nothing to do with Truman's conduct of economic policy but which distort his economic averages and trends, these averages and trends are calculated beginning from no later than year-end 1946. Beginning with 1946 is consistent with the criterion for presidents who served partial years (their total tenure being rounded to the nearest year). Because Truman took over from Roosevelt in April 1945 and because a one-year lag is applied to the economic indicators (explained below), it is appropriate that Truman's record begin with 1946. In the few cases where a different starting point may be used, the reason is fully explained and usually hinges on data availability or the distorting effects of the inclusion of 1946. Last, it should be observed that although the nature of the economy immediately following World War II may make it difficult to assess Truman's performance, the data do translate clearly the effects of the transition from a worldwide war to a peacetime economy into economic terms.

Use of Averages and Trends

In the illustration of economic performance, averages and trends must be considered together, because each measure compensates for the other's weaknesses. For example, a president inheriting high inflation or high unemployment may record a relatively mediocre performance in terms of his average inflation and unemployment levels, even if the inflation and unemployment were lowered during his administration. Somehow, the president also needs to be credited with mitigating the adverse economic indicators. Conversely, a president who inherited low unemployment or low inflation must accept responsibility for increased unemployment or inflation, even if his overall averages are relatively good. These effects are captured through trend analysis, thus, overcoming a critical weakness of averages. The trend variable is calculated by subtracting the value of the indicator from the administration's first year from the value of the indicator for the first year of the next administration, thus, incorporating a one-year time lag. In the text, this trend variable is usually referred to as the "trend change."

Partly because of the inevitability of economic cycles, that is, trends over which policy makers may have little control, averages also are important. Whether a president is successful in simply maintaining desirable levels (averages) of economic indicators during his administration is also telling of his performance. For example, if a president were able to maintain historically high growth rates of GDP or historically low poverty rates, then a small worsening of the trend change would not diminish the good performance. With averages, one has a reasonable idea as to whether good economic conditions prevailed during a given administration, which also may be important to a president's political fortunes. It is not known with certainty whether averages or trends are more closely linked with presidential popularity. However, because indicators in the later years of an administration seem to have the greatest impact on popularity, the trend appears more closely linked and may be more valuable than averages in explaining why a president, or party, was or was not reelected.

The informational value of averages and trend changes varies by indicator. The determination of and the information content of the trend indicator is driven by the choice of the type of average for the indicator, which is the primary basis for ranking the presidents. If the average is an average *level*, as in the case of the saving and investment rates or the real interest rate, then the trend change is the change in those rate levels from the beginning to the end of the administration. If the average is a *growth rate*, as in the cases of GDP and the stock market indicators, then the trend change is the change in the growth rates. Regardless of the type of average, indicator volatility is centrally important and bears an inverse relationship to the information value of an indicator. This relationship holds especially true for the trend change. If an indicator fluctuates substantially even within an administration, then the trend change has rather modest informational value with regard to performance, because it indicates no lasting trend. In the case of the stock market, because of the high volatility of stock market growth, the trend or change in the growth rate is of minimal value. For example, if the administration ended on a down year in the stock market and had started on an up year, then the trend change would be sharply negative. However, because of the observed volatility of stock market growth during 1946–93, the prospect of recovery to significant growth in the next year would be as likely as a continued decline, and, therefore, the trend change is not indicative of any major turnaround of the stock market. GDP growth, on the other hand, is not as volatile, and, therefore, its trend change has much more information value with respect to performance. For each indicator for which volatility is an issue, the limitation on the value of the trend as an indicator of performance is noted.

Types of Indicators

Because two main types of indicators are used to rate presidential economic performance, growth rates, and shares of total, two types of averages must be defined. In addition, because there are delayed effects of policies on economic variables, a one-year lag has been assumed for all administrations for all indicators in Part I, except for the policy variable, money supply (further explanation of the one-year lag is given in the next section). There are two types of averages: type 1 — for indicators for which growth rates are used, for example, GDP, employment, inflation/consumer price index, money supply, the averages are calculated by taking the indicator's value at the end of the administration's first year and computing the average annual growth rate forward to the end of the first year of the next administration (thus, incorporating a one-year lag) and type 2 — for indicators for which either shares or other rates, for example, the real prime interest rate, are used, the averages are the sum of the shares or rates during the administration, lagged by one year, divided by the number of years of the administration. Every indicator has either a type 1 average or a type 2, but not both. The one-year lag applies only to the general indicators of Part I. Because Part II deals with government budget data, these indicators do not require a lag. They are calculated on a fiscal year basis, which implicitly carries a nine-month lag.[2] All data presented are annual. Part I data are based on the calendar year, and Part II data are based primarily on the government fiscal year. One weakness of using annual average data is that the actual increases and decreases in the indicators that occur within years, that is, *intra*year trends, are concealed. For example, such phenomena as the peak inflation and interest rates under Carter at the end of 1980 and the recession of 1960 are muted by the process of averaging over an entire year.

Another important aspect of the indicators is the distinction between real and nominal values. Nominal values are the values that actually occurred; real values are adjusted for inflation. For example, the nominal GDP for 1957 was $449 billion, whereas the real level was $1,838 billion (with a base year of 1987). The reason that the real level is more than four times as high is that the dollar was more than four times as valuable in 1957 as it was 30 years later in 1987. In other words, 449 billion 1957 dollars was equal to 1,838 billion 1987 dollars. It is vitally important to make this inflation adjustment when evaluating economic performance. Growth rates must be based on inflation-adjusted figures in order to capture the actual growth of indicators such as GDP, the federal budget, and federal debt. If the adjustment is not made and the purchasing power of the dollar is not taken into account, then the growth rates of these indicators will be simultaneously accounting for inflation, which will create confusion, because it will not be clear how much of the growth is attributable to inflation and how much to the *real* value of the indicator. It is better to examine inflation separately, as is done in Chapter 4.

In converting indicator values from nominal to real values, it is important to adjust for the type of inflation that is applicable to the indicator. For example, indicators dealing with the government budget require a government budget deflator. Because the government purchases goods at both wholesale and retail prices, its deflator takes into account both wholesale and retail inflation. GDP has its own deflator as well. Some indicators also may be deflated by the consumer price index. If the indicator is viewed from the standpoint of benefit to individuals, such as in the case of social security outlays or growth in the stock market, the consumer price index may be a useful deflator. Indicators that represent shares of totals are not deflated for the purposes of this book; they are current, or nondeflated, shares. Shares may be computed on the basis of real numbers as well but will differ from current shares if the numerator is adjusted by a deflator that is different from that of the denominator, for example, the federal budget share of GDP.

CAPTURING THE DELAYED EFFECTS OF ECONOMIC POLICY — A ONE-YEAR LAG

Presidential economic policies have delayed effects on most general indicators that should be taken into account when assessing presidential performance. For example, the indicators for 1981, the first year of the Reagan administration, are attributed to Carter, just as the first year of Bush, 1989, was attributed to Reagan. Similarly, the economic performance in 1993 is part of Bush's final record. It is contended that the momentum or inertia, depending on how the performance is viewed, of the four years of the Bush administration influenced economic indicators of 1993 more than the economic policies of the newly arrived Clinton administration, which did not even begin implementation until late 1993. Although the news media seemed eager to evaluate Clinton's economic performance before he even took office, it is rather pointless to attribute changes in economic indicators to his policies in any significant way until at least 1994.

All of the indicators in Part I are lagged except money supply growth. Money supply growth, like the indicators discussed in Part II, results directly from policy choice and is, therefore, contemporaneous. Most indicators take time to respond to economic policies while the economy reallocates resources optimally (in theory) in response to these policies. Arguably, the stock market and the interest rate indicators might not be lagged as well, given that they adjust quickly and depend on expectations that have lead rather than lag effects. However, these indicators also depend on the current general health of the economy (which provides a basis for economic expectations) over which the policies of the outgoing president have more influence during the new president's first year than do the policies of the new president.

In any case, it is very difficult to pinpoint exactly how long the lag should be for each indicator. In some cases, a one-year lag may be insufficient. Certainly, the effects of the Viet Nam War on the economy were felt much longer than one year after its conclusion. Today's structural budget deficits and their effects will, likewise, undoubtedly persist for years to come. However, to customize the lag periods for each indicator for each circumstance would require substantial analytical judgments and would make the review of the major economic indicators since 1946 difficult to follow. Clarity of this survey of economic indicators would be sacrificed, making it difficult to establish a starting point for economic analysis, which is what a sourcebook should do.

PRESENTATION OF ECONOMIC INDICATORS

In order to facilitate comprehension and enhance usefulness as a sourcebook, chapter format is more or less uniform throughout (with the exceptions of the first and last chapters). Each chapter begins with an introduction containing the rationale for selecting the indicators and the definition and statistical source of the indicator. Additional explanation of the indicator is needed in such cases as the money supply, the real prime interest rate, and the poverty line. The next section of each chapter, "Overview of Trends in the Long Run," is a discussion of the entire (usually 1946–93) Truman-to-Bush time period. This section refers to indicators as they are presented pictorially in bar graphs. Presidential administrations are delineated on these graphs, taking into account the one-year time lag. In the discussion of these graphs, events that are described in Chapter 1 are brought to bear, where appropriate, on the behavior of the indicators. Inferences can also be drawn, with respect to the changing nature of the economy since 1946, when indicators behave in a distinct way in particular time periods. For example, GDP growth was faster in the first half of the time period. Similarly, productivity gains were more rapid in the first half of the time period but slowed down in the 1970s. Indicators also follow different patterns: GDP growth fluctuated from year to year, while percent of the population below the poverty line moved in "waves" over much longer time spans.

In presenting the indicators graphically, a choice must be made on how to present the indicator, whether as a growth rate, a level, or some other measure. In cases like the real interest rate, there is no decision to make, because it makes little sense to present the growth rate of the interest rate. In other cases, this decision can best be made by illustrating indicator behavior over the time period in its several forms and ascertaining which illustration most clearly answers the specific questions that are raised about the indicator.

For instance, the long-run trend in productivity during 1946–93 (which deals with the controversy of whether there has been a decline in productivity) is much clearer when the level of the productivity index is displayed rather than the changes in or growth of the index. In illustrating saving and investment data, there are three choices: the level, the growth rate, and the rate, that is, as a share of disposable income or of GDP. Examination of the behavior of savings and investment growth rates on a year-to-year basis shows a great deal of volatility, making it difficult to sort out what the trends were. The actual levels of savings and investment, even when adjusted for inflation, neither depict relative year-to-year changes very effectively nor give an idea of the share of resources set aside, either through savings or investment, needed to maintain future income, which is a major concern of policy makers.

RANKING ADMINISTRATIONS FOR EACH INDICATOR

Following the section on overview of trends in the long run, the presidential administrations are individually ranked according to the averages over the President's time in office and changes in the indicator's trend. The relative value of the average versus the trend change is assessed in cases where one is clearly of greater informational value than the other, especially when the trend is of limited value. The rankings are, where applicable, from best (1) to worst (9), and whenever there is a question as to what is best and what is worst, as in the case of money supply growth, an explanation is given. The administration's recorded average and trend improvement are included with each ranking for each indicator.

It is important to notice that in some of the chapters the form of the indicator *illustrated* is different from the form of the indicator *ranked*. A common case is when levels are illustrated but growth rates serve as the basis for ranking. The reason is that, although graphing the level of an indicator may provide a clearer illustration of an indicator's behavior than growth rates, levels carry a weakness in that they may be more dependent than growth on the historical period in which they occurred. Hence, the value of levels as a measure of relative presidential performance is undermined. For example, the real level of GDP increased for every administration, as did employment (the amount, not the growth) and the index (not the rate) of inflation. Thus, a best-to-worst ranking of presidents according to the levels of GDP and employment would be only a chronological listing of presidents from most recent to earliest and would not serve as a meaningful basis for ranking, and, hence, growth rates are preferred for ranking.

A unique example that deserves mention is the percent below the poverty line indicator. In the year for which the indicator was first available, 1959, the U.S. government had a long way to go to eliminate poverty, which stood at over 22 percent. However, poverty declined for the next 14 years (all or part of four administrations), as economic growth was generally steady and the government waged a strong battle to reduce poverty. In the mid-1970s, reduction in poverty seemed to hit against a lower limit of 11 percent, below which it has not been reduced. Naturally, a president's average percent below the poverty line was higher the earlier he was in office during the 1959–74 period, which was through no fault of his own. In light of this fact, the amount which a president reduced poverty is more important than the average level during this period, and as poverty approached its apparent lower limit, the average level resumes greater importance after 1974.

An earlier point deserves reiteration here. In considering these rankings, it is essential to realize that not all of the administrations took place in similar economic worlds but, rather, in a variety of economic time periods in which substantially different economic conditions prevailed. Therefore, the strict comparisons of these administrations implied by rankings cannot be accepted at face value. However, the rankings do contain important information as they proceed from a factual basis using official data and simple and straightforward computations of averages and trends. Any thoughtful economic critique inspired by these rankings undoubtedly will lead to a better understanding of the evolution of the U.S. economy and, thus, of today's economy.

The chapters conclude with a discussion of selected issues regarding the indicator. The issues are often selected because they involve counterintuitive conclusions from the data and/or if the data contradict popular conceptions.

ORGANIZATION OF THE BOOK

One organizational approach to a book entitled, *An Economic Record of Presidential Performance from Truman to Bush* is for individual chapters to be based on presidential administrations rather than on economic and budget indicators. Under such an approach, it would be easier to delve into the policy-making process of each president and to make judgments as to whether the right choices were made by each president. However, because the purpose of this book is not just to compare presidents but also to provide a resource to measure all of the postwar economic period and to show distinct subperiods, each indicator should be viewed at once over the entire time period. This approach would not be possible if chapters were based on individual presidential administrations. Chapters driven by individual indicators offer presidential rankings according to specific indicators, not simply one composite, multiindicator ranking. This method provides additional flexibility to the analyst of assigning the levels of importance (weighting scheme) to specific indicators with which he or she agrees in order to determine his or her own composite ranking. This approach is consistent with that of a sourcebook.

The book is divided into two parts: Part I on the general economy and Part II on the federal government. Part I deals with the performance of general economic indicators that are primarily determined in the private sector. The broad range of indicators presented is designed to capture this performance. GDP is often viewed as the bottom line of presidential performance, but it must be qualified by the full array of indicators, each of which embodies distinct and important elements of overall economic performance.

Chapter 1 contains brief descriptions of the major events leading up to and during 1946–93. These descriptions provide a background against which to view the indicators' behavior. The subsequent chapters in Part I present trends and averages for the most important economic indicators that are not specific to the government budget but that affect all sectors, that is, the macroeconomy. The chapters are devoted to GDP (Chapter 2), employment growth and the unemployment rate (Chapter 3), inflation (Chapter 4), money supply and the real prime interest rate (Chapter 5), saving and investment rates (Chapter 6), productivity and compensation indexes (Chapter 7), the percent of the population below the poverty line (Chapter 8), and the stock market — Dow Jones Industrials Averages (Chapter 9).

Part II presents data on the government sector, an area more under the control of the president and Congress than most of the indicators in Part I. Part II deals with such indicators as the federal budget growth and share of GDP (Chapter 10) and budget deficits and growth in national debt (Chapter 11). Chapter 12 discusses the composition of the government budget during 1946–93. Government sector data are especially important in examining the president's performance because the president has more control over the public sector and, therefore, more responsibility and the government budget reveals the chief executive's (as well as Congress's) spending priorities through the various categories of public expenditure such as national defense and health. Thus, government budget data reflect the president's attitude toward the balance between the public and private sectors and between categories of government expenditure. Presidential policy regarding Social Security, although an off-budget item, is also of critical importance and is treated in Chapter 13. In addition to federal outlays, revenues also must be discussed. Taxation (Chapter 14) is a critical policy tool at the disposal of the president and Congress. A breakdown of tax shares by source as well as tax receipt growth are provided.

Finally, Chapter 15 provides an overall ranking of the presidents' economic performances by bringing together all the economic indicators into one composite ranking. This synthesis is simply a conscientious attempt to provide the reader with a bottom-line evaluation. The value of this synthesis along with its analytical strengths and weaknesses have no bearing on the validity or the usefulness of the indicators as presented in previous chapters. The postscript provides preliminary performance data for the Clinton administration.

Appendix A provides more technical explanations of the indicators and the data underlying the graphs and rankings. The statistics which underlie the graphs and the rankings are presented in Appendix B.

SUMMARY COMMENTS

Of necessity, Americans continuously make rational economic decisions on a household level without a full understanding of their ramifications for the national economy. This book certainly is not needed to aid in these daily economic decisions, nor does this book provide a rigorous treatment of complex economic issues. It is, rather, intended as a resource that takes the interested observer of the U.S. economic scene a critical step further in acquiring a more accurate picture of the national economy, beyond what is available from the popular media on a day-to-day basis. As a result, the reader may find many common perceptions about economic performance in general, and as they pertain to this or that administration, at odds with the actual figures. The attempt here is to minimize political predisposition, thereb, increasing the usefulness of *An Economic Record of Presidential Performance* as an objective guide to and starting point for discussions of economic events. The desired result is that exploration of economic issues can proceed more productively, without fear of initial bias or of manipulation or tampering with the official figures.

NOTES

1. This timeline is especially important because it provides historical background to the indicators. The identification and description of events also serve to qualify presidential responsibility for economic performance by showing that many influential factors were beyond the President's control.

2. Until 1976, the fiscal year ended on June 30, yielding a built-in six-month lag for government budget indicators. Since then, the fiscal year has ended on September 30, yielding the nine-month lag.

I

GENERAL ECONOMIC INDICATORS

FIGURE 1.1
Major Events: Timeline 1945–93

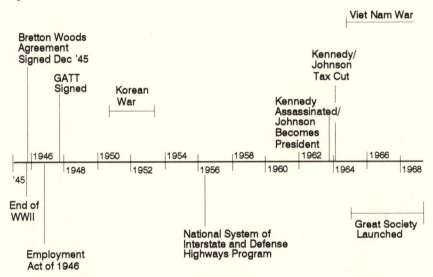

Pres	Truman				Eisenhower				Kennedy	Johnson		
Sen	Dem	Rep	Dem	Dem	Rep	Dem	Dem	Dem	Dem	Dem	Dem	Dem
Hse	Dem	Rep	Dem	Dem	Rep	Dem	Dem	Dem	Dem	Dem	Dem	Dem

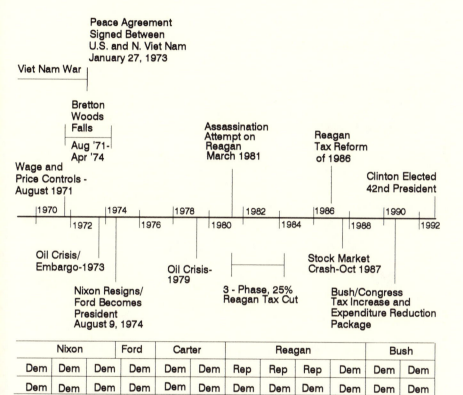

Peace Agreement
Signed Between
U.S. and N. Viet Nam
January 27, 1973

Viet Nam War

Bretton
Woods
Falls

Aug '71-
Apr '74

Assassination
Attempt on
Reagan
March 1981

Reagan
Tax Reform
of 1986

Wage and
Price Controls -
August 1971

Clinton Elected
42nd President

1970		1974		1978		1982		1986		1990	
	1972		1976		1980		1984		1988		1992

Oil Crisis/
Embargo-1973

Oil Crisis-
1979

Stock Market
Crash-Oct 1987

Nixon Resigns/
Ford Becomes
President
August 9, 1974

3 - Phase, 25%
Reagan Tax Cut

Bush/Congress
Tax Increase and
Expenditure Reduction
Package

Nixon			Ford	Carter		Reagan				Bush	
Dem	Dem	Dem	Dem	Dem	Dem	Rep	Rep	Rep	Dem	Dem	Dem
Dem	Dem	Dem	Dem	Dem	Dem	Dem	Dem	Dem	Dem	Dem	Dem

17

1

Major Events and Timeline

A president's control over economic performance is far from complete, even in areas where his influence is the strongest, and it is more often rather tenuous. There are too many variables beyond his control, including the personal economic decisions of 250 million Americans, to be able to influence key economic variables with much certainty. The lack of control is particularly evident when there are major events that are exogenous to the domestic economy, such as wars, oil embargoes, and global economic cycles, all of which have profoundly and repeatedly influenced the U.S. economy. However, there also are important aspects of the economy well within the control of the president (and Congress), such as major economic legislation, controls, liberalization, and reforms. To help develop economic policy and influence economic variables, the president also has the Treasury Department, the Office of Management and Budget, and the Council of Economic Advisors at his disposal. Whether the president has a high degree of responsibility for the economic performance during his reign or not, he is judged by what is perceived to have transpired "on his watch." It is important for that reason and for historical accuracy to have a record of what actually transpired economically, complemented with a background of events that influenced the economic indicators.

To provide context for the economic performance of the administrations from Truman to Bush, major events that occurred during 1945–93 are briefly discussed. This discussion includes both economic and noneconomic events, because both affect the indicators. The intent is to point out coincidence of major events with changes in the indicators; however, the reader should explore additional sources for an assessment of the impact of these events, and suggestions for further reading are provided at the end of each chapter. A timeline of events during 1945–93 is also presented at the beginning of this historical summary.

The events of the post-war era themselves should also be placed in a historical context. A brief overview of the economic policies pursued and the lessons learned during the Depression and World War II provides this context along with insights into prevailing economic thought in the post-war United States and into the policies practiced by the presidents from Truman to Bush. The following section presents some economic historical interpretations of the significance of the Depression and World War II for economic policy since 1945. As such, this chapter is distinguished from the more statistics-based chapters in the rest of the text.

THE GREAT DEPRESSION, 1929–42

Because it jolted the U.S. economy so severely, the Great Depression permanently changed economic thinking. Prior to the Depression, economies of the United States had rebounded regardless of the business shocks and returned to their full-employment levels of gross domestic product (GDP). However, the shock of the 1930s was beyond any other in the U.S. experience; real income fell by 18 percent in 1931 alone. Unemployment skyrocketed from 3.2 percent in 1929 to 24.9 percent in 1933. When the economy bottomed out in March 1933, national income was 36 percent below the 1928 level. As Milton Friedman and Anna Schwartz pointed out in *A Monetary History of the United States*, per capita income had fallen to 1908 levels, thus, erasing a quarter century of improvement in the nation's standard of living. The U.S. economy did not emerge from its depressed state until well after the start of World War II.

Depression Theories

There are many theories as to how such an unprecedented economic decline came about. A few of the more well-known ones are presented here. Each theory offers its own perspective on the causes of the Depression and contributes to understanding the economics of the post–World War II era. The divergence in the explanations of the causes of the Depression parallels the difficulties in establishing an economic policy consensus in the post-war economy.

1. The restrictive fiscal and monetary policies that were pursued primarily out of the fear of increasing budget deficits precipitated a severe recession and turned a banking crisis into full-scale financial collapse. Persistence with these perverse policies throughout the 1930s deepened and prolonged the Depression. This view reflects the "Friedman-Schwartz" or monetarist view.
2. The Federal Reserve intervened too much in not allowing the nominal money supply to fall to its natural level. Therefore, prices did not fall far enough to spark the recovery that would have occurred, ostensibly because demand would have reignited because of lower prices. This

"Austrian"/Schumpeter view notes that with the radical deflation of 1920–21, prices were allowed to fall completely and a recovery did occur.
3. The increasing concentration of wealth that was allowed to develop during the 1920s resulted in a very high saving rate. The correspondingly low consumption rate was gradually outpaced by rising productivity until industry and industrial employment no longer could be supported by consumer demand. This theory also contends that the surplus saving of the rich was used in stock market speculation, which, in turn, contributed to the stock market crash in 1929.
4. "Secular stagnation," a term coined by Keynesian economist Alvin Hansen, stated that because the United States had reached its geographical frontier, population growth had slowed, and because there were fewer investment opportunities and less innovation, the economy was led inexorably into depression (Hughes, 1983, p. 505).
5. With the consumption binge of the 1920s concluding with the stock market crash in 1929, consumers simply decided to be much more cautious and spend less. Proponents of this view note that consumption declined by 41 percent between 1929 and 1933.
6. The standard Keynesian scenario for recession or depression, as presented in *The General Theory of Employment, Interest and Money* (1936), was as follows: For whatever reason (e.g., "animal spirits"), a sudden collapse of the marginal efficiency of capital (or return on capital) occurred. As a result, investors revised their estimates of future returns of current investment plans downward; therefore, investment demand dropped, and recession followed. The Keynesian solution to the recession was called "compensating fiscal policy," which was designed to smooth out the peaks and valleys in the business cycle through compensating tax and spending programs.

An additional Keynesian observation of the Great Depression contended that the large cash surplus that some banks held indicated that they were hoarding cash and, thus, inhibiting demand for securities and investment. This phenomenon later came to be known as the "liquidity trap."

Theories 1 to 3 suggest errors of economic policy, while theories 4 to 6 suggest forces largely beyond control of the policy makers. Ironically, many of the tools of monetary, fiscal, and foreign trade policy were already in place in the 1920s and, in all probability, could have been used to assuage or, possibly, avoid the Depression if they had been correctly understood.

Errors in Economic Policy Leading to and during the Depression

The description of events leading up to and during the Great Depression here follows the line of the first theory, that is, that poor monetary and fiscal policies were to blame. This hypothesis is, perhaps, the most highly supported theory of the Depression, and it focuses on factors within the control of policy makers. It is also more reflective, among the theories presented, of the type of economic thinking that emerged after World War II. International factors contributing to the Depression are also discussed.

Although both monetary and fiscal policy blunders contributed to the Depression, monetary policy was probably the more culpable. The most serious fiscal policy errors were committed well *after* the Depression was under way. Faulty monetary policy was central to engineering the financial crises during 1929–33 that precipitated the Depression. From 1929 to 1933, the money supply was substantially reduced, a counterstimulative policy that was exactly the opposite of what would be prescribed for a recession. In 1929, the M1-measured money supply (a narrow measure of the money supply that includes only cash and transactions deposits — see Chapter 5) stood at $26.4 billion, and by 1933 it had fallen to $19.8 billion,[1] a drop of 25 percent in nominal terms.

The tight money policy certainly aggravated and perhaps was the primary cause of the rapid deflation (over 8 percent annually) that was occurring in the economy. Thus, even though the nominal interest rate was only 1–2 percent, the real interest rate soared to over 10 percent. This high real interest rate had a strong depressing effect on the economy. In addition, in September 1931, Britain left the gold standard. Other countries that held U.S. dollars feared the United States was going to follow Britain. With the low and declining nominal interest rates in the United States, these foreign countries decided to cash in their dollars for gold. The ensuing run on U.S. gold exacerbated the Depression because the Federal Reserve Board, concerned about the gold drain, actually increased the rediscount rate to member banks. The timing of this move was particularly destructive, because it occurred during a wave of bank failures. This perverse policy continued as the rediscount rate was also increased in 1933 and 1937, the latter contributing to the major recessionary setback of 1938.

There was another international policy error that also contributed to the Depression. With economic conditions suddenly declining in other countries as well, there was a clamor for protectionism. Each country, including the United States, was desperate to maintain a favorable trade balance in order to improve its employment situation. Tariffs were raised, and quotas were instituted. In 1930, the Smoot-Hawley Tariff was passed. The collective result of this tariff and the high barriers to imports imposed by other countries further curtailed what employment relief might have been realized from the expansion of international trade.

On the fiscal side, a tax *increase* actually was instituted in 1932 in an attempt to eliminate budget deficits. Because of the fear (especially Herbert Hoover's) of budget deficits, tax rates were increased to a level

TABLE 1.1
Federal Government Receipts and Expenditures, 1929–45
(billions of dollars)

Year	Receipts	Expenditures	Expenditures as Percent of GDP	Surplus or Deficit (–)
1929	3.9	3.1	3.0	0.7
1933	2.0	4.6	8.3	–2.6
1934	3.2	7.0	10.8	–3.6
1935	3.8	6.7	9.3	–2.7
1936	4.2	8.7	10.6	–4.4
1937	5.6	7.9	8.7	–2.8
1938	6.5	6.6	7.8	–1.2
1939	6.3	9.1	10.4	–2.8
1940	6.5	9.5	9.9	–2.9
1941	8.7	13.7	12.1	–4.9
1942	14.6	35.1	24.8	–20.5
1943	24.0	78.6	44.8	–54.6
1944	43.7	91.3	45.3	–47.6
1945	45.2	92.7	43.7	–47.6

Sources: Economic Report of the President (Washington, D.C.: U.S. Government Printing Office, 1994); U.S. Department of Commerce, Bureau of Economic Analysis, *Survey of Current Business* (Washington, D.C.: U.S. Government Printing Office, 1993).

that effectively doubled full employment tax yields. As Table 1.1 shows, this tax increase was not successful in eliminating budget deficits. Tax increases occurred not only at the federal level but also at the state and local levels. At the time, state and local taxes accounted for substantially more revenue than did federal taxes. Although the errant tax increases occurred well after the Depression had started and after national income had already fallen by 30 percent, they served to deepen and prolong the Depression and indicated a further lack of understanding of how economic variables respond to economic policies.

In the decade of the 1930s, government spending increased most years under both Hoover and Roosevelt, and budget deficits were run every year (Table 1.1). In 1935 and 1937–38, however, government spending actually constricted as a share of GDP. Thus, it was more the slow growth in revenues, rather than excessive spending, that was the cause of deficits. In fact, spending fell far short of what was needed for recovery. The 9–10 percent or so of GDP accounted for by federal expenditures, a common level in the 1930s, did not come close to the magnitudes of wartime spending of over 40 percent of GDP.

The taxing and spending structure that continued throughout Franklin Roosevelt's administration in the 1930s was designed more to eliminate the deficits than to nurture the economic recovery. The tax increase of the early 1930s, which, as mentioned, would have doubled revenues at the full employment level of national income, was not rescinded by Roosevelt. Moreover, in 1936, in order to finance the new Social Security programs, additional taxes had to be imposed. Thus, taxes grew faster than expenditures, which held down economic recovery long before full employment was attained. This view is supported by the course of unemployment during the remainder of the 1930s. The level of unemployment did improve to 14.3 percent by 1937 from its 1933 high of 24.9 percent, but it then shot up to 19.0 percent in 1938, almost nine years after the Depression began. Unemployment continued at historically high rates of 17.2 and 14.6 percent during 1939–40. What recovery did occur in the 1930s appeared to come more from a struggling private sector than from fiscal (especially tax) policy, the proliferation of government programs notwithstanding.[2] In conclusion, the economic policies, both monetary and fiscal, that were pursued in the 1930s not only precipitated the Depression but also prolonged and deepened it.

WORLD WAR II

War Financing

At the onslaught of World War II, the policy decision was made to finance the war through additional borrowing as well as taxes. In 1940, individual income taxes were 20 percent of revenues, and in 1945, they were 43 percent. In all, it is estimated that 46 percent of the war expenditures was paid for by current taxation. Thus, most of the incremental war costs were met through borrowing, primarily through bonds sold to the banking system and the public. That the war was heavily financed by borrowing is reflected in the budget deficits in Table 1.1. In 1943 and 1944, government expenditures' share of GDP reached 44.8 and 45.3 percent, respectively. By 1945, government revenues were still less than half of expenditures, and the federal deficit reached a quarter of GDP (today, the federal deficit is roughly 5 percent of GDP). The huge increases in government spending for the war profoundly reduced the unemployment rate. In 1940, the unemployment rate stood at 14.6 percent, 0.3 percent higher than the rate three years earlier in 1937, but as the preparations for war began in 1941, the unemployment rate dropped to 9.9 percent and then to 4.7 and 1.9 percent in 1942 and 1943, respectively.

In the final analysis, it was deficit spending that hauled the economy out of the Depression. The combination of taxing and spending followed a Keynesian blueprint: increased government expenditures generated the output needed for war and for civilians. The money or production cost of war goods meant income for civilians, but war goods did not enter the economy, which meant increased income without increased goods on which to spend it. Taxation and war bond sales played the role of absorbing the excess income and, therefore, avoided inflation. However, there were also pervasive price controls. Whether these price controls had more to do with controlling inflation than the absorption of excess income by war financing needs is the subject of further study.

Wartime Changes in the Economy

The exigencies of the war and the need to pay for it ushered in new features to the economy that remain today. For example, changes were made to revenue collection to facilitate the financing of the war. The pay-as-you-earn individual income, or withholding, tax was instituted in accordance with the Revenue Act of 1943. The timing of revenues and expenditures was improved and the costs of collection were avoided, because employers would perform the tax collection function for the Internal Revenue Service (IRS). Tax paying also became an act of patriotism.

Another interesting development in economic policy practiced during World War II and important to future economic policy was the discovery of the revenue side of fiscal policy as a tool for economic stabilization.[3] The realization emerged that returning spending power to the economy through lower taxes had advantages over deficit spending. The enhancement of aggregate demand through lower taxes would be more evenly distributed throughout the economy and be less distortive and inflationary than government deficit spending, which would be confined to public works projects. Although wartime tax rates did not return to pre-war, peacetime levels when the war ended, the idea of stimulating aggregate demand through tax cuts gradually gained support and culminated in the Kennedy-Johnson tax cut of 1964, which is discussed below.

At the end of World War II, the Depression experience was still fresh, several new institutions of the Roosevelt administration — the Social Security Administration (1936), the Securities and Exchange Commission, and the Federal Deposit Insurance Corporation — were more firmly established, U.S. manufacturing had been built up tremendously, and the United States was ready to assume the leadership role in the world economy. Thanks to some painful lessons learned in the Depression, U.S. presidents could pursue macroeconomic policies with a better understanding, which was infused, to a large extent, with Keynesian economics. The economic framework of today has many basic similarities to that of 1945, in spite of the dramatic changes between 1945 and 1993, thus, leaving a basis for presidential comparison during this time period.

MAJOR EVENTS, 1945–93

Transformation to a Peacetime Economy

The United States emerged from World War II with the only intact industrial base in the world, a currency that was preferred to gold, and virtually no international competition. Yet, in the transformation to a peacetime economy, many economists predicted a massive recession with high unemployment. The reason for this dire prediction was the tremendous reduction that was about to occur in the government's military expenditures, which could not reasonably be expected to be compensated for by increased government expenditures in other sectors. Government expenditures fell from $93 billion in 1945 to $30 billion in 1948 (nominal terms), a drop in outlays as a share of GDP from 43.7 percent to 12.1 percent. In real terms, government expenditures declined by rates of 43, 50, and 16 percent, respectively, during 1946–48. The newly demobilized military personnel also were not expected to be absorbed by the private economy.[4] However, although the fall in government outlays did occur without compensating government outlays elsewhere, the private sector responded, and the recession was much milder and shorter than expected.

Some economists attribute the milder than expected recession to the pent-up purchasing power that consumers had accumulated during both the Depression and the war, a period of almost 17 years. Consumer demand, thus, could pave the way for the transition not only from a wartime to a peacetime economy but also from a government-run to a private economy. However, the prospect of inflation because of this demand was strong. In addition to the pent-up domestic demand, there was great demand in Europe and elsewhere, especially for U.S. goods needed to rebuild. Ultimately, both foreign and domestic demand fueled a successful transformation to a peacetime economy. The manufacturing and housing sectors quickly geared up for this demand and created millions of new jobs. In addition, the Serviceman's Readjustment Act of 1944, better known as the G.I. Bill, facilitated the transition back into civilian life with loans, educational subsidies, and other benefits.

It could be said that Truman's performance bore the burden of the economic transition but also had the advantage of the purchasing power that had accumulated during the Depression and the war years and the benefit of international demand in meeting the rebuilding needs of Europe. With the tremendous demand, both foreign and domestic, for U.S. output, it turned out that it was not the greatly feared return to high unemployment that threatened the transition but, rather, the control of inflation (as Chapters 3 and 4 show).

Employment Act of 1946

The Employment Act of 1946 represented the philosophical consensus for the post-war economy in terms of redefining, or, at least, reexamining, the relative economic roles of the government and the private sector. The act also is significant for the debate that ensued during and after its drafting. Initially, the Keynesians in Congress wanted the act to be called the Full Employment Act. Their idea was to emphasize the government's commitment to achieve full employment, because they felt that the primary objective of economic policy was to avoid a return to the high unemployment of the Great Depression. Central to this view was that the government had the primary responsibility to achieve full employment. This view maintained, moreover, that if there was unemployment, then the government could run a budget deficit that would achieve full employment and that this deficit could be estimated by economists.

After debate in Congress, however, the act was modified to replace the goal of "full employment" with "maximum employment, production and growth," to delete references to the government's deficit as the exclusive tool of economic management, and to reaffirm that economic measures must be consistent with the free market system. The act also created the Council of Economic Advisors to assist the president in formulating economic policy.

From this congressional debate, it was clear that Keynesianism was strong but that it did not have full reign over economic policy. The government's power, or mandate, to achieve full employment had limits, and the goal of full employment had to accommodate policies that encouraged economic growth as well. Thus, the U.S. economy remained essentially a free market system with the intended role of the government as an enabler rather than a regulator of economic growth.

The Post-War International Economic Order

As the post-war economic framework took shape within the United States, the United States also was working with other nations in sculpting the international economic framework. There were three important components to the framework that helped achieve and maintain international economic order. The three components were the Bretton Woods System, the General Agreement on Tariffs and Trade (GATT), and the Marshall Plan. The new international system departed from the protectionist philosophy of the 1930s and created an environment conducive to a rapid expansion of trade. The expansion of trade, in turn, contributed to the historically high growth rates in the United States and the rest of the industrial world from World War II through the 1960s. From the U.S. viewpoint, the emerging Cold War placed particular urgency and political importance on the establishment of an international economic order based on Western principles of free trade and competition.

The Bretton Woods System — Exchange Rates, The World Bank, and International Monetary Fund, 1945-71

The Bretton Woods Agreement was signed on December 27, 1945, in Washington, D.C., following the United Nations (UN) Monetary and Financial Conference at Bretton Woods, New Hampshire, in July 1944. The agreement established the International Bank for Reconstruction and Development, commonly known as the World Bank, and the International Monetary Fund (IMF). The purpose of the World Bank, which began operation on June 25, 1946, was to make loans for development projects, primarily infrastructure, in war-torn countries and in developing countries for the benefit of poor people, while the IMF was to maintain exchange rate stability and facilitate exchange rate adjustment. The Bretton Woods agreement also attempted to establish a stable international environment through fixed exchange rates, currency convertibility, a gold standard that maintained a gold price of US\$35 per ounce, and provision for orderly exchange rate adjustment in the event of "fundamental disequilibrium" between major currencies.

The IMF would oversee the system and provide medium-term loans to countries with temporary balance of payments difficulties, which would, therefore, help preserve the system of fixed exchange rates and provide more stability. As mentioned, the IMF would also facilitate adjustments to a country's exchange rate if the country was in "fundamental disequilibrium," that is, the value of its currency had simply changed with respect to the other currencies such that currency transactions would not be able to sustain the current fixed exchange rate. Currency convertibility meant that one major currency could buy or be bought with another at the fixed exchange rate. However, although the fixed exchange rates component of Bretton Woods was implemented from the beginning, currency convertibility did not come about until the end of the 1950s. Currency convertibility was a precondition for freedom of capital mobility and ultimately led to the integration of global financial markets, as shown later by, among other things, the rise of the Eurodollar market. Balance of payments crises also were worked out at the IMF through ad hoc arrangements.

General Agreement on Tariffs and Trade, 1947

Although the Bretton Woods system did not become fully operational until well into the 1950s, another major feature of international trade was introduced in October 1947, the GATT. GATT was important in setting up the rules of trade, especially for industrial countries. GATT consolidated a series of bilateral trade agreements and created a liberal trade regime based on nondiscrimination in trade, in that a privilege extended to one signatory was extended to all (i.e., "the most-favored nation clause"); industry protection through tariffs rather than quotas or other non-tariff barriers; and a mechanism to work out trade disputes. Much of the rapid growth of international trade following the war has been attributed to the principles on which GATT was based. The rapid trade expansion, in turn, is cited by many economists as the engine of both European recovery and sustained growth in the United States.

Marshall Plan, 1948–52

The Marshall Plan for European Reconstruction (officially called the European Recovery Program) was carried out from 1948 to 1952 and was the largest foreign aid program ever launched by the United States. The plan cost US$13.2 billion over the four-year period. Another US$1 billion went to East and Southeast Asia. The primary recipients of aid were the United Kingdom (US$3.2 billion), France (US$2.7 billion), West Germany (US$1.4 billion), and Holland (US$1.1 billion), followed by (in order of amount received) Greece, Austria, Belgium, Denmark, Norway, Turkey, Ireland, and Sweden. There were four additional recipients that received modest amounts. The plan helped to rebuild these countries by financing raw materials, semifinished goods, agricultural inputs, machinery, vehicles, fuel, and so on.

The Marshall Plan played an important role in the rapid recovery of Europe. Europe's human capital and know-how were intact after the war, but its physical capital lay in ruin. Thus, the infusion of capital from the Marshall Plan could be absorbed effectively. The economic success of the recipient countries, especially West Germany, is consistent with this view. Economic historians also note that the Marshall Plan supplanted the World Bank in its role as an "International Bank for Reconstruction." Rather, the World Bank became a development institution for Third World countries, many of which were still waging battles for independence after the Marshall Plan was implemented.

Korean War, June 1950–July 1953

The Korean war lasted a little over three years. Hostilities broke out in June 1950 when a force of Soviet-supported North Koreans crossed south of the thirty-eighth parallel and invaded South Korea. President Truman acted immediately and gained a UN Security Council Resolution (the Soviets were boycotting the UN at the time) to resist the aggression. The vast majority of fighting occurred during the first year of the war, which is reflected in the trend in U.S. government expenditures. Huge swings in the tide of battle characterized the war, with the

UN forces driven almost into the sea, followed by General MacArthur's counterattack, which pushed the North Koreans almost to the Chinese border. When the Chinese entered the war, UN troops were forced back to the thirty-eighth parallel. Thereafter, a stalemate ensued and many lengthy rounds of truce talks were conducted, with the war finally concluding on July 27, 1953, as President Eisenhower signed the armistice drawing the border at the thirty-eighth parallel. At its peak, U.S. troop strength in Korea was 350,000. There were 33,600 U.S. soldiers killed in action and approximately $18 billion (noninflated) was spent by the United States on the war.

The Korean War, economists argue, had two effects on the economy. The first was the economic boom, especially in 1950 and 1951, which was triggered by a major increase in defense spending, partially restoring the massive defense cuts following World War II. The second was the worsening of inflation, particularly in 1951. In its concern over inflation, Congress gave Truman broad power over the economy, including that of wage and price controls. The end of the war was followed by the brief 1954 recession. An interesting sidelight to the Korean War is that the United States ordered thousands of military trucks for the war effort from a relatively unknown Japanese company named Toyota, a transaction that some analysts contend provided an important post–World War II boost to the Japanese vehicle manufacturer.

Tax Cut of 1964

The tax cut of 1964 was the largest tax cut in history up to that time and is attributed to Kennedy but was actually passed and implemented after his assassination. Kennedy had originally promised such a tax cut in June 1962, but the first stage of the two-stage tax cut was not enacted until February 1964. Congress had delayed in passing the tax cut because of fears of higher budget deficits, and some suggest that the tax cut was approved only on a wave of sympathy from Kennedy's assassination. The second stage occurred the following year. The purpose of the tax cut, according to Kennedy, was to favor temporary increases in budget deficits in order to promote fuller use of resources and more rapid economic growth rates over the environment of slower growth rates and small, but chronic, deficits of previous years.[5]

The tax cut entailed across-the-board reductions of individual tax rates, with the top rate reduced from 91 to 77 percent in 1964 and to 70 percent in 1965. It also reduced corporate taxes to 22 percent on the first $25,000 of taxable income, and the tax rates on the remainder went from 52 to 50 percent in 1964 and to 48 percent in 1965. Capital depreciation was also enhanced. The estimated total tax reduction effectively represented $11–14 billion transfer from the public to the private sector.

The tax cut was considered a milestone in that it was not only Keynesian, because government expenditures rose relative to revenues, but also a "supply side" measure, as resources were shifted from the government to the private sector. On balance, the tax cut was conservative in nature, because it relied on tax reduction rather than expenditure increases, gave benefits to wealthier individuals, and lowered the tax burden on corporations.

The New Frontier and the Great Society, 1964–69

The tax cut of 1964 was followed quickly by the Great Society programs of Johnson. Prior to Johnson's own programs, he secured passage of several New Frontier bills initiated by Kennedy, the most important of which was the Civil Rights Act of 1964, which survived a 57-day filibuster from Southern senators. In addition to enactment of New Frontier initiatives, Johnson also declared his "War on Poverty" and established the Economic Opportunity Act, the Job Corps, and Vista Volunteers (a domestic peace corps), all in 1964.

In his 1965 State-of-the-Union address, Johnson presented his plan for the Great Society. It expanded federal programs to cover the poor and elderly, the rural and urban areas, and the middle class. Benefits to the middle class were viewed as a means to gain support for the Great Society program as a whole. The main components of the Great Society passed in 1965 and 1966 and included the Housing and Urban Development Act, creating a cabinet-level department to coordinate federal housing programs; Medicare to provide health care for the elderly; the Appalachian Regional Development Act, which provided aid to that area; the Elementary and Secondary Education Act and the Higher Education Act, which provided funds and scholarships; the National Teachers Corps; the Immigration Act; the Voting Rights Act; the Demonstration Cities and Metropolitan Area Redevelopment Act; and a general expansion and increase of other programs such as Social Security and minimum wages. The budgetary implications of these programs are dealt with in Part II.

The Viet Nam War, March 1965–January 1973 (U.S. Involvement)

Although the groundwork for U.S. involvement in Viet Nam was laid in the Eisenhower and Kennedy administrations, it was under President Johnson that sustained, large-scale war was waged. When Johnson assumed office in November 1963, there were 17,000 U.S. troops in Viet Nam, mainly serving as advisors to South Vietnamese army units. In August 1964, the North Vietnamese attacked U.S. ships in the Gulf of Tonkin, after which the Gulf of Tonkin Resolution was passed by Congress, paving the way for greater military involvement.

After several other escalations, Johnson sent the first combat troops to Viet Nam in March 1965. Table 1.2 charts the yearly course of the war.

TABLE 1.2
Viet Nam War: Cost, Troop Strength, and Fatalities

Year	Cost (fiscal year, $ millions)	Estimated Number of Troops Deployed	Estimated Number of Troops Killed
1965	103	175,000	2,100
1966	5,812	400,000	6,400
1967	18,417	475,000	11,100
1968	20,012	540,000	15,900
1969	21,544	470,000	11,600
1970	17,373	284,000	7,800
1971	11,542	150,000	2,200
1972	7,346	27,000	400
Total	102,149		57,500

Source: Allan R. Millet, ed., *A Short History of the Vietnam War* (Bloomington: Indiana University Press, 1978).

Table 1.2 shows that the war had two distinct phases that corresponded exactly with the tenures of the two presidents in charge, Johnson and Nixon. Under Johnson, what started as a few skirmishes and tens of millions of dollars by 1968 had turned into a full-fledged war with troop strength at 540,000 and tens of billions of dollars spent annually. The peak troop level was reached in March 1968 at 541,500. Government expenditures on the war reached 13–14 percent of the total U.S. budget (unified on- and off-budget) for fiscal 1969 and 1970.

In 1969, newly elected President Nixon changed the character of the war by undertaking a policy of "Vietnamization," whereby the burden of ground combat would be shifted from U.S. forces to those of South Viet Nam. U.S. troop levels were steadily reduced, along with U.S. casualties, although the policy proved unsuccessful in winning the war. Although there was a steady downward trend in the number of U.S. military personnel, Nixon waged a vigorous bombing campaign in Viet Nam as well as an "incursion" into Cambodia. In January 1973, a peace agreement was signed, and the remaining U.S. troops and prisoners of war returned. In the final tally, the Viet Nam war had cost almost 58,000 lives and over $100 billion,[6] not including the costs to the other participants in the war. Through both the Johnson and the Nixon phases, the waging of the war coincided with sustained economic growth and low unemployment on the one hand and larger budget deficits and increasing inflation on the other. Additional details of the effects of the war on the government budget are found in Part II.

Wage and Price Controls, August 15, 1971–April 10, 1974, and the Fall of Bretton Woods

Wage and price controls and changes in the rules of international economic exchange were instituted by President Nixon beginning in August 1971 in response to persistent and relatively high inflation along with the concern, which had been brewing since the 1960s, of a run on the U.S. dollar in the foreign exchange markets. In addition to temporarily freezing wages and prices, the measures rescinded dollar-gold convertibility and fixed exchange rates, thus, removing two pillars of the Bretton Woods system. Also as part of the program, Nixon levied a surcharge on imports as a means to force other major countries to revalue their currencies with respect to the dollar, created an investment tax credit, deferred certain government expenditure increases, and eliminated the excise tax on automobiles. A new cabinet committee, the Cost of Living Council, was also created to manage the program, which lasted almost three years.

The Nixon wage-price controls were enthusiastically received by the public, with the Dow Jones Industrials Average rising 32.9 points the day after the program's unveiling, the largest one-day increase in history up to that point. This response is interesting in that it suggests rather shallow public support (as represented by the stock market), in principle, for the basic characteristics of a free market economy. The public's acceptance of the controls did not change for the nearly three years that the controls were in effect. The actual price and wage freezes lasted only about 90 days, and the program as a whole lost the battle with inflation.

Key features of Bretton Woods were eliminated by President Nixon because they did not reflect the economic reality of the time. For example, Bretton Woods was a fixed exchange rate system in a world where economic forces required exchange rates to change constantly. This phenomenon, as mentioned, was known as "fundamental disequilibrium" because "real" exchange rates differed from the fixed exchange rate. Different inflation rates between countries, as well as other factors, made it impossible to maintain the value of some currencies with respect to others. Fixed exchange rates could not be maintained even with substantial interventions from major central banks. Furthermore, on average, countries felt more pressure to devalue than to revalue their currencies with respect to gold and, therefore, the dollar. Without the other currencies revaluing, the United States could support the exchange rate of the dollar only by selling gold. U.S. gold reserves were depleted from $17.8 billion in 1960 to $11 billion in 1971, a decline of 38 percent. The result was a deterioration of the balance of payments and a dollar crisis in the United States, giving rise to a liquidity problem that thwarted the ability of the system to adjust.

Thus, Nixon was forced to sever the dollar-gold link and, later, to cast off the system of fixed exchange rates in 1973. Although Bretton Woods essentially ended as an operational system of international exchange with the delinking of the dollar from gold and the abandonment of fixed exchange rates, its legacy lives on in the two institutions it created, the IMF and the World Bank.

The Oil Crises of 1973 and 1979

The energy crisis of 1973–74 was many years in the making. In the 1950s and 1960s, most of the industrialized countries had become dependent on oil imports for sizeable portions of their energy consumption. The immediate crisis in 1973 was precipitated by the Organization of Petroleum Exporting Countries oil embargo of countries supporting Israel in the Arab-Israeli war of that year. The embargo was in effect against the United States from October 1973 to March 1974 and led to a tripling of the U.S. price of oil. A number of measures were taken by the United States to manage the scarcity, including voluntary lowering of thermostats, restrictions on gasoline purchases, and a standby authority for rationing.

The second oil shock of the 1970s occurred as a result of the overthrow of the shah of Iran. During the turmoil leading up to the shah's flight from his country in January 1979, Iranian oil workers went on strike. Iranian oil exports, which accounted for 12 percent of the noncommunist world's oil supply, were severely disrupted. Taking advantage of this situation, Organization of Petroleum Exporting Countries raised the price of crude oil by almost 15 percent during 1979. Increases in production from such countries as Saudi Arabia probably prevented an even greater crisis.

Within the United States, a series of gasoline shortages swept the nation, beginning in May in California and extending to the East coast by summer. Interestingly, some observers laid the blame for this gasoline shortage on the U.S. Department of Energy's allocation methods, citing that supplies of crude oil in the United States were actually higher in 1979 than in 1978, some regions of the country never experienced any shortages, and regional shortages often disappeared quickly.

Reagan Tax Cut of 1981–83

One of the major issues in Ronald Reagan's 1980 campaign was general tax reduction, following the premise that such a tax reduction would increase resources and incentives for production. After surviving an assassination attempt in March 1981, President Reagan pursued his major policy initiatives, which included substantial income tax reduction, cuts in social programs, and accelerated defense spending. The plan was codified in the Economic Recovery Act of 1981.

One important, and often thought to be the most important, element of this act was an across-the-board reduction in individual income tax rates phased in over three years. The income tax rate reductions amounted to 5 percent in 1982, 10 percent in 1983, and 10 percent in 1984, for an overall rate reduction cut of 25 percent over the three years, although, because of technicalities in the process, the total cut worked out to only 23 percent over the three years.

Perhaps an even more important aspect of the tax package was the indexing of income tax rates. For years leading into the Reagan administration, individuals' income rose rapidly in money terms, largely because of inflation. Although individuals' real wealth and purchasing power had not risen nearly as rapidly, they, nevertheless, found themselves in ever-higher tax brackets, paying higher percentages of their income to the government. In effect, this phenomenon, known as "bracket creep," gave the government automatic tax increases that were geared to the rate of inflation. Moreover, Congress never had to pay the political price for enacting these tax increases. However, starting in 1985, the Economic Recovery Act required the IRS to increase the income tax bracket levels by the increase in the consumer price index, thus, ending years of progressively higher tax rates on inflation-induced increases in income. Consequently, the hidden benefit to the government of inflation-induced tax increases was ended. The budgetary impact of Reagan's tax changes is discussed in Part II.

There were also benefits to businesses in the new laws. These benefits included cuts in tax rates at the lower levels of corporate income and a new system of depreciation, known as the Accelerated Cost Recovery System. This system provided for much faster write-offs of capital expenditures and, consequently, lower taxes to companies making such investments.

Tax Reform of 1986

Some observers termed the 1986 Tax Reform Act the most important piece of financial legislation since 1913, when the sixteenth amendment to the Constitution, authorizing modern-day income taxes, was ratified. It took two years to enact and was signed into law by President Reagan in October 1986.

Perhaps the important aspect of the 1986 tax reform was that it largely eliminated, or at least greatly dulled, the progressive tax system for individuals. It also eradicated many long-cherished tax breaks. Prior to 1987, there were 15 tax brackets for single taxpayers and 14 for married taxpayers. Maximum tax rates were 50 percent in both categories. This system was replaced by a five-bracket system in 1987 (considered a transitional year) and a two-bracket system thereafter. Under the two-bracket system, married and single individuals were taxed at 15 percent up to a certain level of income and 28 percent thereafter. At higher levels of income, the benefits associated with the 15 percent rate were phased out. Among the significantly curtailed or eliminated tax deductions were interest on consumer loans, medical expenses, sales tax, political and charitable contributions, and unreimbursed business expenses (sometimes referred to as the "three martini lunch").

Another important component of the 1986 act was the curtailment of tax shelters. For many years, tax shelters had gained notoriety as unfair tax dodges available only to the very rich. The 1986 act significantly reduced the attractiveness of tax shelters through the following changes in the code: first, the investment tax credit was repealed; second, the generous depreciation schedules of the 1981 Economic Recovery Act were scaled back; and third, losses from tax shelters no longer would be deductible against otherwise regular taxable income. Businesses did receive some benefits in the 1986 act including reduced tax rates on the top corporate tax brackets.

Stock Market Crash of 1987

The stock market crash of 1987 occurred on October 19, "Black Monday," when the Dow Jones Industrials Average dropped 508 points, losing 22.6 percent of total market value, the largest one-day loss ever. An overlooked aspect of this crash is that the market had already fallen over 250 points in the previous week. Over the weekend prior to "Black Monday," investors apparently became increasingly nervous about the rapid decline, and by Monday, the stock market was reeling. The many possible explanations for the crash range from international causes such as Treasury Secretary Baker's announcement that the United States would not prop up the dollar and indications that foreign holders of U.S. debt were becoming uneasy with financing U.S. deficits to technical causes such as think-alike MBAs engaged in programmed trading. The market did recover partially in the following days, and by mid-July 1990 had regained its precrash level.

Omnibus Budget Reconciliation Act of 1990

The desire to avoid Gramm-Rudman automatic spending cuts in 1990 forced President Bush and Congress into dealing more seriously with the budget deficits than they had in the previous year, Bush's first year in office. With the economy slowing down and the estimates of the budget deficit rising, the automatic spending cuts would have had to be enormous in order to meet the Gramm-Rudman targets. Thus, there was a great deal of pressure on Bush to reach a major compromise with Congress that would attack the deficit on both the expenditure and the revenue sides. Democrats, not wanting again to be tarred as "big tax and spenders" would not initiate proposals for increased revenues without the president signing on. On the other hand, for Bush to increase tax revenue meant going back on his central campaign pledge of "no new taxes."

During 1990, two major budget agreements were drafted. The first budget agreement, the result of a budget summit between the president and Congress, was based on excise tax increases on gasoline and home heating oil and spending cuts, largely on Medicare, but was devoid of both the much-discussed capital gains tax cut and upper income tax increases. When this first agreement was resoundingly defeated in the House by a vote of 179 to 254, with many Republicans voting against the summit agreement, a second budget agreement had to be drafted.

Obviously, the second budget agreement needed more votes than the first, and the question became whether votes should be sought from the left or the right of the political spectrum. House Democrats who felt that Bush had already inoculated them against the big-taxers label put together their own plan, which included higher taxes on the wealthy and eliminated the regressive gas tax. The Senate Democrats found the House version desirable but created their own budget plan, which was modified to get the needed Republican support. The choice was shifted considerably to the left compared with the earlier budget agreement as, in the end, greater Democratic support was sought. The agreement that finally passed included an increase in the tax rate in the high income bracket (strongly fought against by Bush) and other indirect tax increases on the better-off (i.e., elimination of some deductions), no capital gains tax cut, a smaller increase in gas taxes, and smaller cuts in Medicare compared with the summit agreement. On October 28, 1990, the final agreement, which purported to decrease budget deficits by $490 billion over a five-year period, was passed in the House and Senate and was later signed by the president under the name of the Omnibus Budget Reconciliation Act of 1990, more commonly known as the Budget Enforcement Act (BEA).

Also noteworthy are the provisions of the BEA that made it more difficult for the president and Congress to dodge the budget deficit targets set by its predecessor in budget legislation, Gramm-Rudman-Hollings (GRH). GRH had required the administration to estimate budget deficits at the start of the fiscal year to see whether the estimate complied with the GRH deficit target. However, it was possible to pass legislation to increase the deficit later in the year as well as in subsequent years, because GRH applied only to the current year. The BEA closed off both of these circumventions by requiring that the administration reveal whether the legislation it signed increased or decreased the deficit. If BEA targets were exceeded, then across-the-board spending cuts would be invoked until the targets were met.

SUGGESTIONS FOR FURTHER READING

Bernstein, Michael A., *The Great Depression*. New York: Cambridge University Press, 1987. Surveys short- and long-run theories of the Depression and offers explanations for the delayed recovery.

Friedman, Milton, and Schwartz, Anna, *A Monetary History of the United States — 1867–1960*. Princeton, N.J.: Princeton University Press, 1963. Provides an in-depth portrayal, but with readable narrative, of monetary developments during the entitled period, including good background on the Federal Reserve and the Great Depression.

Graham, Andrew, and Seldon, Anthony, eds., *Government and Economies in the Postwar World — Economic Policies and Comparative Performance, 1945–85*. New York: Routledge, 1990.

Hughes, Jonathan R. T., *American Economic History*. Glenview, Ill.: Scott, Foresman, 1983.

Millet, Allan R., ed., *A Short History of the Vietnam War*. Bloomington: Indiana University Press, 1978.

Niemi, Albert W., Jr., *U.S. Economic History: A Survey of the Major Issues*. Chicago: Rand McNally, 1975.

Price, Harry Bayard, *The Marshall Plan and Its Meaning*. Ithaca, N.Y.: Cornell University Press (under the auspices of the Governmental Affairs Institute), 1955.

Stein, Herbert, *Presidential Economics*. New York: Simon and Schuster, 1984. Covers presidents from Roosevelt to early Reagan with in-depth, interpretive historical treatment of economic events and policy.

NOTES

1. From Friedman, Milton, and Schwartz, Anna, *A Monetary History of the United States — 1867–1960*. Princeton, N.J.: Princeton University Press, 1963.

2. It should be recognized that, although the sum total of all of the new government programs through 1941 did not comprise a fiscal stimulus sufficient to raise the economy from depression, there were positive intangible effects. Many who lived through the Depression have attested that the myriad of Roosevelt initiatives signaled that the government was fully engaged in trying to end the Depression. This impression probably contributed to political stability in the United States during these years.

3. See Stein, Herbert, *The Fiscal Revolution in America*. Washington, D.C.: AEI Press, 1990.

4. The number of military personnel was reduced from approximately 12 million in 1945 to 1.5 million by 1947. Not all of the demobilized personnel chose to enter the civilian labor force. Actually, the civilian labor force increased by "only" 6.3 million during 1945–47. Chapter 3 provides further discussion of the employment aspects of this transition.

5. Although there were some deficits under Kennedy's predecessor, Eisenhower, nevertheless, recorded 3 of the 8 budget surpluses of the 1946–93 time period.

6. Estimates of total killed vary, as do estimates of total cost. Many sources cite a total cost of $150 billion, but it is not clear whether this is meant to be an incremental cost that is entirely attributable to the Viet Nam War (as is intended here) or whether other military costs that would have been incurred in the absence of the war are included.

2

Gross Domestic Product

Gross domestic product (GDP), accounts for all goods and services produced in the United States in a given year and is probably the most widely reported economic statistic.[1] GDP is commonly broken down into consumption (C), investment (I), government purchases (G),[2] and net exports (X – M, exports minus imports), which yields the equation often found in economics textbooks:

$$C + I + G + (X - M) = GDP$$

GDP is the best known standard of living indicator, and raising it is (arguably) the primary objective of economic policy.[3] However, the temptation should be resisted to regard GDP growth as the all-important measure of economic performance.

To appreciate presidential economic performance, factors that underlie GDP growth must be considered, including the broad range of economic variables that fosters, and inhibits, GDP growth. For example, in addition to the components of GDP (C, I, G, X, and M), GDP growth is also positively correlated with other economic variables presented in Part I, including employment growth, productivity, and saving. The relationship between these variables and GDP can be seen as two-way: these variables not only contribute to but also result from higher GDP. For example, a higher national income, or GDP, will allow a higher level of national consumption, and higher consumption leads to higher GDP. The same is true for many of the other variables. Because these variables lay the ground for present and future GDP growth, GDP, by itself, cannot tell the whole story of economic performance. Thus, although GDP may be viewed by some as the bottom line of economic performance, it is, rather, the components of GDP and other driving economic indicators (e.g., employment rate, productivity) that are the building blocks of economic growth and more closely measure the impact of economic policies.

The main reason that one must look beyond mere average GDP growth rates to an array of indicators is that a broader set of indicators provides insights into whether GDP growth *would* have been higher or lower *under a given set of economic conditions.* If, for example, GDP growth were mediocre for a particular president but savings and investment rates were high, the overall presidential performance rating would have to be raised, because the higher saving and investment rates would have laid the basis for a future GDP growth rate toward the upper level feasible under the prevailing economic conditions (domestic and international). This upward adjustment is especially important if the president would not get credit for the higher GDP growth, that is, if the growth resulting from higher saving and investment occurred beyond the one-year time lag. Yet, it is stressed that without a comprehensive review of economic policy measures, it would remain unknown how much the president had to do with the savings and investment improvements that underlie GDP growth.

Figure 2.1, growth of GDP, is based on annual data from the U.S. Department of Commerce, which is the official source for GDP data. The Department of Commerce also makes the announcements of monthly and quarterly GDP growth, which the news media reports and which pollsters and politicians closely track. As is well-known, these announcements can have significant short-term impact, both political and economic, which is sometimes registered in the stock market (Chapter 9). Figure 2.1, on the other hand, creates a long time-horizon over which to view GDP growth. GDP growth rates rather than levels are used because it is easier to interpret GDP improvements through growth rates, which are relative measures. Growth rates are adjusted for inflation.

OVERVIEW OF TRENDS IN THE LONG RUN, 1946–93

From 1946 to 1993, GDP grew at an average rate of 3.0 percent.[4] Within this time frame, three separate growth periods are evident, as Figure 2.1 illustrates. The first period is of the volatile post-war years, 1946–51 (in which GDP grew at an annual average of 0.2 percent counting 1946 or 4.2 percent if starting with 1947), which gave way to the relatively stable, moderate to high growth years of 1952–69 (average growth of 3.4 percent). The third period, which began with a mild recession, runs from 1970 to the present and has been characterized by moderate growth (an average of 2.5 percent) interrupted by four recessions of varying degrees (an average of one every six years).

Figure 2.1 shows that the growth in GDP fluctuated more sharply during the Truman administration than in subsequent years. In fact, even more volatility would be evident if the full magnitude of the 1946 decline were illustrated. The decline in GDP for 1946 is not fully represented on the graph because the enormous 20.6 percent decline in GDP

FIGURE 2.1
Growth of Gross Domestic Product, 1946–93
(Adjusted for Inflation)

Real GDP Growth Rate

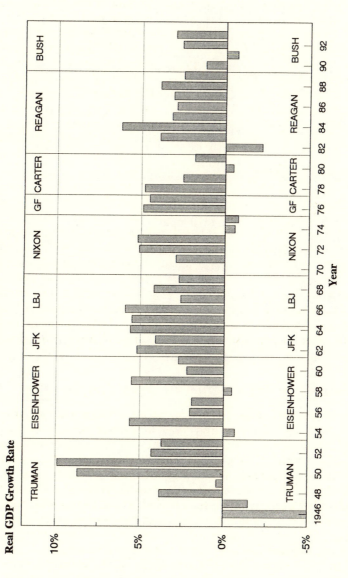

Source: U.S. Department of Commerce.

that occurred in that year would distort the scale of the graph and obscure comparisons of subsequent years.[5] The graph truncates the downward spike in 1946 at 5 percent, a level chosen in recognition of the fact that the next largest decline was only 2.2 percent.

The Truman administration in 1947 continued to experience negative growth, but at a much more moderate −1.5 percent. In 1948, growth recovered to 3.8 percent and, in 1949, there was a mild recession, although overall growth for the year was a positive 0.4 percent.[6] Thereafter, the Truman administration recorded positive growth. Growth rates reached the highest post-war levels before or since, at 8.7 and 9.9 percent in 1950 and 1951, respectively, coinciding with the build-up for the Korean War, which began in June 1950. After the period of relative volatility in growth, the economy gradually settled down, closing out the Truman years with growth rates of 4.3 and 3.7 percent in 1952 and 1953, respectively. The difference between the high and low growth years for Truman was quite large, 11.4 percentage points, from −1.5 percent to 9.9 percent (if 1946 is counted, the difference is 30.5 percentage points). The high level of volatility under Truman was undoubtedly caused by the transition to a peacetime economy, which required a tremendous reduction in military expenditures and, therefore, the government budget and a major retooling of U.S. productive capacity.

GDP growth in the Eisenhower years was still volatile compared with subsequent years but much less so than during Truman. The Eisenhower years began with a moderate recession, −0.7 percent growth in 1954, probably owing a good deal to the end of the Korean War and a reduction of the budgetary outlays needed to sustain it. This mild recession was followed by very strong growth of 5.6 percent in 1955, then a gradual slowing of the growth rate leading to a mild economic downturn in 1958, when GDP fell by 0.5 percent. The 1958 recession was followed by a very strong recovery, though not of the magnitude of 1950, as the economy grew at 5.5 percent. During the last two years of the Eisenhower administration, growth moderated to 2.2 and 2.7 percent for 1960 and 1961, respectively. The administrations that followed did not experience the sharp swings of Truman and, to a lesser extent, Eisenhower, with growth rates remaining within a moderate range of −2.2 percent to 6.2 percent (both of which occurred during the Reagan years).

During Kennedy and Johnson, growth was positive for all years, hovering between 4 and 6 percent from 1962 to 1966, with most years 5.5 percent or more, before tapering off to a 3.2 percent average during 1967–69. In 1970, the first year attributable to Nixon, the GDP growth rate was zero for the year, including a light recession that occurred in the first two quarters (as well as the fourth quarter of 1969), and ended an 11-year run (1959–69) of positive growth years, the longest run since World War II.[7] This period of growth may have been extended, first, by the Kennedy-Johnson tax cut of 1964–65 and, later, by expenditures for the Viet Nam War. The economic slowdown of 1970 was followed by three years of gradually increasing growth that reached 5.2 percent in 1973; a two-year recession hit in 1974–75, during which GDP declined by 0.6 and 0.8 percent, respectively. After Ford took over for Nixon, the economy entered a recovery, growing robustly in 1976 and 1977 at 4.9 and 4.5 percent, respectively.

Under Carter, growth continued at 4.8 percent in 1978 and 2.5 percent in 1979 and fell to –0.5 percent in the recession of 1980. A one-year recovery, attributable to Carter, occurred in 1981, with growth of 1.8 percent. In 1982, under the first year of Reagan, there was a major recession in which the economy declined by 2.2 percent. Excluding the negative growth of 1946, this decline was the largest since World War II. In 1983, the economy emerged strongly from recession with growth of 3.9 percent followed by 6.2 percent in 1984, the highest growth rate since 1951. From 1983 through 1990, on an annual average basis, there was uninterrupted growth of the economy.[8] This eight-year economic expansion was second only to the period of 1959–69 as the longest expansion since World War II. The eight years of steady growth tapered off in 1990 to 1.2 percent, dipping into recession in the third and fourth quarters of that year. The recession continued through the first quarter of 1991, with average growth for the year of –0.7 percent. Positive growth resumed by the second quarter of 1991 and continued through 1993, recording growth rates of 2.6 and 3.0 percent for 1992–93.

PRESIDENTIAL RANKINGS

In ranking the presidents' GDP performances, growth rate averages are well-complemented by the trend improvement indicator. It is not sufficient in the cases of GDP growth to look only at averages; one must also see the direction in which a president "took" economic growth. For some indicators, because of high volatility of trends, for example, the stock market levels, trend changes do not offer much information, because they vary so greatly with the end points of the trend period while not indicating any economic trend beyond that year. GDP behaves differently and trend changes clearly show the change in the rate of economic expansion from the beginning of an administration to its end. However, it is granted that the trend improvement indicator can be very sensitive to the business cycle, over which presidents have only modest influence. Table 2.1 shows the presidents' rankings of average GDP growth rates and trend changes from best to worst.

Although these rankings suggest responsibility for the GDP growth rates as well as comparability between the presidents, it is stressed here and throughout the text that the control by the president of the economy may, at times, be tenuous at best and that each president did operate in a distinct economic world. With that said, a discussion of the rankings follows. The presidents' performances are discussed according

TABLE 2.1
Gross Domestic Product Growth Rates

Average GDP Growth Rate			*Change in GDP Growth Trend*	
President	*Term*	*Percent*	*President*	*Percentage Points*
Kennedy	1961–63	4.8	Ford	5.3
Ford	1974–77	4.6	Truman	5.2
Johnson	1963–69	4.1	Kennedy	3.0
Truman	1945–53	4.0	Reagan	0.8
Reagan	1981–89	2.9	Bush	0.5
Eisenhower	1953–61	2.3	Eisenhower	−1.0
Carter	1977–81	2.1	Carter	−2.7
Nixon	1969–74	1.9	Johnson	−2.9
Bush	1989–93	1.5	Nixon	−3.5
Average, 1946–93		3.0		

to their rankings rather than in chronological order as in the foregoing long-run overview. For each president, the average GDP growth rate is first discussed and then qualified by the growth rate change or trend value.

Presidents Kennedy and Ford had the highest GDP growth rates, but they also had the shortest tenures, with Kennedy in the White House for two years and eleven months and Ford for two years and five months. Kennedy came into office during the early stage of the longest post-war expansion, and Ford's record begins with a robust recovery after two recessionary years. Neither president really endured a full business cycle. Yet, the increases in the growth rate that were achieved under Ford, 5.3 percentage points (the largest improvement of any president) and Kennedy, 3.0, percentage points — indicate that the already good situation that they inherited did improve during their tenures.

Johnson's growth rate of 4.1 percent is impressive because it was over a five-year period and it followed six years of solid growth. However, although he exited office with a significantly positive growth rate, the growth rate itself declined by 2.9 percentage points from an initial 5.6 percent in 1964 to 2.7 percent in 1969.

Truman, Reagan, and Eisenhower round out the middle third of the ranking with growth rates of 4.0, 2.9, and 2.3 percent, respectively. In addition to achieving the higher growth rate, Truman stands out as having increased the GDP growth rate by 5.2 percentage points. However, as mentioned, the results for Truman do not include 1946, because the large drop in GDP growth in that year may yield misleading or exaggerated results for the trend figure. If Truman's performance were measured from 1946 rather than 1947, his average growth rate would be only 0.6 percent, but the growth rate improvement would be 24.4 percent. This radically different result is due to the previously mentioned −20.6 drop in GDP that occurred immediately after World War II. Reagan also increased the GDP growth rate over 1981 by 0.8 percentage points, while Eisenhower slightly reduced the GDP growth rate by 1.0 percentage point.

Carter, Nixon, and Bush recorded the lowest average growth rates of 2.1, 1.9, and 1.5 percent, respectively. While recording rather modest growth rates, Carter and Nixon also left GDP growth rates that were well below what they inherited. Under Carter, GDP growth declined 2.7 percentage points, while under Nixon, the decline was 3.5 percentage points. Bush had the lowest average growth rate, but because he left office during a recovery, the GDP growth rate increased by 0.5 percentage points.[9]

SUMMARY AND SELECTED ISSUES

For many, the performance of the earlier presidents, Truman and Eisenhower, has been forgotten or was never very well-known. In summary, it can be said that growth was respectable, averaging around 3.2 percent for Truman and Eisenhower; however, there *were* recessions and slow growth years as well. In some years, there was quite high, but not astronomical, growth (not exceeding, for example, 10 percent), as some might believe. In fact, growth was higher during the succeeding Kennedy-Johnson period. Historically high growth still has been attainable in recent years, but not quite as high and not as sustained.

In the past 15 years, many strong perceptions about presidential performance have developed. Two examples are discussed here in the context of GDP growth to supplement the previous historical discussion. A more critical look is taken at the Carter-Reagan comparison and the characterization of Bush's economic performance as the worst in 50 years.

What some may find surprising is that Carter's average growth rate of GDP, 2.1 percent, was not all that inferior to Reagan's 2.9 percent. In fact, if calculated without a one-year lag, both Carter's and Reagan's growth rates are 2.8 percent. This fact may be surprising because, as mentioned, it was well-known that under Reagan, the United States had the second longest (sometimes presented as the longest) post-war recovery/expansion in history, beginning in the fourth quarter of 1982 and continuing for eight years. This expansion would suggest that Reagan's average GDP growth would have been considerably higher given that Carter left office during an economic downturn and that he was not perceived as an economic success. In addition, the frequent and largely unrebutted attacks on the Carter economic performance might lead to the perception of a lower average growth rate for his administration.

The question can be resolved by noting that, although the growth rate during the Carter administration was a reasonable 2.1 percent, Carter inherited from the Ford administration an economy already in a rapid recovery, with a 4.9 percent growth rate in 1976. Growth continued strong, recording 4.5 percent in 1977 and 4.8 percent in 1978. However, growth plummeted to –0.5 percent in 1980, the election year, before recovering rather weakly to 1.8 percent in 1981. The growth trend was decidedly downward during his administration, thus, bequeathing to Reagan a more anemically growing economy.

In addition, it must be taken into account that the 2.9 percent growth rate of the Reagan administration bears the burden of the –2.2 percent GDP decline during the major recession of 1982. Many economists believe that one reason for the 1982 recession was the policies pursued (mainly tight monetary policy) to rid the economy of the historically high inflation during the Carter administration. If a two-year rather than a one-year lag were used, thus, attributing the recession of 1982 to the Carter administration, then the average growth rate for Carter would fall to 0.4 percent, while the average growth rate for Reagan would rise to 3.4 percent. However, a one-year lag has been selected as the most appropriate and is applied uniformly as the basis for comparison for all indicators in Part I (except for the money supply).

A second controversy (arising in 1992), that the Bush administration had the worst economic record in 50 years, is an interesting charge and calls for some review of the Bush economic record in comparison with other presidents. During the Bush administration, average GDP growth was indeed the lowest since the World War II era. In the last year for which the Reagan administration was responsible, 1989, the growth rate was 2.5 percent, and for the first year of the Bush administration, it was 1.2 percent. The GDP growth rate was negative for 1991, recording –0.7 percent. GDP turned positive in the second quarter of 1991 and continued positive through 1992, recording an average of 2.6 percent. Economic growth further improved in 1993 to 3.0 percent.

Thus, the charge leveled against the Bush administration that it had the worst economic record in 50 years (i.e., since 1942, during the Franklin Roosevelt administration) is true from the standpoint of the GDP growth rate. However, because GDP is not the all-important performance indicator, the charge must be examined in terms of the other indicators, such as employment, productivity, and inflation. A further evaluation of this charge is carried out in the employment and inflation chapters. As will be seen, the examples of the Carter and Nixon administrations and others with respect to a wider range of major indicators weaken the validity of the charge against Bush's economic performance.

SUGGESTIONS FOR FURTHER READING

Carson, Carol S., and Jaszi, George, "The National Income and Product Accounts: An Overview." *Survey of Current Business* 61 (February 1981): 22–34.

Clayton, Gary E., and Giesbrecht, Martin Gehard, *A Guide to Everyday Economics.* New York: McGraw Hill, 1990. Provides a very readable and concise explanation of some major economic indicators.

"Integrated Economic and Environmental Satellite Accounts." *Survey of Current Business* 74 (April 1994): 33–49 describes a new accounting framework that takes into account the effects of economic activity on the environment. The term "satellite accounts" refers to the fact that the environmental accounting framework is meant to supplement, rather than replace, conventional national accounting.

National Income and Product Accounts of the United States Vols. 1 (1929–58) and 2 (1959–88). Washington, D.C.: U.S. Department of Commerce, Economics and Statistics Administration, Bureau of Economic Analysis, 1992.

Young, Alan H., and Tice, Helen Stone, "Introduction to National Economic Accounting." *Survey of Current Business* 65 (March 1985): 59–76.

In addition, in its September issues, the *Survey of Current Business* publishes historical annual and quarterly data from 1929 to the present of GDP and its components in current and constant dollars.

NOTES

1. Gross national product, which *was* the more-often used concept, has given way to GDP as the preferred indicator of national income among U.S. statisticians. Although the two indicators are very close in concept, there is a slight difference: essentially, gross national product includes net factor income/payments from abroad, which GDP does not.

2. Government purchases is distinguished from government expenditures in that government purchases excludes (in descending order of magnitude of 1993 budget shares) government transfer payments, such as welfare and unemployment compensation (43.6 percent), grants to state and local governments (12.5 percent), net interest paid (12.1 percent), and subsidies (2.2 percent). These exclusions accounted for $1,051.8 billion out of a total budget of $1,495.3 billion or over 70 percent of total federal outlays in 1993. Inclusion of, for example, transfer payments in the computation of GDP would constitute double counting and, thus, overestimate GDP. Total government expenditure, which includes transfer payments, is the subject of Part II.

3. A frequent critique of the GDP concept is that it does not always accurately capture a country's standard of living and is, sometimes, even inversely related. For example, when earthquakes and floods hit, living standards are clearly lowered. In the aftermath, a great deal of rebuilding must take place, which increases GDP. In the end, people have endured major hardships and spent a lot of resources just to get back to their predisaster status, while GDP has recorded an increase. The same is true when a crime is committed. The commission of a crime lowers society's living standard, but dealing with the crime requires law enforcement, court, and prison costs, which increase GDP. A new type of accounting called "Green Accounting" has emerged that attempts to take into account some of the shortcomings of GDP, such as failure to consider environmental quality and depletion of natural resources. However, because this is a relatively new accounting method, it does not offer any historical context and cannot be used for this analysis.

4.   This growth rate is calculated beginning with the constant GDP level at the end of 1946/beginning of 1947, that is, the large drop in real GDP during 1946 is not included. If it were, then the growth rate for the period from the end of 1945 to the beginning of 1946 would be 2.4 percent.

5.   Under an important assumption, an alternative and more "normal" growth rate can be calculated for 1946. The assumption is that, because the deficit was incurred almost entirely for wartime needs, the deficit, therefore, consisted mainly of government purchases of goods and services rather than transfer payments. This assumption is important because purchases are counted in GDP, but transfer payments are not. Thus, if the amount of the huge 1945 budget deficit, which amounted to 22.5 percent of GDP, were excluded from GDP for year-end 1945, then the growth in GDP for 1946 calculated from this adjusted year-end 1945 figure would be a positive 2.4 percent. The 2.4 percent growth rate actually requires a second assumption because it ignores the likely additional growth that would have occurred had the deficit portion of the government resources been allocated to the private sector. As it is, Truman's average and the entire period average are measured from the end of 1946 GDP figure rather than the beginning of 1946/end of 1945.

6.   A recession is defined as two successive quarters of negative GDP growth.

7.   However, there were 5 quarters of negative growth (out of a total of 46 quarters) scattered throughout this period.

8.   The Department of Commerce reported negative growth of 0.3 percent for the second quarter of 1986, although overall growth for 1986 was a positive 2.9 percent.

9.   An interesting feature of government statistics is the revision of previous year' data. For example, in late 1992, Bush's growth rates for 1990–92 were recorded at 0.8, –1.2, and 2.3 percent, respectively, but were all revised upward to 1.2, –0.7, and 2.8 percent after the election.

3

Employment Growth and the Unemployment Rate

Employment indicators, such as the number employed and the unemployment rate, are preeminent measures of economic performance and are closely related to other measures of economic performance. For instance, they correspond fairly closely to gross domestic product (GDP) growth. If employment is growing or unemployment is falling (the distinction is explained below), then it is likely that GDP is increasing. These indicators have, in the past, sometimes been perceived as *inversely* related to inflation by policy makers who view increasing unemployment, or decreasing employment, as a way to counteract higher inflation.[1] Employment indicators also provide a measure of the extent to which people share in whatever growth is occurring by virtue of their being employed. Finally, in today's "safety net" society in which the government makes transfer payments to persons who are unemployed, an increase in unemployment carries a double cost: the lost production from the unemployed worker and the increased expense to the government, and, therefore, to the taxpayer, of unemployment compensation and other transfers. Thus, it is important to national economic health for unemployment to be low.

As alluded to above, two measures are used in this chapter to capture employment performance. The unemployment rate is the most commonly used labor market indicator and represents the percentage of workers in the labor force (i.e., those working and seeking work) that are unemployed and, in this way, measures the underutilization of a productive resource. However, as a measure of presidential economic performance, the unemployment rate does not take into account that, for the past 30 years, an ever-higher percentage of the population has been seeking employment.

The *participation rate*, that is, the percentage of the noninstitutional population that is part of the labor force, has risen since the early 1960s from around 59 percent to over 66 percent in the 1990s. This increase may be somewhat smaller than that suggested by often-heard political rhetoric that claims that two income earners are required to support a household where before one sufficed. Nevertheless, this increase in the participation rate poses a greater challenge to the economy to meet the demand for jobs and keep the unemployment rate low. With the growth in the participation rate, the unemployment rate can increase even though the economy is creating more jobs. Because of the increase in the participation rate as well as in the overall population, the growth in employment indicator is needed to compliment the unemployment rate because it captures the actual increase in the total number of jobs in the economy, a key criterion of economic performance. Growth in employment, or the net creation of jobs, is, therefore, chosen as the second indicator for measuring employment performance and is one that often has been the focus of political campaigns.[2]

Employment data for Figures 3.1 and 3.2 are from the U.S. Department of Labor, Bureau of Labor Statistics (BLS). The labor market statistics of the BLS are reported on a monthly basis, as well as quarterly and annually, and always attract the attention of the news media, pollsters, and politicians. The graphs use annual data of the BLS and create a longer time horizon over which to view changes in the unemployment rate and employment.

OVERVIEW OF TRENDS IN THE LONG RUN, 1946–93[3]

The unique circumstances immediately following World War II affected the behavior of both unemployment and employment growth during 1946–47 in ways that, on the surface, might be puzzling. Paradoxically, it is surprising that, for the years 1946–47 the *civilian* unemployment rate was as low as it was but also that it was as high as it was. Either high or low unemployment rates reasonably might have been expected, given the extraordinarily large demobilization of U.S. military personnel after 1945 and the economy's response. In 1946 alone, the shift to a peacetime economy transferred almost 9 million people out of military and into civilian life. Another 2.8 million followed in 1947. The economy responded by raising civilian employment by 2.4 million (4.6 percent) in 1946 and 2.5 million (4.6 percent) in 1947. The effect on the unemployment rate was a 2 percentage point *increase* from 1.9 to 3.9 percent during 1946, which held through 1947. However, it would have been reasonable to assume that the unemployment rate would have risen much higher because of the release of 11.5 million people into civilian life and that, at least initially, the unemployment rate would have soared. On the other hand, with the growth of employment at a rate that has yet to be surpassed, the unemployment rate well might have held at its low wartime level. (Employment statistics are illustrated in Figure 3.1, for the civilian unemployment rate, and Figure 3.2, for the civilian employment growth rate.)

FIGURE 3.1
Unemployment Rate, 1946–93

(Percent of Civilian Labor Force)

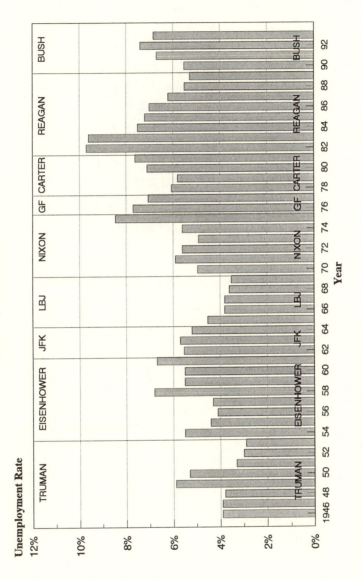

Source: U.S. Bureau of Labor Statistics.

FIGURE 3.2
Employment Growth, 1946–93   (Annual Percent Change)

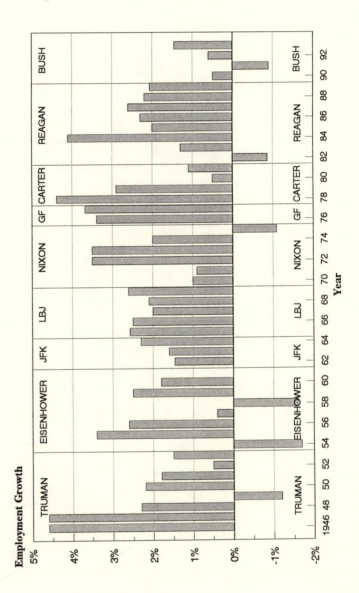

Source: U.S. Bureau of Labor Statistics.

The reconciliation of these observations is in the fact that almost half (about 46 percent) of those demobilized did not seek civilian employment after the war.[4] Almost 5.3 million of the 11.5 million demobilized personnel, a large proportion of which were female, chose not to join the civilian labor force and, perhaps, the ranks of the unemployed. That work seekers were fewer than might have been helps explain the less than astronomical (albeit post-war high) civilian employment growth rate. The decision of so many not to seek civilian unemployment softened the increase in unemployment. The explanation for the doubling of the unemployment rate from a very low 1945 level in the face of sharply growing civilian employment is that, although not all demobilized personnel joined the labor force, the labor force still grew even faster, a 3.6 million increase (6.8 percent of the total), than the number employed in 1946, a 2.4 million increase. The changes in the labor participation rate, defined as the civilian labor force divided by the civilian noninstitutional population 16 years old and older, played only a minor role in muting the increases in unemployment and employment growth, falling only 1.5 percentage points in 1946 to 57.3 percent and rising 1 percentage point to 58.3 percent in 1947 (see Appendix B).

Unemployment Rate

The peak unemployment rates shown in Figure 3.1, as would be expected, track very closely with the recessionary troughs identified in the GDP growth graph (Figure 2.1). Substantial increases in unemployment coincide with the recessions of 1949, 1954, 1958, 1970, 1975, 1980, 1982, and 1991. In addition, there is a perceptible trend upward in unemployment rates, that is, both the peaks and the troughs are higher as time passes from the 1940s to the early 1980s. Thereafter, this trend flattened out, and the unemployment trough of 1988–90 and the peak of 1991–93 were lower than the trough of 1978–79 and the peak of 1982–83. The average unemployment rate for the 1946–93 period was 5.8 percent.

Under Truman, unemployment rates start at 3.9, 3.9, and 3.8 percent during 1946–48, rise to 5.9 percent in 1949, and drop to around 3.0 percent for the next three years. Unemployment rates were higher under Eisenhower, starting with the 1954 recession, in the aftermath of the Korean War, at 5.5 percent dropping to slightly above the 4 percent level for three years, and reaching 6.8 percent in the 1958 recession. The unemployment rate then dropped to 5.5 percent for 1959–60 before hitting the next slow growth year, 1961, when unemployment climbed back up to 6.7 percent.

The unemployment rate fell fairly steadily throughout the Kennedy and Johnson years, from around 5.6 percent to 3.5 percent. This downward trend continued for seven of the eight years, at the end of which the economy was still at a higher level of unemployment (0.6

percentage point higher) than at the end of the Truman administration. Under Nixon, unemployment jumped to 4.9 percent of the labor force in 1970, then flirted with the 6 percent level for several years (although, in 1973, the rate was only 4.8 percent) before vaulting to 8.5 percent in the 1975 recession. Unemployment improved substantially over the next four years, and the rate fell to 5.8 percent in 1979. However, unemployment took off again and increased for the next three years, reaching a post-war high of 9.7 percent (on an annual average basis) in the 1982 recession, remaining near that level in 1983 (9.6 percent), although prior to year-end 1983, the trend was well on its way downward. Some may recall that unemployment topped 10 percent during 1982, which is true, but the *average* for the year was 9.7 percent.

Over the next six years, under Reagan, unemployment plummeted from 9.6 percent to 5.3 percent in 1989, which was the lowest level since 1973. The economy slipped back into recession in 1990, although unemployment was only 5.5 percent for the year, and remained in recession until early 1991, as the unemployment rate rose to 6.7 percent in 1991. By 1992, the unemployment rate had increased to 7.4 percent, although at year-end, unemployment had fallen back to 7 percent and edged down further to 6.8 percent in 1993.

Growth in Employment

As previously discussed, the growth rate of employment is also included in the discussion, because it does not penalize a president's employment performance record because of the increasing participation rate (i.e., the rise in the percentage of the population in the labor force, employed and unemployed) as does the unemployment rate. The long-term trend in the civilian labor force participation rate was an increase from 55.8 percent in 1946 to 66.2 percent in 1993. This increase is largely because of the increasing participation of women, whether electively or out of economic need, in the workforce. The large influx of women into the labor force started in the 1960s. With the participation rate rising, it has become more difficult for the economy, or the president, to keep the unemployment rate low, because a higher percentage of people are seeking work. The growth rate of employment takes this phenomenon into account by simply measuring the net increase in the total number of jobs in the economy and, thus, provides a useful compliment to the unemployment rate.

The general observations over the entire 48-year period depicted in Figure 3.2 are the high degree of fluctuation of employment growth during the Truman and Eisenhower administrations relative to those of succeeding presidents (as was observed in the case of GDP growth), the moderate and sustained growth during 1962–74, and the moderate to high growth occasionally interrupted by declines from 1974 to 1993. The average growth rate for 1946–93 was 1.8 percent.

By 1948, the shock of demobilization largely had subsided, and employment recorded a growth rate of 2.3 percent. In the 1949 recession, the number employed fell 1.2 percent, but it increased for the next four years, 1950–53, at rates of 2.2, 1.8, 0.5, and 1.5 percent, respectively. During Eisenhower's two recessions of 1954 and 1958, employment dropped substantially, at rates of 1.7 and 1.6 percent, respectively. Between the 1954 and 1958 recessions, employment growth was, on average, strong, including growth rates of 3.4 and 2.6 percent during 1955–56. After the 1958 recession, total employment grew at 2.5 and 1.8 percent, with a negligible decline (–0.05 percent) in the last year of the Eisenhower period.

With the arrival of Kennedy, employment growth picked up and maintained steady and mostly significant growth throughout his administration, the Johnson years through 1969, and the first five years of Nixon's administration. It was not until the recession of 1975 that the employment level declined. For the three-year Kennedy period, employment growth was in the 1.5 to 2.3 percent range, while for Johnson, it was in the 2.0 to 2.6 percent range. Under Nixon, the first two years of growth were a modest 1.0 and 0.9 percent, respectively, but then accelerated to 3.5 percent for both 1972 and 1973. In 1974, as recession set in in the second half of the year, employment growth fell to a still-respectable 2.0 percent before tumbling to –1.1 percent in 1975, thus, ending 13 straight years of positive employment growth, 10 of which outpaced population growth.

Fortunately, during the two-year Ford administration and the first two years of the Carter administration, employment growth recovered very strongly. Ford recorded growth rates of 3.4 and 3.7 for 1976 and 1977. Under Carter, growth rates were 4.4 percent in 1978, the highest since 1947, and 2.9 percent in 1979. The Carter period closed with employment growing at 0.5 and 1.1 percent for 1980 and 1981.

The Reagan period began with a drop in employment of –0.9 percent, reflecting the deep recession of 1982. However, employment growth was substantial for the remaining seven years of the Reagan period. In 1983, growth recovered to 1.3 percent, then leaped to 4.1 percent in 1984, the second highest employment growth rate since 1947, and remained in the 2.0 to 2.6 percent range for the next five years through 1989. Under Bush, growth slowed to 0.5 percent in 1990, declined by 0.9 percent in 1991, and recovered modestly to 0.6 percent in 1992 and further to 1.5 percent in 1993.

PRESIDENTIAL RANKINGS

Unemployment Rate

The presidents' unemployment rates and trend improvements rankings are given in Table 3.1. As unemployment is undesirable,[5] the

TABLE 3.1
Unemployment Rates

Average Unemployment Rate			Change in Unemployment Rate — Trend	
President	Term	Percent	President	Percentage Points
Johnson	1963–69	3.8	Reagan	−2.3
Truman	1945–53	4.0	Johnson	−1.7
Eisenhower	1953–61	5.4	Kennedy	−1.5
Kennedy	1961–63	5.5	Ford	−1.4
Nixon	1969–74	5.9	Truman	−1.0
Bush	1989–93	6.6	Carter	0.6
Carter	1974–77	6.7	Bush	1.6
Reagan	1981–89	7.2	Eisenhower	3.8
Ford	1974–77	7.4	Nixon	4.9
Average, 1946–93		5.7		

lowest values of averages and trend changes are rated highest. The fact that the economy was in a lower unemployment environment in the first half of the 1946–93 period is not factored into the rankings.[6] Examining both the change in the unemployment rate as well as the average rate for each president is particularly informative in the cases of Reagan, Eisenhower, Nixon, and Ford, whose records on unemployment averages were significantly different from their records on unemployment trends.

Johnson and Truman had the lowest average unemployment rates while also reducing the rate they inherited. Eisenhower recorded the third lowest unemployment rate, averaging 5.4 percent while in office, but left with the unemployment rate 3.8 percentage points above the rate he inherited. Kennedy, who averaged a 5.5 percent unemployment rate, on the other hand, recorded a reduction of 1.5 percentage points. Nixon's average unemployment rate was 5.9 percent. Although a desirable rate by today's standards, there was a strong upward trend under Nixon. The unemployment rate was raised almost 5 percentage points (from 3.5 to 8.5 percent) during his tenure, mainly because he resigned in the midst of a recession, which worsened his overall unemployment rate record.

The unemployment rate was a relatively high 6.6 percent during the Bush administration, on average, and the trend change was a 1.5 percentage point increase. Carter's unemployment was about the same, and he also raised unemployment, although to a lesser degree than did Bush. Reagan had the second highest unemployment rate, but he also reduced unemployment more than any other president, 2.3 percentage points, again showing the importance of the trend change as a compliment to averages in measuring performance. This large improvement in the trend also attests to the high rate of unemployment during Carter's last year. Finally, although unemployment was the highest under Ford, he also must be credited with decreasing unemployment by 1.4 percentage points.

Employment Growth

The presidents' rankings of employment growth rates and trend changes from best to worst are shown in Table 3.2, with the higher positive values for the indicators obviously commanding the higher rating. Because employment growth rates were somewhat volatile, often fluctuating between positive and negative values, the trend change indicator should be assigned limited value as an indicator of a president's economic performance.[7]

President Ford ranked the highest both in the rate of growth, 3.6 percent, and in the improvement in the growth rate, 4.8 percentage points. Johnson had the next highest average growth rate, 2.3 percent, and a slight improvement in the growth rate. Carter was third at 2.2 percent but decreased the growth rate by 2.6 percentage points (similar to his GDP performance). Reagan ranked fourth with a 2.0 percent employment growth while also increasing the growth rate by 0.8 percentage points. Kennedy follows with 1.8 percent and a significant improvement in the trend of 2.3 percentage points. Nixon recorded moderate employment growth, 1.6 percent, but the growth rate fell 3.7 percentage points from what he inherited, which was the largest decrease.

TABLE 3.2
Employment Growth Rates

Average Employment Growth Rate		Change in Employment Growth — Trend	
President	Percent	President	Percentage Points
Ford	3.5	Ford	4.8
Johnson	2.3	Kennedy	2.3
Carter	2.2	Reagan	1.0
Reagan	1.9	Johnson	0.3
Kennedy	1.8	Bush	−0.6
Nixon	1.6	Eisenhower	−1.6
Truman	1.6	Carter	−2.6
Eisenhower	0.9	Truman	−3.1
Bush	0.4	Nixon	−3.7
Average, 1946–93	1.7		

Although he began with fairly rapid employment growth, Truman, somewhat surprisingly, had only a 1.6 percent growth rate and a sharply declining trend (by 3.1 percentage points). Eisenhower, also somewhat surprisingly, had a low growth rate of 0.9 percent and reduced the growth rate by 1.6 percentage points. Eisenhower's average was especially hurt by the recessions of 1954 and 1958. Bush, who spent much of his tenure struggling out of recession and into a hesitant recovery, had only slight growth in employment, 0.4 percent, accompanied by a mild worsening in the growth rate of 0.6 percentage points.

SUMMARY AND SELECTED ISSUES

Summary

Although employment and GDP growth are closely correlated, as shown by correspondence of declining employment with recessions,[8] employment did not grow as fast as GDP. This phenomenon is understandable because employment can grow only to the point where everyone in the labor force is employed. GDP growth does not have this limitation and can rise rapidly at times because of technological innovations or other productivity increases or with the discovery and opening of new markets. This constraint on employment growth explains why the presidents' average growth rates of employment tended to be considerably lower than they were for GDP.

Similarly, the lower limit on unemployment reduction may explain why some presidents had especially modest employment growth rates. Because unemployment during their tenures was already so low, it was difficult to attain employment growth that was any higher than labor force growth. Economists widely acknowledge that it is virtually impossible to eliminate all unemployment considering that there are always people changing jobs and that it takes time for workers to switch from economic sectors that are declining to those that are expanding.

Over the long run, it was observed that unemployment rates were substantially reduced during the administrations of Reagan, Johnson, Kennedy, and Ford but that unemployment increased by a greater amount in the Eisenhower, Nixon, Carter, and Bush administrations, such that there was a general increase in unemployment over time. Although the Nixon and Carter administrations had some years of good employment growth, the average employment growth over their full tenures did not keep pace with the growth of the labor force and resulted in higher unemployment. Some have contended that the higher unemployment rate observed in the latter half of the 1946–93 period was because of the divergence between that portion of the labor force that made the transition to the more modern and expanding sectors of the economy and the growing portion of the labor force that did not.

Employment statistics, it is sometimes argued, mask this underlying phenomenon.

Recent Performance Issues

Some of the other recent performance questions deserving a closer look include the disparate performances of Nixon and Ford, the Carter-Reagan comparison, and the characterization of the Bush economic record as the worst in 50 years. On the Nixon/Ford issue, the main reason for the top performance of Ford and the below average performance of Nixon, simply stated, is that Ford took office shortly before the economy began to recover, while Nixon had to resign during a recession, more than two years before the end of his administration. Ford, considering the one-year lagging effect of economic policies, was president only during recovery years. Because Nixon's last year was during a recession, his trend changes were very unfavorable for both the unemployment rate and employment growth. An accounting of the overall Nixon performance under the scenario that he completed his term is presented in Chapter 15.

The comparison of the performances of Reagan and Carter on employment supports the results of the comparison of their performance on the basis of GDP. To assess the relative performances of the two presidents, trend changes and averages for both unemployment and employment growth rates must be compared. Carter recorded good employment growth, although he presided over a sizeable reduction in that growth, 2.6 percentage points. Reagan's average employment growth rate was slightly less than Carter's, 2.0 versus 2.2 percent, although his performance was aided, to some degree, by his increase in the growth rate of employment, 1.0 percentage point. With respect to the unemployment rate, Carter ended with a high rate of unemployment of 7.6 percent and averaged 6.7 percent for his administration. Reagan's average unemployment was higher at 7.3 percent, however, he reduced the unemployment rate more than any other president, 2.3 percentage points, while Carter raised unemployment 0.6 percentage point. Reagan's high average unemployment was mainly because of his first two years, in which unemployment averaged 9.7 and 9.6 percent. In summary, with Reagan's better performance with respect to the unemployment rate and comparable performance on employment growth, his overall employment performance was superior to that of Carter.

Continuing the examination begun in the previous chapter of the charge that Bush had the worst economic record in 50 years, Bush did, in fact, have the lowest employment growth rate, 0.4 percent. On other aspects of employment, he was not the worst. Although Bush's record is poor, both Carter and Nixon reduced employment growth by substantially greater amounts. Nixon and Eisenhower also increased unemployment rates more than Bush. In addition, three presidents, Carter,

Reagan, and Ford, averaged higher unemployment than Bush, although Reagan and Ford actually ended up substantially reducing unemployment. Thus, although it may not be too bold an assertion that Bush did have the worst performance with respect to employment, certainly Carter and Nixon are strong competitors for the distinction of the worst employment performance.

SUGGESTIONS FOR FURTHER READING

Employment and Earnings. Washington, D.C.: U.S. Department of Labor, Bureau of Labor Statistics. Monthly publication offers current updates on employment estimates as well as historical data on employment.

Labor Force Statistics Derived from the Current Population Survey — 1948–87. Bureau of Labor Statistics, August 1988. Provides a comprehensive data set on employment and explanatory notes on historical comparability and estimating methods.

NOTES

1. Economists sometimes refer to this controversial relationship between inflation and employment as the Phillips Curve trade-off, in which inflation rises as the economy reaches full employment. The level of unemployment "required" to keep inflation under control is called the "natural rate of unemployment."

2. Actually, it is the change in the number of "non-farm payroll jobs" that receives more press coverage than the change in total employment.

3. BLS data for 1946 and before are based on the labor force that is 14 years old or older, while data for 1947–93 are based on the labor force that is 16 years old or older. However, data from both definitions of the labor force are available for 1947, the overlap year. The 1946 data are adjusted using a scalar based on the overlap year (see Appendix A, Technical Notes).

4. The total number employed, that is, civilian and military personnel, dropped 5.4 million, or 8.7 percent of the total number employed.

5. Some unemployment may actually be desirable when it represents the share of the labor force that is in the process of voluntarily changing jobs. This form of unemployment is called "frictional unemployment," which is a minimum level of unemployment that arises because of a mismatch between unfilled vacancies and suitable labor. This mismatch is caused by economic growth combined with the inevitable time lags in the functioning of labor markets, such as these job search delays. Frictional unemployment is short-term in nature. There is also usually some structural unemployment in the economy (which is undesirable), which arises from changes in demand or technology that lead to an oversupply of labor with particular skills or in a particular location. There is no implication of unfilled vacancies with structural unemployment, and it tends to be longer-term.

6. This rule — not to attempt to incorporate interperiod changes in the U.S. economic environment in ranking presidents — is followed throughout the text.

7. A formal weighting scheme that assigns relative importance to indicators in measuring presidential economic performance is discussed in Chapter 15.

8. Although many indicators, including employment indicators, are used to determine whether the economy is in recession, typically, a recession is defined as two successive quarters of negative growth, or decline, in GDP.

4

Inflation

Inflation completes the trio of the most prominent economic indicators (which includes gross domestic product (GDP) and employment indicators). The inflation measure used here is the annual change in the consumer price index — all urban consumers (CPI-U), a broad index of prices of goods and services purchased by households for consumption.[1] Among the many price indexes released by the Bureau of Labor Statistics, this CPI-U (CPI is used hereafter) is the index most widely reported by the media. The quantity weights associated with prices of the goods and services in the index are periodically revised to reflect changing relative expenditure patterns in national consumption. The rate of inflation is a critical determinant of the consumer's purchasing power and in both short- and long-term investment decisions.

Inflation has real costs. It is not simply a rise in the level of prices matched by a simultaneous rise in nominal wages and interest rates that preserve real wages and returns. Wages, prices of goods, and, to a lesser extent, interest rates may be slow to adjust to inflation. There is a period during which wages, prices of goods, and interest rates adjust, and this period, or delay, represents costs to the wage earner, consumer, and investor, respectively. Thus, real purchasing power and real return on investment can be, at least temporarily, eroded by inflation. Relative prices of goods and services, which are signals to the economy on how to allocate consumption and investment, also change, again, at least temporarily. In a high-inflation environment, because prices are rising more rapidly, it is also more difficult for people to accurately evaluate price information needed to make consumption and investment decisions. Because of the greater difficulty in processing information, mistakes are more frequent in allocating expenditures between today and tomorrow and between this product or that, and additional real costs are incurred. Furthermore, during particularly high or unstable inflationary periods, investment is riskier and the investment level tends to shrink because a higher real return is required for the same level of investment.

Therefore, keeping inflation as low as possible is one of the most important objectives of economic policy, and, fortunately, inflation appears to be an economic indicator that can be more closely controlled than other major indicators, if policy makers choose to do so. Inflation is also a particularly valuable indicator of presidential performance, because, unlike employment, savings, investment, productivity, compensation, and, to some extent, the stock market, it is *not* correlated with GDP. Thus, by itself, inflation captures the important aspects of economic performance mentioned above.

In order to keep inflation low, its causes must be understood, and economists do not all agree on what those causes are. However, most will agree that rapid expansion of the money supply is the easiest way to cause inflation. This expansion could take the form of printing money or one of the more sophisticated tools of monetary policy that are described in the next chapter. Economists adhering to the monetarist school of economics stop there; they contend that inflation is strictly a monetary phenomenon. Other economists view nonmonetary events, such as the oil crises, as inflation causing. Monetarists would view such events as temporary increases in the price level that would not meet their definition of inflation. Thus, one can define inflation as broadly or as narrowly as needed in order to conform to a given set of causes of inflation. The policy goal remains to keep sustained increases in the price level to a minimum.

Inflation data are published by the U.S. Department of Labor, Bureau of Labor Statistics, which is the official source for inflation data, in this case, the CPI. These data are published on a monthly basis and are reported on by the news media as are GDP growth rates and employment indicators. Figure 4.1 uses the change in the annual average CPI data, as opposed to the December to December CPI change. For example, the inflation rate for 1958 is measured here as the growth, or decline, from the *average* 1957 CPI to that of 1958. The inflation that occurred between December 1957 and December 1958 is a different concept of inflation. Some might suggest that because the annual average is an average of inflation occurring from January 1 to December 31, the annual average implicitly carries a six-month lag. Strictly speaking, a six-month lag would mean using the CPI recorded on June 30. December to December CPI changes have some quantitative differences from annual averages but would not materially affect the results presented here.

OVERVIEW OF TRENDS IN THE LONG RUN, 1946–93

Over the 48-year time span depicted in Figure 4.1, at least four separate inflationary periods can be discerned. The first extends from 1946 to 1955 and displays high volatility with very high inflation combined with a couple of years of deflation. The second period is of low, stable

FIGURE 4.1
Inflation, 1946–93

(Annual Changes in the Consumer Price Index)

Inflation Rate

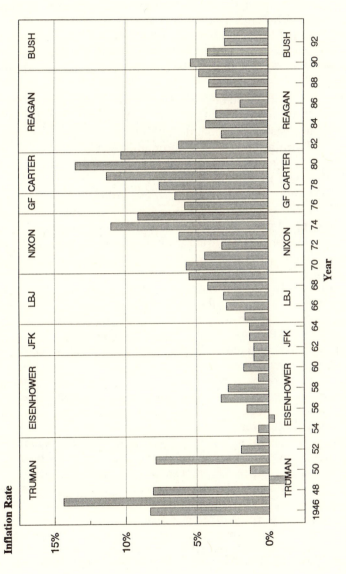

Source: U.S. Department of Labor.

inflation rates and runs from 1956 until 1972. However, even though
the inflation rate never exceeded 5.7 percent, it did increase for ten
straight years from 1961 through 1970, evoking the concern of policy
makers and ultimately resulting in major policy changes, most notably
the abandonment of the Bretton Woods system. The third period was
characterized by high and somewhat volatile inflation, beginning with
a surge in 1973 and continuing until 1982. In the fourth period, high
inflation was broken, and inflation remained relatively low and steady
during 1983–93. The average inflation rate for the period 1946–93 was
4.3 percent.

The 1946–93 period began with a three-year period of high inflation.
Because the unemployment rate remained fairly low (Chapter 3), the
more severe post-war economic problem, contrary to the fears of many,
was clearly inflation rather than unemployment. Inflation reached levels of 8.3, 14.4, and 8.1 percent for the years 1946–48. Inflation tumbled
to −1.2 percent in 1949 (one of only two years in which there was price
deflation) and was 1.3 percent in 1950. Inflation shot up to 7.9 percent
in 1951, a likely consequence of Korean War expenditures, but thereafter remained very low, not exceeding 3.3 percent until the late 1960s,
including the second deflation year of −0.4 percent in 1955. Thus, for 16
years, including the last two years of the Truman administration, all
eight years of the Eisenhower administration, the Kennedy administration, and the first three years of Johnson's administration, the United
States did not have an inflation problem.

However, inflation began to climb steadily under Johnson, reaching
4.2 percent in 1968 and closing the Johnson period at 5.5 percent. Nixon
began with a 5.7 percent inflation rate in 1970 but reduced it to 4.4 and
3.2 percent over the next two years. In 1973, following a year of relatively high growth in the money supply, inflation began to take off
again, reaching 6.2 percent, jumping to 11.0 percent in 1974 following
the oil embargo, and easing somewhat to 9.1 percent in 1975. Because
the high inflation years of 1974–75 coincided with recession, the economy was said to be in a state of "stagflation," that is, stagnation, or recession plus inflation. Under Ford, an economic recovery began, and inflation abated in 1976 to 5.8 percent and 6.5 percent in 1977.

As the Carter period began, inflation was on its way back up, reaching 7.6 percent in 1978, 11.3 percent in 1979, and a 23-year high (and
second highest of the entire period) of 13.5 percent in 1980, before closing out the Carter years at 10.3 percent. In the first year attributable to
Reagan, inflation plummeted to 6.2 percent in 1982, the big recession
year. As the economy began recovering in 1983, inflation continued
downward to 3.2 percent, then moved up to 4.3 percent in 1984, back
down to 3.2 percent in 1985, and then dropped to 1.9 percent in 1986, a
21-year low. The Reagan years ended with moderately low inflation of
3.6, 4.1, and 4.8 percent during 1987–89. Under Bush, inflation rose to

5.4 percent in 1990 but fell to a moderately low 4.2 percent in 1991 and closed out the administration at 3.0 percent for both 1992 and 1993.

PRESIDENTIAL RANKINGS

Rankings of presidential administrations by average inflation rates and trend changes from best to worst are given in Table 4.1. The trend change in inflation is probably as meaningful as, or more than, the average in evaluating economic performance. The reason is that inflation is difficult to "wring out" of the economy, and it is, therefore, critical to performance evaluation to know in which direction the president "took" the inflation rate. In keeping with convention, the average indicator is used as the primary basis for ranking, but it should be recognized that, in this case, the trend change is of more or less equal importance.

Kennedy and Eisenhower clearly had the lowest average inflation rates at 1.2 and 1.4 percent, respectively, and each only slightly increased the inflation rates they inherited. The major difference was that Eisenhower maintained the low inflation for eight years, compared with Kennedy's two years and ten months. Although Johnson is in third place at 3.3 percent, he increased inflation by more than any other president, 4.2 percentage points. Bush is next with a 3.8 percent average and a 1.8 percentage point reduction. Reagan follows closely with a 3.9 percent average inflation rate but, more impressively, with an inflation rate reduction of 5.5 percentage points from that of his predecessor.

Truman is sixth with a somewhat higher average inflation rate of 4.5 percent, but because he presided over the period in which the economy and inflation settled down, he is credited with the largest drop in

TABLE 4.1
Inflation Rates

Average Inflation Rate			Reduction in Inflation Rate — Trend Change	
President	Term	Percent	President	Percentage Points
Kennedy	1961–63	1.2	Truman	−7.5
Eisenhower	1953–61	1.4	Reagan	−5.5
Johnson	1964–69	3.4	Ford	−2.6
Bush	1989–93	3.8	Bush	−1.8
Reagan	1981–89	3.9	Eisenhower	0.2
Truman	1945–53	4.5	Kennedy	0.3
Ford	1974–77	6.0	Nixon	3.6
Nixon	1969–74	6.4	Carter	3.8
Carter	1977–81	10.1	Johnson	4.2
Average, 1946–93		4.3		

inflation, 7.5 percent. Rounding out the bottom of the list are Ford, Nixon, and Carter. Ford's relatively high average inflation of 6.0 percent is substantially assuaged by the fact that inflation fell by 2.6 percentage points during his tenure. Nixon, on the other hand, although recording an average inflation of 6.4 percent, raised inflation by 3.6 percentage points. Carter has, by far, the worst inflation record, with an average of 10.1 percent while also raising inflation by the second highest amount, 3.8 percentage points.

SUMMARY AND SELECTED ISSUES

The surge in inflation during the three years immediately following World War II is an important event in the history of inflation and one that is probably not widely known or remembered. Although the circumstances under which it occurred were unusual, that is, the unleashing of 17 years of pent-up purchasing power, this three-year period still provides the historical perspective that the U.S. economy did experience extremely high inflation after World War II, long before the stagflation years of the 1970s, and recovered rather rapidly from it. It is also probably not well-known that the 14.4 percent average annual inflation of 1947 was even higher than Carter's inflation average of 1980. The three years immediately following World War II, as was pointed out, demonstrated that inflation was a more serious economic concern than the return to high unemployment that many economists had predicted. Understandably, most people view the 1950s and 1960s as years when inflation was not a problem. It is, in fact, true that the U.S. economy enjoyed low inflation almost every year between 1949 and 1968.

The Johnson administration ushered in a sustained, higher level of inflation to the economy, as rates rose from the 1 percent to the 5 percent level. After ten more years of inflation ranging from nearly 6 percent to 13.5 percent, added under Nixon, Ford, and Carter, it appeared that the days of inflation rates of 5 percent or less were gone forever. The inflation rate even rose as high as 20 percent in late 1980 (monthly data), a level that is smoothed out by averaging inflation over the entire year (the method used here). Yet, inflation rates were lowered under Reagan and Bush, and the inflation levels of today average close to those of the mid-1960s. However, with the exception of Reagan's 1.9 percent inflation rate in 1986, the economy has never been able to resume pre-Johnson inflation rates.

How inflation was defeated is an important performance question, one that cuts across two presidential administrations. A decision was made by the Federal Reserve in 1979 to beat inflation by refocusing monetary policy on the size of bank reserves (see Chapter 5). This policy, clearly, was initiated during the Carter administration, but inflation was not "broken" until 1982–83. Many observers attribute the defeat of inflation not only to the change in monetary policy but also to the deep recession that occurred under Reagan in 1982. Thus, although Reagan's average GDP growth rate bears the burden of the recession, his inflation record reaps the benefit. Once defeated, inflation remained relatively low, dropping to, as mentioned, as low as 1.9 percent in 1986 and not exceeding 4.8 percent for the rest of Reagan's term.

In evaluating the charge against Bush as having the worst economic record in 50 years, with respect to inflation, it must be noted that in Bush's first year, inflation did exceed 5 percent for the first time in 8 years. However, inflation subsequently fell to 4.2 percent in 1991 and was only 3 percent by 1992 and 1993, yielding an average inflation rate of 3.8 percent and an improvement in the inflation trend of 1.1 percentage points. This performance is better than average for the nine presidents surveyed and, therefore, far from the worst. Thus far, the charge against Bush's economic record has been examined with respect to the three most prominent economic indicators: GDP growth, employment, and inflation. In the case of GDP growth, the charge has been found to be true; in the case of unemployment, arguably but not unequivocally true; and false in the case of inflation. Chapter 15 provides an overall ranking of the presidents taking into account all of the indicators that affect economic performance, thus, rendering a more complete and definitive verdict on the charge against Bush.

SUGGESTIONS FOR FURTHER READING

The BLS Handbook of Methods. Washington, D.C.: Department of Labor, Bureau of Labor Statistics, 1992. Chapter 19. Contains more detailed information on the CPI's structure and history.

Fender, John, *Inflation — Welfare Costs, Positive Theory and Policy Options.* Ann Arbor: University of Michigan Press, 1990. Discusses real costs of inflation and ways to deal with it.

Fixler, Dennis, "The Consumer Price Inedx: Underlying Concepts and Caveats." *Monthly Labor Review* 116 (December 1993): 3–46. Presents mathematical, but largely readable, approaches to the CPI.

Hall, Robert E., ed., *Inflation and Its Causes and Effects.* National Bureau of Economic Research Project Report. Chicago: University of Chicago Press, 1982. A collection of 12 authors' discussions of the causes and effects of inflation rather than policy recommendations.

Paarlberg, Don, *An Analysis and History of Inflation.* Westport, Conn.: Praeger, 1993. Provides a history of U.S. inflation during 1933–87; also provides examples from other countries in other historical time periods.

"Understanding the Consumer Price Index: Answers to Some Questions." Washington, D.C.: U.S. Department of Labor, Bureau of Labor Statistics, revised April 1993. A pamphlet that provides clear and concise answers to 21 key questions about the CPI.

NOTE

1. The consumer price index, as defined in "Anatomy of Price Change" (*Monthly Labor Review* 116 [December 1993]: 4) is "a Laspeyres fixed-quantity price index [i.e.,

the weights are derived from a specific base year] that measures the price change of a fixed market basket of goods and services of constant [not improved] quality bought on average by urban consumers (CPI-U). The CPI-U focuses on urban consumers and the CPI-W focuses on urban wage earners and clerical workers. It is the ratio of the value of a market basket in two periods: the numerator is the value of the market basket at, say, current prices and the denominator is the value of the market basket at base period prices." The CPI is distinguished from the cost of living index, which is "a ratio that measures the impact of price change on consumer well-being. The numerator is a hypothetical expenditure — the lowest expenditure level necessary at current prices to achieve the base period's living standard. The denominator is the lowest expenditure at base period prices to achieve the base period's living standard."

5

Money Supply and the Real Prime Interest Rate

Money supply growth and the real interest rate are presented together because the money supply is often changed with the intent of altering interest rates. In fact, influencing interest rates (and ultimately gross domestic product [GDP] and employment) and managing inflation are the main objectives of monetary policy. Although, theoretically, changes in the money supply do not affect the long-term *real* interest rate, they can substantially influence the short-term *nominal* rate on which the real prime rate is based. The nominal prime rate is the actual rate quoted by commercial banks to the lowest-risk corporate borrowers for very short-term loans. The real prime rate is this nominal rate adjusted for expected inflation.[1] The real interest rate is important to the economy because it influences the levels of saving and investment (Chapter 6), which, in turn, drive economic growth. The official source of the nominal money supply data is the Federal Reserve Board of Governors. The nominal prime rate data are also from the Federal Reserve but are then adjusted for inflation using the consumer price index, which is published by the Bureau of Labor Statistics.

MONEY SUPPLY GROWTH

The three most commonly cited measures of the money supply are M1, M2, and M3. Each measures the amount of cash and near-cash in the U.S. economy. M1 is the narrowest concept of money supply, including coin and currency and transactions, or demand deposits (e.g., checking accounts). M2 is a broader concept, including everything in M1 plus broker/dealer money market funds, consumer savings and time deposits, and overnight Eurodollars and repurchases. M3 includes everything in M2 plus large time deposits, institutional money market funds, and term Eurodollars and repurchases.[2] Clearly, the measures from M1 to M3 become progressively broader, with the money supply measured by M3 being greater but less liquid than that measured by

M2, which is greater but less liquid than M1. M2 is selected as the indicator of money supply mainly because the Federal Reserve has more control over it than M3 and because it has maintained a more stable relationship with respect to GDP than has M1.[3] Further explanation of the M2 concept and its behavior is given in the Overview of Trends section below.

The money supply differs from the other indicators presented in this book in that its fluctuations are neither inherently good or bad; the money supply is, rather, a policy tool to achieve certain ends.[4] As such, monetary targets are considered "intermediate targets" designed to achieve more fundamental goals. Monetary policy, or control of the money supply, usually seeks either to lower (raise) interest rates by raising (lowering) the money supply or to curb inflation by restricting the money supply. Because of its effect on other indicators, especially inflation and interest rates, money supply growth is an ingredient to economic performance and provides additional context in which to view that performance. For example, Chapter 1 showed how strong the effects of monetary policy were in the 1930s, when a very restrictive, even perverse monetary policy, plunged the United States into a deep depression.

The growth rate, or percent change in the money supply, as opposed to its absolute level, is chosen as the money supply indicator, because growth rates are what the Federal Reserve actually targets and because they are more easily related to GDP growth rates and inflation rates. The money supply growth rates are not adjusted for inflation, because it is the nominal growth rates to which inflation is most closely related. Adjusting the money supply for inflation would neutralize the relationship between inflation and money supply growth. Growth rates also show the increment to the money supply relative to its current base, which absolute levels do not. As shown in the next chapter, the effect on savings and investment of changing the money supply also can be seen more easily through growth rates. Therefore, Figure 5.1 depicts M2 growth rates as opposed to M2 levels.

REAL PRIME INTEREST RATE

The real prime rate is important in large measure because it reflects the real cost of capital to the banking sector's preferred customers, that is, those with the lowest risk of loan default. In this sense, it is also a measure of perceived risk in the economy — that is, the interest rate to the lowest risk borrowers in the market incorporates the lowest risk premium and is the lowest interest rate in the market. The prime rate may be represented by the following: $r_p = r_f +$ risk premium, where r_p is the prime interest rate and r_f is the risk-free (no default risk) interest rate. The prime interest rate also serves as a barometer of risk for the economy as a whole (private treasury spreads are another). For

FIGURE 5.1
Growth of Money Supply (M2), 1949–92

M2 Growth

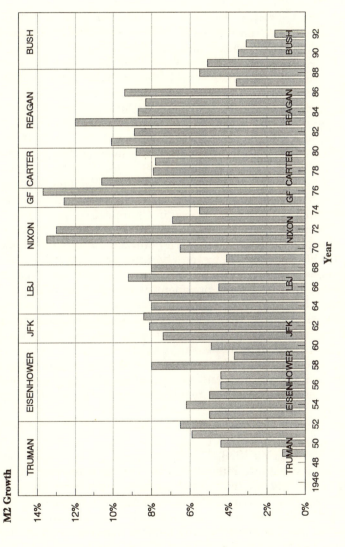

Source: Federal Reserve 1959–92, Rasche 1949–58.

example, a rising real rate of interest may suggest that the level of confidence in the country's economic future is falling and that the riskiness of investment is increasing.

The banking sector's preferred customers, who are financially sound, mainly large investors, base their level of investment in the economy, in part, on the real interest rate (the cost of borrowing adjusted for expected inflation). Clearly, lower interest rates offer these investors a lower borrowing cost and encourage more investment. An increased investment level, in turn, raises national output (GDP) and employment. Thus, the real interest rate is an important factor in achieving and sustaining economic growth. The real interest rate also acts as an important inducement for saving, although in the opposite direction. Increased saving rates are fostered, all other things being equal, by higher real interest rates, which mean greater rewards for saving. Saving provides funds for growth-sustaining investment. The supply of loanable funds (saving), in its various forms, and the demand for loanable funds (investment) determine the interest rate. The interest rate is the financial "price" at which investment and saving are equal. The effects of the real interest rate on investment and saving for the 1946–93 time period are described in Chapter 6.

Numerous interest rates prevail in the market, all of which are determined by the risk and maturity of the underlying financial instrument. Of all the rates, however, the prime rate is the most trackable over the post-war era and, therefore, provides the most consistent long-term series and long-term presidential comparability. The prime rate provides a base on which other rates are set. Other market rates, for example, 10- and 30-year Treasury securities, longer-term corporate borrowing, etc. either follow to some degree or are tied to (as in the case of mortgages) the movements in the prime rate.

One caveat on this latter point is that short-term interest rates (e.g., the prime interest rate) and long-term interest rates do not *always* move together, nor do they maintain exactly the same ratio to each other from year to year. Longer-term interest rates do not mirror current economic conditions as closely as do short-term interest rates. For example, long-term interest rates were much lower than short-term interest rates during 1979–81, suggesting that, over the long term, people expected substantial improvement over the prevailing economic conditions. Similarly, as real prime interest rates declined in the early 1990s, long-term interest rates increased slightly, possibly because of large budget deficits or other factors (discussed further below). "Yield curves," which measure the relationship between the maturity (long, medium, and short term) of financial instruments (e.g., bonds and Treasury bills) and their interest rates, may also shift and/or change in steepness over time. Nevertheless, long-term interest rates do tend to move in the same general direction as the prime rate, although, again, not always on a year-to-year basis. Hence, the prime rate does capture much of the behavior of long-term interest rates. Experience has shown that monetary policy more strongly and predictably affects interest rates with the shorter maturities, whereas longer maturity interest rates are driven more by the market's expectations of future inflation and time-varying risk premiums.

Another qualification to the value of the prime rate as an economic indicator is that it may no longer be the lowest lending rate on the market. In recent years, banks have been providing an increasing volume of loans at *below* prime rates. Three-month Treasury bill rates may, therefore, have become a better indicator of the lowest rate on the market.

The real prime rate indicator is best viewed as a level, not as a growth rate. Because it represents a rate of return, percent changes from year to year would have little meaning and would obscure the behavior of the indicator. Thus, Figure 5.2 depicts actual real prime interest rates. The prime rate is adjusted for inflation, that is, the inflation component of the nominal interest rate, as measured by the consumer price index, is removed in order to arrive at the real prime interest rate.[5] Finally, although the prime rate is lagged one year, there is also an argument not to lag the interest rate. The main reasons are that, as a financial variable, the interest rate moves quickly and that the market, through the interest rate, also anticipates what the economic effects of an event *will be*, for example, the election of a new president, and, so, would call for *leading* rather than *lagging* the interest rate variable. Although these reasons are valid, it is maintained here that the foundation of interest rate expectations is laid by the events and policies of prior years, and, thus, the real prime interest rate should be lagged.

THE FEDERAL RESERVE

A brief discussion of the Federal Reserve may facilitate understanding of the importance of the money supply to the economy and how monetary policy works.

Established during the Woodrow Wilson administration, the Federal Reserve, or "Fed," as it is commonly called, has been running U.S. monetary policy since 1914. Through his power to appoint the Fed's governors as well as the chairman of the Fed (with the consent of Congress), the president has some control over the Fed and, therefore, monetary policy.[6] The Fed's policy actions are independent thereafter, because they do not have to be approved by either the president or the Congress. However, the president can register his monetary policy preferences in communications to the Fed. The Fed chairman is also frequently called to make presentations and answer questions before Congress. Nevertheless, the Fed enjoys a high degree of independence relative to monetary authorities in other countries, enabling it to pursue low,

FIGURE 5.2
Prime Interest Rate, 1946–93   (Adjusted for Inflation)

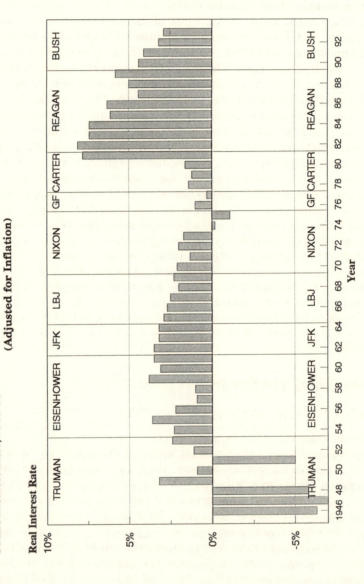

Source: Board of Governors, Federal Reserve.

stable inflation,[7] without the periodic disturbances of short-term political considerations.

Monetary policy is actually conducted by two major bodies of the
Federal Reserve System: the already described 7-member Federal
Reserve Board, which sets the discount rate and has jurisdiction over
many aspects of bank regulation, and the Federal Open Market
Committee, which consists of the 7 members of the Fed Board and 5 of
the 12 presidents of the Federal Reserve Banks throughout the United
States. The Federal Open Market Committee makes decisions affecting
interest rates, the money supply, inflation, and economic growth.

The Fed has essentially three ways of controlling the money supply:
open market operations in which the Fed can sell (buy) securities in
order to reduce (increase) the money supply; regulating the discount
rate at which the Fed lends to member banks; and changing the
required reserve rate, that is, the percentage of total deposits a bank is
required to have on hand in the form of cash. In open market operations, the Fed may lower the money supply by selling its bonds to the
public in exchange for cash. Likewise, it raises the money supply by
buying bonds from the public for cash, thus, injecting more money into
the banking system. By lowering the discount rate, the Fed encourages
member banks to borrow more from the Fed, an act that releases more
money into the banking system and increases the money supply.
Conversely, raising the discount rate lowers the money supply. The Fed
also may increase the money supply by lowering the required reserve
rate, because banks can lend a higher portion of their cash.[8] Finally, the
Federal Reserve may act as a lender of last resort in the event of national liquidity crises, such as arose after the 1987 stock market crash.

OVERVIEW OF TRENDS IN THE LONG RUN[9]

Money Supply, 1949-92

Before examining the behavior of the money supply as measured by
M2, certain of its aspects should be reviewed. As a long-run time series,
M2 is problematic mainly because its monetary aggregate contents
changed in 1980, largely because of legislative changes, that is, the
deregulation of interest rates and thrift institutions. Moreover, the Fed
did not always target M2, but, rather, targeted M1 (currency and transactions or demand deposits). The reason the Fed switched from M1 to
M2 (M1 plus broker/dealer money market funds, consumer savings and
time deposits, and overnight Eurodollars and repurchases) was that in
the late 1970s and early 1980s, the relationship between M1 and GDP
became unstable,[10] such that the Fed came to the conclusion that M1
was an ineffective policy tool. In order to preserve monetary policy's relevance to ultimate economic goals such as output, employment and

inflation, changes in the aggregates that the Fed targets are required from time to time:

The evolution of the Federal Reserve Board staff's definitions of monetary aggregates primarily has been governed by economists' changing empirical perceptions of the appropriate concept of money. In the 1960s, economists' focus on the medium of exchange function of money made M1 the principal aggregate. As empirical relationships for M1 appeared to break down in the 1970s and attention turned once again to the role of liquid near-moneys, some suggested that multiple monetary aggregates might collectively reveal more information about the stance of monetary policy with respect to economic activity. The Federal Reserve responded by creating the monetary aggregates M2 and M3 in 1971, and M4 and M5 in 1975. (Anderson and Kavajecz, 1994)

Anderson and Kavajecz further caution that, "a failure to appreciate the interdependence of time, data, [monetary aggregate] definitions and procedures may adversely affect or vitiate research and policy conclusions." For the purposes of developing the long-run trend (time series), the change in monetary policy target poses a potential problem in that neither M1 nor M2 provides consistent comparison across all presidential administrations and because neither has been *officially* calculated prior to 1959. In addition, M2 was redefined in 1980 to include balances at savings and loan institutions, which it had previously excluded.[11] Fortunately, the official series from the Fed is revised and applies a consistent definition for 1959–93. In addition, a series for M2 levels has been calculated back to 1948, which, although not official, does use the methodology for M2 employed by the Fed. Because M1 is known to be unstable after 1980 and the Fed ceased to target M1 thereafter, M1 is rejected, here, as the measure of money supply growth in favor of M2. It is also fortunate that the ratio between M2 and M1 is fairly stable between 1948 and 1958 (ranging from 1.6 to 2, see Appendix B), the period over which the *unofficial* M2 data is used, and, thus, this M2 series can serve as a proxy for M1, which the Fed *was* targeting during that period.

Because the earliest year for which data are available for the level of M2 is 1948, growth rates can be calculated from 1949. It is necessary to extend the time series for money supply only to 1992 (Bush's last year in office) rather than to 1993, because the money supply indicator is not lagged. For the 44-year time period, the average growth rate of M2 was 6.8 percent. Within this period, five subperiods of monetary growth are apparent in Figure 5.1: moderate/low growth through 1960, moderately high growth during 1961–70, very high growth from 1971 through 1977, moderately high growth from 1978 to 1986, and low growth after 1986. In general, surges in M2 growth preceded increases in GDP growth until the late 1980s.

M2 grew at only 1.2 percent, the lowest ever, in 1949, perhaps over concern about the high inflation of 1947–48. By 1950, however, M2 growth reached moderate levels, remaining within the range of 3.7 to 6.5 percent throughout the Eisenhower administration until the end of 1960, with the exception of 1958. In 1958, there was a recession, and, in response, the Fed may have opted for a stimulative monetary policy because M2 grew at 8.0 percent. Between 1961 and 1968, M2 entered a higher growth range of 7.4 to 9.2 percent, with one dip to 4.5 percent in 1966. M2 growth dropped to 4.1 and 6.5 percent in 1969 and 1970, respectively, before soaring to 13.5 and 13.0 percent in 1971 and 1972, respectively. In 1973–74, M2 growth dropped below 7 percent before shooting up to very high levels for the next three years at 12.6, 13.7, and 10.6 percent.

By 1978, M2 growth rates returned to lower levels, recording 7.9, 7.8, and 8.8 percent during 1978–80. In spite of the success in fighting inflation during 1981–83, M2 growth was relatively high at 10.1, 8.9 and 12.0 percent for the three years. Yet, Paul Volcker's monetary policy appeared to beat inflation. For the rest of the 1980s, M2 growth rates generally fell. There was an upsurge to 9.4 percent in 1986, but in the following year, growth dropped to only 3.6 percent. Since then, the M2 growth rate has not exceeded 5.5 percent, and growth during the Bush administration did not exceed 3.5 percent.

Real Prime Interest Rate, 1946–93

The average real prime interest rate was 2.2 percent for 1946–93. Two general observations are made with respect to the real interest rate as shown in Figure 5.2: the long-term trend in the real interest rate displays less fluctuation than most other indicators, and there are three distinct interest rate environments. The first is contained within the Truman administration and generally is characterized by grossly negative real interest rates (although the real rates for 1949–50 were positive), which were as low as –11.3 percent in 1947. This phenomenon was a result of low, nominal interest rates, combined with 14.4 percent inflation, hence, the sharply negative real interest rate.[12] By 1952, as interest rates increased modestly and inflation abated, the second real interest rate period emerged. In the second period, which lasted from 1952 to 1980, the range of interest rates was rather narrow, between –1.1 and 3.8 percent. This period included a 16-year stretch, 1959–75, in which rates declined fairly steadily from 3.8 percent to –1.1 percent. The second period closed out with the real prime rate in the 1.2–1.6 percent range for the three years from 1978 to 1980. The third period began with a quantum leap in 1981 (actually beginning in late 1980) when the real interest rate jumped to 7.8 percent and peaked at 8.1 percent in 1982. Thereafter, there was a steadily declining trend from the 8.1 percent peak down to 2.9 percent in 1993.

Figure 5.2 exhibits its shape, in large part, because of the behavior of the underlying nominal prime rate. The nominal prime rate tended to adjust in steps, remaining at one level for a period before moving to another level. One reason for this behavior was that banks also could determine their lending terms through what is known as a *compensating balance*, in which borrowers are required to leave a deposit with the lending bank (often at a zero interest rate). Thus, the effective rate of the loan was higher than the stated prime rate. For example, if a top corporation wants to borrow $1 million at 10 percent but must also maintain a $100,000 compensating balance, the effective loan amount is $90,000, on which the corporation pays $10,000; therefore, the effective interest rate is $10,000/$90,000, or 11.1 percent. Thus, a reason why the prime rate did not fully respond to various inflationary environments in the 1940s, 1950s, and 1960s is that banks would also (in fact, were more inclined to) vary the size of the compensating balance and, therefore, the *effective* prime rates. A second reason that the prime rate moves stepwise is that the official prime rate is recomputed only when a majority (15) of the 29 banks that the Fed follows establishes a new prime rate.

Until 1971, the prime rate essentially was set by a few large New York banks, with other banks following suit. However, in response to inflationary concerns in 1971, banks began to set the prime rate based on a formula that was geared to open market rates on commercial paper and certificates. In practice, this formula was followed by bankers only when it was advantageous for them to do so.

PRESIDENTIAL RANKINGS

Money Supply

As noted previously, it is not necessarily good or bad to have a higher money supply growth rate, and, therefore, the presidents' rankings thereof are not especially important. In addition, with the changing definition of M2 and rapid development of financial markets, presidential comparisons are not as valid as for other indicators. However, it is important not to have excessive monetary growth, because it leads to inflation and increased economic uncertainty, as occurred in the 1970s. For this reason, presidents are ranked in ascending order, implying a preference for lower monetary growth (Table 5.1). The trend change has even less meaning in terms of performance because of its higher degree of year-to-year fluctuation.

Bush and Truman, the last and first presidents of the time period, had the lowest M2 growth rates, at 3.2 and 4.4 percent, respectively. Eisenhower, Johnson, Kennedy, Nixon, and Reagan follow, ranging from 5.1 to 8.0 percent. Ford stands out as having by far the highest average

TABLE 5.1
Money Supply Growth Rates

Average M2 Growth Rate			Change in M2 Growth Rate — Trend	
President	Term	Percent	President	Percentage Points
Bush	1989–93	3.2	Carter	−4.9
Truman	1945–53	4.4	Bush	−4.0
Eisenhower	1953–61	5.1	Reagan	−3.3
Johnson	1963–69	7.3	Nixon	−2.5
Kennedy	1961–63	7.7	Eisenhower	−1.6
Nixon	1969–74	7.9	Johnson	−0.4
Reagan	1981–89	8.0	Kennedy	3.5
Carter	1977–81	8.4	Truman	5.2
Ford	1974–77	12.4	Ford	8.2
Average, 1949–92		6.8		

M2 growth rate at 12.4 percent. Although unimportant in terms of evaluating performance, trend changes are presented for completeness' sake.

Real Prime Interest Rate

Table 5.2 shows the presidential ranking by average real interest rate. To rank the presidents, it must be decided what is a desirable interest rate, yet, it is not clear what that interest rate is. It must be high enough to offer a reasonable return on saving but low enough not to discourage investment under prevailing economic conditions. A further complication is the fact that compensating balances as well as the nominal prime rate determine the effective prime rate, making it more difficult to assign presidential responsibility for real interest rate levels. However, it is reasonable to assume that when compensating balances increased to their upper limit, the prime rate was increased to relieve the pressure. Hence, the prime rate may have been only somewhat slower to respond than the effective interest rate, while long-run interest rate trends were unaffected. The trend change is important because it reveals the change in the climate of confidence in the economy as measured by the change in the rate at which the economy discounts the future (also a measure of risk). For example, the faster the real interest rate increases, the greater is the loss in investor confidence. For the purpose of ranking, it is assumed that a lower average real interest rate is preferred. For the trend change, reduction in the real interest rate is preferred.

Table 5.2
Real Prime Interest Rates

Average Real Interest Rate		Change in Real Interest Rate — Trend	
President	Percent	President	Percentage Points
Truman	−2.6	Nixon	−3.5
Ford	0.6	Bush	−2.9
Nixon	1.0	Reagan	−2.0
Johnson	2.5	Johnson	−0.8
Eisenhower	2.5	Kennedy	−0.3
Carter	3.0	Eisenhower	1.1
Kennedy	3.3	Ford	1.4
Bush	3.6	Carter	7.5
Reagan	6.3	Truman	8.6
Average, 1946–93	2.2		

Truman's average is, by a wide margin, the lowest at −2.6 percent, which is because of the combination of high inflation and very low interest rates. The inflation rate declined sharply. Therefore, it came as no surprise that Truman raised the real interest rate more than any other president, by 8.7 percentage points, from −6.3 percent to 2.4 percent. The adjustment of the real prime rate under Truman brought the rate close to the long-run average for the period of 2.2 percent. Ford and Nixon follow at real prime rates of 0.6 and 1.0 percent, respectively. They were also in power during fairly low nominal interest rate environments and experienced relatively high inflation. However, under Ford, the real interest rate rose by 1.4 percentage points, while under Nixon, it fell by 3.5 percentage points. Johnson is fourth, but at a significantly higher 2.5 percent, reflecting the low, albeit rising, inflation level during his presidency. Eisenhower is also at 2.5 percent, reflecting a low inflation rate, but with an increase in the real rate of 1.1 percentage points, contrasting with Johnson's lowering of interest rates by 0.8 percentage point.

Carter's average is 3.0 percent, but it is notable that under Carter, the real interest rate first soared, by 7.5 percentage points, from 0.3 percent to 7.8 percent (year average). Although Truman's increase in the real interest rate was higher, it was an aberration because of the correction for the highly negative real interest rate immediately after World War II. Kennedy and Bush are next at 3.3 and 3.6 percent, respectively. Kennedy's average, like Johnson's, reflects the low average inflation level combined with gradually rising interest rates. Bush's 3.6 percent average is rather remarkable, not because it was the continuation of a trend already started under Reagan, but because it fell rather than rose. If the link made by many economists between interest rates and the deficit were true, then the rapidly growing budget deficits under Bush should have driven the real interest rate up substantially. Instead, it *dropped* substantially, by 2.9 percentage points, second among presidents only to Nixon. Reagan, who inherited very high interest rates (both real and nominal) by historical standards, had, by far, the highest real interest rates at 6.3 percent. Yet, he also recorded a reduction in the interest rate, 2.0 percentage points (the third largest).

SUMMARY AND SELECTED ISSUES

Money Supply

A perennial issue surrounding monetary policy is the degree of true independence of the Fed. Some have suggested that the money supply typically surges during election years (the independence of the Fed notwithstanding) in order to pump up the economy and increase the chance of the incumbent president/party remaining in power. The average M2 growth rate for all election years (i.e., every four years starting in 1952 and continuing through 1992) is 7.6 percent compared with an average for the entire period of 6.8 percent. Election-year M2 growth is higher than the overall average, but it is not at all clear that unusually expansionary monetary policy was pursued (ostensibly for political purposes). Average inflation rates following election years average 4.2 percent, compared with 4.3 percent for the entire period. Thus, judging by postelection inflationary impact, monetary policy to achieve short-term economic stimulus for potential political gain was pursued to no unusual degree during election years.

The Fed may enjoy relative political independence, but there is clearly interdependence of financial markets and, therefore, monetary policy, given the increasing globalization of financial markets. Globalization is facilitated by growth of the Eurodollar market and through technological improvements in making international financial transactions that create opportunities for "end-running" domestic monetary policy. These developments and the breakdown in the relationships, first, between M1 and GDP and, later, between M2 and GDP, raise questions as to how much control the Fed really has over the money supply. Yet, the short-term effects of monetary policy are undeniable.

A final point on the Carter-Reagan comparison is that, as mentioned, it was Carter who appointed Volcker as the Fed chairman who is credited with shifting the Fed's attention to bank reserves rather than interest rates, a policy that is widely believed to have defeated inflation. This policy was announced on October 6, 1979. Inflation was finally defeated during 1982–83, but not before the major recession of 1982, which has also been attributed largely to restrictive monetary policy. Thus, although Carter can be credited with appointing a true inflation fighter to head the Fed, the real pain of beating inflation was felt under Reagan and his GDP record shoulders the burden of this recession.

Real Interest Rate

From the beginning of the post-war period through the 1970s, the highest real interest rate was 3.8 percent. In only 8 of the 35 years during 1946–80 did the real prime rate exceed 3.0 percent. Throughout this period, as interest rate changes were slow and steady, the main avenue by which the president could maintain real returns as represented by the real interest rate was by the control of inflation. The pattern of low or even negative interest rates changed in the 1980s. Suddenly, in 1980–81, the combination of high nominal interest rates, high inflation, and pessimistic expectations at the end of the Carter presidency drove real interest rates far higher than they had ever been and even higher than in subsequent years when budget deficits were a much higher percentage of GDP.

Some economists attributed the high real interest rates of the 1980s to the deficits. It is true that Carter racked up consistently large deficits, which may have weakened investor confidence leading into the 1980s; however, the truly large deficits were yet to come. As the deficits doubled in the early 1980s, fell in the mid-1980s, and rose again in the late 1980s and early 1990s, the real interest rate remained on a steady downward trend from 1982 to 1993, dropping from 8.2 to 2.9 percent, lower than the average during the Kennedy administration. The doctrine that the high real interest rate was caused in large part by the deficit would have undoubtedly forecast a real interest rate in 1993 that was at least as high as it was in 1982 and probably much higher, given the larger deficits. However, the opposite happened.

Certainly, the deficit plays a role in determining real interest rates, and very high deficits must, all else being equal, lead to a shakier economy, because the government must increase borrowing and absorb more resources from financial markets, spend more of its budget on interest payments, and contemplate interventions to reduce the deficit, all of which have potentially economically depressing effects. In addition, the public's anticipation of future deficits may affect real rates. Nevertheless, the notion that budget deficits are dominant in determining the real interest rate is contradicted by the historical record. The growth in the national debt and federal deficits are dealt with in detail in Part II.

SUGGESTIONS FOR FURTHER READING

Board of Governors of the Federal Reserve System, *The Federal Reserve System — Purposes and Functions*. Washington, D.C.: Board of Governors of the Federal

Reserve System, 1984. A good, concise overview of the Federal Reserve System and monetary policy.

Federal Reserve Bulletin. Washington, D.C.: The Federal Reserve. A monthly periodical that delves into recent and historical monetary, interest rate, and inflation developments, as well as data issues concerning the measurement of monetary aggregates.

Friedman, Milton, and Schwartz, Anna, *A Monetary History of the United States — 1867–1960.* Princeton, N.J.: Princeton University Press, 1963. Looks at money supply behavior and its effects on the economy prior to and for the first third of the 1946–92 time period.

Money Stock Revisions (M1, M2, M3). Washington, D.C.: Board of Governors of the Federal Reserve. A data source which provides an annual update of monetary aggregates (M1, M2, and M3 and their components) and explains the changes that were made to the data series from the previous year.

NOTES

1. The term "expected inflation" is used because borrowers and lenders, by whose actions the prime interest rate is determined, make judgments as to what they "expect" inflation to be, in order to decide whether, how much, and for how long to borrow or lend. Actual current inflation is used here as the estimate of expected inflation. Thus, the implied assumption is that the expectation of inflation is accurate.

2. The precise definitions of M1, M2, and M3 are found in Appendix A, Technical Notes.

3. The Advisory Committee on Monetary Statistics (1976) laid down general criteria for selecting the appropriate monetary aggregate to target, "the Federal Reserve should use as an intermediate target that monetary total (aggregate), or those totals, through which it can most reliably affect the behavior of its ultimate objectives — the price level, employment, output, and the like. Which total or totals best satisfy that requirement depends, in turn, on (1) how accurately the total can be measured, and (2) how precisely, and at what costs, including unwanted side effects, the Fed can control the total; and (3) how closely and reliably changes in the total are related to the ultimate policy objectives" (Anderson & Kavajecz, 1994). As shown in Appendix B, the relationship between M1 and GDP is less reliable than that between M2 and GDP.

4. Economists of the Rational Expectations School would be quick to point out, however, that unanticipated fluctuations in the money supply could have some real effects on the economy.

5. The conversion from the nominal rate to the real rate is $r_{rp} = (1 + r_p) / (1 + $ inflation rate), where r_{rp} is the real prime rate and r_p is the nominal prime rate. Additional notes pertaining to the real interest rate are given in Appendix A.

6. Each of the seven governors of the Fed serves a 14-year term. Therefore, no president can appoint all of the governors but, rather, appoints an average of only one governor for every two years as president. The Fed chairman, on the other hand, serves a four-year term, and, usually, every president has an opportunity to appoint a Fed chairman.

7. The government is obliged to do so by the Employment Act of 1946 as amended by the Full Employment and Balance Growth Act of 1978.

8. For example, if a member bank takes in a deposit of $100 and is required to hold $12.50 in cash on hand (implying a required reserve rate of 12.5 percent), then the banking system can lend a total of $800 based on the original $100 deposit. This multiplier effect is made possible by the fact that the bank has to keep only 12.5 percent of the deposit in cash on hand or in liquid instruments. The "money multiplier," which is eight in this case, is calculated by dividing the required reserve rate, 12.5

percent, into 100 percent. If the Fed lowers the required reserve rate at member banks from 12.5 to 10.0 percent, the money multiplier is then increased from eight to ten, and a $100 deposit now allows the banking system to lend $1,000, rather than $800, thus, increasing the money supply.

9.   The period examined for the money supply extends only to 1992 because this variable is not lagged but, rather, coincides exactly with the president's term of office.

10.   The relationship between a measure of the money supply (whether M1, M2, or M3) and GDP, which is defined as GDP divided by the money supply measure, is called the "velocity" of money. In order to provide a reliable target for monetary policy, the monetary measure should have a stable velocity. In the case of M1, the velocity did not remain constant but rose steadily from 1970 until 1981, when it dropped sharply. M1 has had an unstable relationship with GDP ever since. By contrast, M2 fluctuated around a fairly constant velocity during 1970–93.

11.   Anderson and Kavajecz point out that, "While the change [in definition] has a strong footing in the increased similarity between banks and thrifts that arose after 1980, the counterfactual restatement of all past data on the same basis at least suggests caution in the intrepretation of results from long run studies." It is valid to aggregate financial assets only to the extent that they are close substitutes in either demand or supply.

12.   The prime rate should not be confused with deposit rates, which were strictly controlled under interest rate ceilings. These interest ceilings meant that deposit rates were essentially determined by the inflation rate, because there was only very limited possibility for the regulated nominal rate to adjust. Only the low and moderate inflation of the 1950s and 1960s guaranteed "reasonable" real returns on deposits. As nominal deposit rates were gradually deregulated during the 1970s and early 1980s, nominal deposit rates were initially quite volatile and high, because of the deregulation and the perceived increased risk level in the economy caused by high inflation followed by a deep recession, which combined to raise nominal interest rates to historically high levels.

6

Saving and Investment Rates

Saving represents the supply of and investment represents the demand for loanable funds. The two are linked, as shown in the previous chapter, by the interest rate. The investment referred to in this chapter is the gross private investment, while two measures of saving are used: gross private saving, which is all private sector saving, that is, from individuals and corporations, but excluding the government, and personal saving, which captures only individuals' saving behavior and accounts for less than half of the total supply of loanable funds. Thus, only the minor share of investment depends on the level of personal saving. In only nine of the 42 years for which data are available does personal saving account for even one-third of investment funds, and in no year did the share of savings in total investment sources exceed 44.4 percent. The corporate sector had to bear the burden of declining personal saving and increasing government dissaving to supply the economy with investment funds. In addition, in recent years, investment funds have come increasingly from abroad. Yet, the personal saving rate is worth examining separately because it provides separate insights into the percentage of income that individuals are willing to set aside in order to bolster future income and security.

The interest rate represents the "financial price" at which total saving and investment are equal.[1] However, there are numerous other factors that determine saving and investment. For investment, the interest or borrowing rate is the "opportunity cost of capital" against which the expected return on investment[2] must be compared. If the expected return on investment is greater than the opportunity cost of capital, then the investment under consideration has met the minimum criterion and is viable. This investment must still be ranked among a list of possible competing investments before it is determined that it should be carried out. Keynes, in his *The General Theory of Employment, Interest and Money*, posited that investment was driven not so much by financial variables as by "animal spirits" (akin to human urges) that take on a collective momentum throughout the economy. For saving, the level of income is most often cited as the determinant. The higher an individual's income, the higher is not only the level but also the rate of saving. The percentage saved of each additional dollar earned is higher, that is, the marginal saving rate rises with income. The "permanent income hypothesis," developed by Milton Friedman,[3] offers another explanation of saving behavior. This hypothesis maintains that individuals change their saving in order to preserve a steady rate of consumption, implying that individuals' saving decisions are not particularly sensitive to the interest rate.

GROSS PRIVATE INVESTMENT RATE

The broad components of investment, as reported in the National Income and Product Accounts (NIPA), are residential, nonresidential, and change in business inventories. Government spending is not part of investment. As shown in Chapter 2, investment is a component of gross domestic product (GDP) in the equation $C + I + G + (X–M) = GDP$. Investment, I, is divided by the GDP to yield the investment rate. Investment is not as direct a measure of economic performance as is GDP, but it is what propels economic growth. The entrepreneur, willing to risk his own capital to pursue an activity with the expectation that it will provide a return that is superior to that of risk-free assets, makes economic growth and higher living standards possible. It is true, as the above equation shows, that increases in both consumption and investment add to GDP. However, although consumption is the ultimate goal of economic activity, it is investment and saving that provide for the future and enhance economic security. Although the right balance between investment or saving and consumption is uncertain, it has never been the consensus that there was too much investment or saving in any year since World War II. Thus, the investment rate is an important measure of presidential performance because it creates employment and economic growth both in the present and for years after the administration has ended, that is, long after the one-year time lag on which the averages and trends are based. The rate of investment was chosen over either the investment growth rate or the real level of investment because it more clearly illustrates performance. Investment growth rates fluctuate so sharply that they sometimes exaggerate and other times mask performance trends, while real investment levels do not capture relative changes in investment. Investment rates also illustrate the percentage of the GDP that the economy is willing to devote to investment in order to increase future employment and consumption. Official investment data are provided by the U.S. Department of Commerce.

SAVING RATE

Gross Private Saving

As stated, two saving measures are used: the gross private saving rate and the personal saving rate. Gross private saving closely approximates the level of gross private investment, while personal saving focuses on individuals' saving behavior. Gross saving, which includes the government sector, is omitted here because the government sector saving is amply dealt with in Chapter 11. The components of gross private saving are personal saving, corporate and noncorporate consumption of fixed capital, and undistributed corporate profits. Gross private saving data are provided by the U.S. Department of Commerce, Bureau of Economic Analysis. The rate of gross private saving is determined by dividing gross private saving by GDP.

Personal Saving

The personal saving rate is provided to compliment the gross private saving rate, because it gets at the saving behavior of individuals, around which much of the saving controversy centers. The personal saving concept used here consists of the increase in financial assets (including securities and private life insurance reserves) plus the net increase in tangible assets (e.g., homes, factories, inventories) minus the net increase in liabilities (e.g., mortgage debt on homes and other property, consumer credit). All saving rates are ex post, that is, actual. This formulation of the saving rate follows the NIPA definition. Another version of the personal saving rate is calculated according to the flow of funds (FOF) definition, which is similar to the NIPA but includes government pension and insurance reserves, net investment in consumer durables, and net saving by farm corporations. The NIPA version is used because it is the more restrictive definition of the two measures of saving and because gross private saving already covers a broad saving concept. The personal saving rate is calculated by dividing personal saving (NIPA version) by disposable income (rather than GDP).

The personal saving rate is a valuable indicator of a major source of investment funds and for examining the longstanding belief that Americans are poor savers who are unwilling to postpone current consumption for greater security and consumption in the future. It is important to address this controversy, because if the charge is true, then Americans are establishing a weak saving base on which to build an improved future living standard. A weak saving culture could also mean a more difficult adjustment for Americans if austerity measures are needed. Certainly, the unpopularity of austerity measures to reduce the dissaving represented by recent federal deficits lends credibility to the belief that Americans, in the aggregate, are not good savers. The answer to the related question of whether Americans are becoming ever larger spendthrifts over time can also be ascertained from the data.

The saving rate also provides information on the changing importance of saving as a source of investment funds over time. If savings are considered insufficient by some measure(s), then, to the extent that inadequate savings incentives are to blame, the president's performance evaluation suffers. The implication is that policies that create incentives to save, such as tax policy, could have been better. Therefore, the saving rate can be viewed as a presidential performance measure. A consistent data series for saving is available back to 1929 for the NIPA version. Saving rates, as opposed to saving growth rates, which are highly volatile, or real savings levels, are preferred as a performance measure, because saving rates, like investment rates, provide a clearer picture of the trends in saving over time. Thus, saving rates are depicted in Figure 5.2. The NIPA personal saving rate is provided by the Department of Commerce, Bureau of Economic Analysis.[4]

OVERVIEW OF TRENDS IN THE LONG RUN, 1946–93

Gross Private Investment Rate

The investment rate is available from the beginning of the post-war period and is illustrated in Figure 6.1. The average investment rate for the entire period is 16.2 percent. As is characteristic of the Truman years, volatility was high with the first two years of the period at about 15 percent, then jumping to 18.5 percent in 1948, and plummeting to 14.2 percent in 1949 before shooting up again to 18.9 and 18.2 percent in 1950–51, the highest levels until 1978. For the last two years of the Truman administration, investment fell back to 15.4 and 15.2 percent. Eisenhower started off with a further decline in 1954 to 14.5 percent and a substantial increase to 17.0 and leveling at 16.9–17.0 percent during 1955–56. Investment rates then fluctuated between 14.2 and 15.9 percent during 1957–61. Kennedy began with a 15.4 percent investment share in 1962, which inched up to 15.7 percent by 1964. In 1965 and 1966, Johnson realized higher investment rates of 16.8 and 17.0 percent, respectively, before the rates dropped to the 15.7 to 16.2 percent range during 1967–69.

Nixon's administration began with a substantial drop to 14.9 percent but then recorded three substantial increases to 16.0, 17.0, and 18.0 percent by 1973. His administration ended with a substantial drop over two years to 14.3 percent by 1975. Under Ford, the rates recovered to 16.2 percent in 1976 and 18.1 percent in 1977. Carter enjoyed even higher investment rates, beginning at 19.4 percent in 1978, 19.3 percent in 1979, dropping to 17.3 percent in 1980, and closing out the

FIGURE 6.1
Gross Private Investment Rate, 1946-93

(Percent of GDP)

Investment Rate

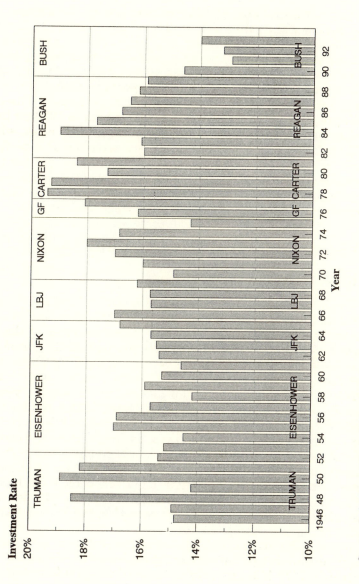

Source: U.S. Department of Commerce.

administration in 1981 at 18.4 percent. The Reagan administration began with a large drop to the 16.0–16.1 percent level in 1982 and 1983. In 1984, under full economic recovery, the rate of investment leaped to 19.0 percent. Over the next five years, the investment rate declined to 15.9 percent, first with substantial decreases to 17.7 percent in 1985 and 16.8 percent in 1986 and then more gradually to 16.8, 16.2, and 15.9 percent during 1987–89. Under Bush, the downward trend resumed but at a faster rate with investment dropping to 14.6 percent in 1990 and 12.9 percent in 1991 (the low for the period) before recovering to 13.2 percent in 1992 and 14.0 percent in 1993.

Saving Rate

Gross Private Saving

For the period as a whole (Figure 6.2), private saving rates varied only within a narrow range, 15.3–19.7 percent, with the exception of 1946 and 1947, when the rates were only 14.3 and 12.0, respectively. Within the 1946–93 period, three subperiods can be identified: 1948–69, which was typified by moderate and steady saving rates ranging between 15.3 and 17.0 percent; 1970–84, characterized by sharply increasing and high saving rates (11 of the 15 years had rates of 18 percent or higher and a peak of 19.7 percent in 1984); and 1985–93, in which saving generally declined until 1990 and remained near 16 percent through 1993. The average for the 1946–93 period was 16.9 percent.

As is often the case with the indicators immediately following World War II, the overall period began with the two lowest saving years of the period, 14.3 and 12.0 percent. In 1948, the saving rate recovered strongly to 16.3 percent, fell a percentage point to 15.3 percent the following year, and then increased for the next three years to 16.1 percent by 1952. The gross private saving rate fell to 15.6 percent in 1953, then rose for another three years to 17.0 percent, and remained at that level for three years (1956–58). In 1959, the saving rate dropped slightly to 16.7 percent, then to 15.9 percent the following year. During 1961–63, saving rates rose to 16.4 percent, then to 16.8 percent, and fell back to 16.4 percent. For the next four years, saving rates were relatively high, exceeding 17 percent. Over the next two years, the rate dropped sharply from 17.7 percent in 1967 to 15.6 percent in 1969.

The second period of saving rates began in 1970 and led off the first two years with large increases to 16.4 and 17.5 percent. The rate dropped to 17.0 percent in 1972, increased to over 18 percent for the first time in 1973, fell to 17.6 percent in 1974, and then remained at 18 percent or higher for the next 11 years. It was over 19 percent for the first time in 1975. The rate was above 18 percent for all of Carter's administration and reached peaks of 19.6 and 19.7 percent under

FIGURE 6.2
Gross Private Saving Rate, 1946–93

Percent of GDP

Savings Rate

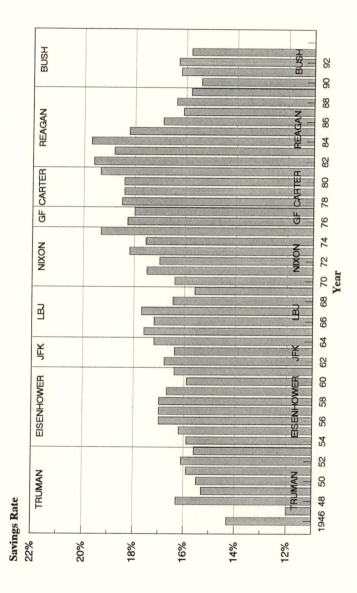

Source: U.S. Department of Commerce.

Reagan in 1982 and 1984, respectively. After 1984, the saving rate entered the third subperiod with three substantial percentage drops to 18.2, 16.9, and 16.1 in 1985, 1986, and 1987, respectively. For the next six years, gross private saving remained within the range of 15.4–16.4 percent, comparable to the first period but lower than the second.

Personal Saving

In general, the pattern of personal saving rates is not regular, although the peaks and troughs tend to be spaced about three to five years apart (Figure 6.3). There are no trends that last more than four years in either a positive or negative direction, and the lower and upper bounds of saving rates are 4.0 percent and 9.0 percent, respectively. For the period 1950–86, unlike the case for most other indicators, the saving rate levels in the earlier years do not appear systematically different from those of the latter periods, that is, individuals' inclination to save did not change significantly during 1950–86. However, from 1987 to 1993, personal saving rates were substantially lower than in previous years. The average saving rate for 1946–93 was 6.6 percent.

For the first five years under Truman, personal saving rates were quite volatile, starting in 1946 at 8.5 percent, dropping to 3.0 percent the following year, back up to 5.7 percent in 1948, down to 3.7 percent in 1949, and to 5.9 percent in 1950. Thereafter, rates settled down to the 7.2–7.3 percent level during 1951–53. Early in the Eisenhower administration, saving rates fell to 6.3 in 1954 and to 5.7 percent by 1955. The saving rate increased to 7.2 percent for two years and to 7.5 percent in 1958 before beginning another two-year drop to 5.7 percent by 1960, which proved to be the lowest rate until 1987. Eisenhower closed out his administration with a 6.6 percent saving rate. Under Kennedy, the saving rate dropped to 6.5 and then 5.9 percent but increased to 6.9 percent in 1964. During Johnson's term, saving rates oscillated between 6.5 and 8.1 percent, closing with 6.5 percent in 1969. The Nixon administration witnessed higher saving rates, ranging from 7.0 to a historically high 9.0 percent in 1973. Rates fell to 7.4 and 6.3 percent under Ford.

During Carter's administration, the saving rate increased all four years, reaching 8.8 percent in 1981. Under Reagan, the saving rate fell slightly in 1982 to 8.6 percent and then sharply to 6.8 percent in 1983 but by 1984 had recovered to 8.0 percent. Thereafter, it was downhill for saving rates, as the Reagan administration closed out with a historical low of 4.0 percent. The Bush administration improved personal saving rates somewhat to 5.3 percent by 1992 and closed with 5.0 percent in 1993.

FIGURE 6.3
Personal Saving Rate, 1946–93

(Share of Disposable Income)

Savings Rate

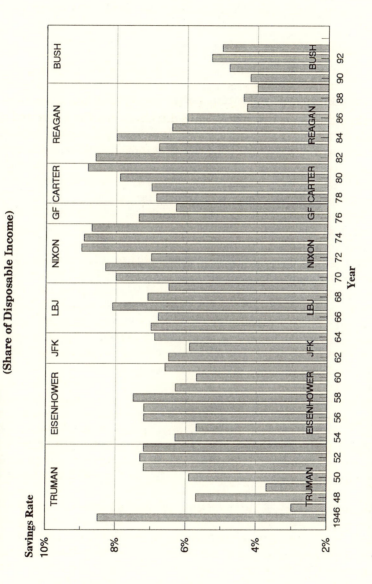

Source: U.S. Department of Commerce.

PRESIDENTIAL RANKINGS

In ranking both types of saving rates and investment rates, it is clear that the higher the indicator value, the better. Hence, the presidents are ranked in descending order according to average rates and trend improvement. Although the degree of fluctuation of saving and investment rates occasionally was rather high, the trend changes within administrations contain important information on performance, although generally not as important as the averages.

Gross Private Investment Rate

The presidential rankings of gross private investment rates are shown in Table 6.1. Carter had the highest average investment rate, 18.6 percent. However, he recorded only a modest improvement in the rate (0.3 percentage points), having inherited a high (18.1 percent in 1977) rate of investment from Gerald Ford. Ford ranks second at 17.2 percent and has the sharpest rate improvement at 3.9 percentage points. After Ford comes Reagan at 16.8 percent but with the largest reduction of the investment rate, 2.6 percentage points. Truman is in fourth place at 16.5 percent, with a 0.3 percentage point improvement, followed by Johnson and Nixon with rates of 16.3 and 16.2 percent, respectively. Under Johnson, the rate increased by 0.5 percentage point, while under Nixon, the rate declined by 1.9 percentage points. Eisenhower and Kennedy at 15.5 percent and Bush at 13.7 percent round out the bottom third, but Kennedy's performance rating is aided by the improvement in the rate of 1.1 percentage points, whereas

TABLE 6.1
Gross Private Investment Rates

Average Investment Rate			Increase in Investment Rate — Trend Change	
President	Term	Percent	President	Percentage Points
Carter	1977–81	18.6	Ford	3.9
Ford	1974–77	17.2	Kennedy	1.1
Reagan	1981–89	16.8	Johnson	0.5
Truman	1945–53	16.5	Truman	0.3
Johnson	1963–69	16.3	Carter	0.3
Nixon	1969–74	16.2	Eisenhower	−0.6
Eisenhower	1953–61	15.5	Nixon	−1.9
Kennedy	1961–63	15.5	Bush	−1.9
Bush	1989–93	13.7	Reagan	−2.6
Average, 1946–93		16.2		

Eisenhower and Bush both lowered the rate by 0.6 and 1.9 percentage points, respectively.

Saving Rate

Gross Private Saving

As with investment, a higher saving rate is considered better, and the presidents are ranked in descending order in Table 6.2. Gross private saving is conceptually closely linked with gross private investment, and the two rankings are similar, with the exception of Truman's and Nixon's. Also, as in the case of investment, the trend change may be as important as the average to saving performance. Carter, Ford, and Nixon recorded the highest private saving rates of 18.7, 18.1, and 17.7 percent, respectively. Nixon raised the saving rate by far more than the other presidents, 3.7 percentage points, which, combined with his high average, suggests that he had the best saving performance. Carter is a close second with the highest average and an increase in the rate of 1.3 percentage points, but still 2.4 percentage points below Nixon. Ford reduced the saving rate by 1.3 percentage points and is not a contender for the top rank.

Reagan, Johnson, and Kennedy are next, but Kennedy is clearly the superior because he raised the rate while the other two lowered it. Although Reagan recorded a relatively high 17.7 percent (the same as Ford), he reduced saving by the second most of any president, 3.6 percentage points. Johnson also reduced the rate but by a lesser amount,

TABLE 6.2
Gross Private Saving Rates

Average Gross Private Saving Rate		Increase in Saving Rate — Trend Change	
President	Percent	President	Percentage Points
Carter	18.7	Nixon	3.7
Ford	18.1	Carter	1.3
Nixon	17.7	Eisenhower	0.8
Reagan	17.7	Kennedy	0.8
Johnson	16.9	Bush	0.0
Kennedy	16.8	Ford	−1.3
Eisenhower	16.5	Johnson	−1.6
Bush	15.9	Reagan	−3.6
Truman	15.1	Truman	−5.7
Average, 1946–93	16.9		

1.6 percentage points. Eisenhower, Bush, and Truman recorded the lowest average gross private saving rates, with 16.5, 15.9, and 15.1 percent, respectively. Eisenhower, however, increased the saving rate by 0.8 percentage point. Bush left the saving rate unchanged, while Truman lowered the saving rate by more than any other president, 5.7 percentage points. Overall, Truman clearly had the weakest saving performance.

Personal Saving

The presidential rankings of personal saving rates are shown in Table 6.3. Nixon recorded the best personal saving record as well, with the highest saving rate at 8.3 percent and an increase in the rate of 2.2percentage points. Carter was second at 7.7 percent and increased the saving rate by 2.5 percentage points. Johnson was third at 7.1 percent but slightly reduced the rate by 0.4 percentage point, and Ford was fourth with an average of 6.8 percent but with a substantial decrease in the saving rate of 2.4 percentage points.

TABLE 6.3
Personal Saving Rates

Average Personal Saving Rate		Increase in Saving Rates — Trend Change	
President	Percent	President	Percentage Points
Nixon	8.3	Carter	2.5
Carter	7.7	Nixon	2.2
Johnson	7.1	Bush	1.0
Ford	6.8	Kennedy	0.3
Eisenhower	6.6	Johnson	−0.4
Kennedy	6.4	Eisenhower	−0.6
Reagan	6.1	Ford	−2.4
Truman	6.1	Reagan	−4.8
Bush	4.8	Truman	−11.9
Average, 1946–93	6.6		

Eisenhower, Kennedy, Reagan, and Truman are close together at 6.6, 6.4, 6.1, and 6.1 percent, respectively. Kennedy improved the personal saving rate slightly, and Eisenhower reduced it slightly. Reagan recorded the second largest drop in the personal saving rate of 4.8 percentage points, and Truman recorded by far the largest personal saving rate decline at 11.9 percent. As is often the case, Truman's numbers are distorted by the post-war economic transition. If 1947 is taken as his first year, rather than 1946, then Truman's trend change would be a positive 1.3 percentage points. Bush's weak average savings rate is bolstered somewhat by his improvement of the savings rate by 1.0 percentage point (third best).

SUMMARY AND SELECTED ISSUES

Investment Rate

In general, the behavior of investment rates appears to be one of continuous fluctuation, although within a narrow range (14.5 to 18.0 percent, with the exception of the very beginning and very end of the 1946–93 period) without any particular time dependency — that is, there does not appear to be any long period of high investment rates or low investment rates; high and low rates are scattered throughout the period. The presidential rankings are consistent with the observation that a president's average investment rate had little to do with the historical period in which he held office. The top three investment rates were from Carter, Truman, and Ford, and the bottom three were from Eisenhower, Kennedy, and Bush.

There does appear to be some relationship between investment and the cost of borrowing, that is, the real interest rate. Presidential rankings of average investment rates bear some resemblance to those of real interest rates. For example, Ford had the second highest investment rate and the second lowest real interest rate. Johnson ranks in the middle of the nine presidents in both real interest rates and investment rates. Bush and Kennedy recorded the second and third *highest* average real interest rates and the first and second *lowest* average investment rates. However, Reagan and Carter seem out of place in terms of the investment/interest rate relationship. Carter had a relatively high (fourth highest) real interest rate but by far the highest investment rate. Reagan had by far the highest real interest rate but was only 0.4 percentage point from second place in average investment rate.

An interesting statistical linkage is that between gross private investment and gross private saving, which display similarities in the presidential rankings. In terms of these rankings, it is notable that four presidents (Carter, Ford, Johnson, and Eisenhower) occupy the same positions in the rankings for both private saving and investment, while two others (Reagan and Bush) have only a one-notch difference in their respective gross private saving and investment rankings. This observation lends support to the idea that saving and investment generally move together, if not on a year-to-year basis. However, there is some general similarity among the major subperiods for private saving and private investment as well. The fluctuations in private investment are more radical and, in some years, move in opposite directions to those of private saving.

In point of fact, gross private saving and gross private investment are not the best match to demonstrate equality between saving and investment, as Table 6.4 shows. Gross private saving and gross private investment differ statistically and/or conceptually in three ways: (1) gross *private* investment omits net foreign investment, (2) gross *private* saving omits all government (federal and state and local) surpluses and deficits, and (3) a statistical discrepancy exists, which is defined as the amount by which gross investment exceeds gross saving. Because the magnitude of government saving (surpluses and deficits) bears no relationship to that of foreign investment, the size of the omissions from gross private saving and gross private investment may be quite different and, therefore, so will be gross private saving and gross private investment. The concepts of gross saving and gross investment actually track each other much more closely because they include items (1) and (2). Thus, they differ only by the statistical discrepancy. To clearly illustrate the difference, the atypical example of 1945 is presented in which there was an extremely large budget deficit. In that year, gross private saving was $45.5 billion, while gross private investment was only $10.9 billion. However, gross saving and gross investment were

TABLE 6.4
Components of Saving and Investment
(billions of current dollars)

	1945	1988
Gross saving	5.6	704.0
Gross private saving	45.5	802.3
Personal Saving	28.6	155.7
Undistributed corporate profits with inventory valuation and capital consumption adjustment	4.5	112.6
Undistributed profits	4.7	95.2
Inventory valuation adjustment	−0.6	−27.3
Capital consumption adjustment	0.4	44.7
Corporate consumption of fixed capital	6.5	327.6
Noncorporate consumption of fixed capital	5.9	206.4
Wage accruals less disbursement	0.0	0.0
Government surplus or deficit (−), national income, and product accounts	−39.9	−98.3
Federal	−42.5	−136.6
State and local	2.6	38.4
Capital grants received by the United States (net)	0.0	0.0
Gross investment	9.5	675.6
Gross private domestic investment	10.9	793.6
Net foreign investment	−1.3	−118.0
Statistical discrepancy	3.9	−28.4

Source: National Income and Product Accounts of the United States, Vols. 1 and 2 (1929–88). Washington, D.C.: U.S. Department of Commerce, 1992.

much closer together, at $5.6 and $9.5 billion, respectively, leaving a statistical discrepancy of $3.9 billion. This discrepancy is far above typical statistical discrepancies for the 1946–93 period. Most are 3 percent or less of gross investment. The year 1988 is added to Table 6.4 to show a more representative and recent breakdown of the major components of saving and investment under the NIPA.

On the performance side, certainly one of the more unexpected observations is that, Carter, in contrast to below par performance in most other indicators, had by far the highest investment rate. Despite a declining economy, high interest rates, and high inflation, investment remained high during his administration, not falling below 17.3 percent. Yet, GDP growth under Carter was weak during his last years, 1980–81. Moreover, as shown in the next chapter, Carter's productivity growth was the lowest for any president. In contrast, in 1982 and 1983, investment rates were low, but GDP growth took off shortly thereafter during 1983–84. The explanation for these observations may be the comparative lack of consumer confidence during the Carter administration and, with the defeat of inflation, the restoration of consumer confidence under Reagan. The thesis that the expansion in the 1980s was consumer driven might explain the lower investment but higher growth levels under Reagan compared with Carter. A consumer-driven expansion is also consistent with the declining saving rates observed after 1984.

Gross Private and Personal Saving Rates

For many years, Americans have been chastised as poor savers by the Europeans and Japanese, both of whom save a higher percentage of their disposable income. Compared with these groups, Americans do have an inferior savings record, as shown by the personal saving rates during 1946–93. Moreover, concern has been raised that for decades, saving rates have been going down, leaving the impression that they actually have. This concern is valid only after 1986. In the years leading up to 1987, saving rates were not appreciably lower than those of the 1940s and 1950s. Saving rates did, however, reach historically low levels in the 1990s. There was an upward trend at the end of the period, but it is uncertain whether saving will be restored to previous levels or if it will remain depressed for a prolonged period.

Another important observation with respect to saving is that saving rates demonstrated little or no relationship to real interest rates. Certainly, saving depends on other variables such as income and individuals' efforts to maintain steady consumption based on their estimated lifetime income. However, the interest rate constitutes a "reward" for saving and would be expected to exert some visible influence on saving. For example, it would seem, at least intuitively, that very low real interest rates would be associated with low saving rates. Sometimes, even the opposite was true. The very low real interest rates of the 1970s, especially 1974 and 1975, saw among the highest saving rates of the entire 1946–93 period. Conversely, when real interest rates were still very high, around 5 percent during 1987–89, gross private and personal saving rates fell to around 15.4–16.4 percent and 4.0–4.4 percent, respectively, their lowest levels during the period. Thus, it is clear that other factors were stronger in determining saving rates.

Finally, in spite of some similarity, gross private saving and personal saving did display different patterns of behavior. Clearly, the main reason for this difference was that corporate saving behaved differently from personal saving. For example, although gross private saving, like personal saving, dropped substantially during 1985–87, the decrease in gross private saving was not nearly as severe, and, unlike the case of personal saving rates, the levels of gross private saving rates of the early 1990s were still higher than those of the late 1940s and early 1950s. In general, gross private saving fluctuations were of a smaller magnitude than those for personal saving. Thus, at several points (1949, 1954–56, 1959–60, 1976–80 and 1986–91), as can be inferred by comparing Figures 6.2 and 6.3, changes in corporate saving appeared to compensate for the decreases (and sometimes the increases) in personal saving. This observation supports the thesis that policies aimed at increasing overall saving must take into account the different saving behaviors of the corporate and individual sectors.

SUGGESTIONS FOR FURTHER READING

Adams, Gerard F., and Wachter, Susan M., *Savings and Capital Formation.* Lexington, Mass.: Lexington Books, 1986. Authors address problems of saving measurement and interpretation of post-war saving, disparate saving rates of United States and Japan, saving policies, and so on.

Walker, Charls E., Bloomfield, Mark A., and Thorning, Margo, eds., *The U.S. Savings Challenge — Policy Options for Productivity and Growth.* Boulder, Colo.: Westview Press, 1990. Evaluates the concern over saving and investment rates and offers strategies for increasing them. Provides both economist and policymaker perspectives.

NOTES

1. Of course, there is no unique interest rate but, rather, a range of interest rates that reflects the various risk and maturity combinations of the different forms of saving and investment. In the aggregate, gross saving equals gross investment.

2. The term "marginal efficiency of capital" is sometimes used and refers to the return realized by an additional dollar of investment.

3. Bransen, William H., *Macroeconomic Theory and Policy,* (2d ed.), p. 196. Philadelphia, Pa.: Harper & Row, 1979.

4.   Although the Federal Reserve primarily relies on the FOF concept of personal savings, it also calculates the NIPA concept of personal savings using FOF data. The Fed's method is to convert the FOF savings figure into a NIPA savings figure by subtracting, among other things, net investment (new minus depreciation) in consumer durables. The Fed uses a distributed lag to estimate the net investment in consumer durables.

7

Productivity and Compensation in the Business Sector

GROWTH IN PRODUCTIVITY INDEX

Closely linked to the hot topics of international competitiveness and the U.S. worker's standard of living is labor productivity. In political debates, the position is sometimes taken that the productivity of the U.S. worker is either declining or stagnating and, therefore, so is the U.S. standard of living. With productivity rising in competing countries, the argument goes, international competitiveness of the United States declines and so do exports, the trade balance, and so on. By examining the productivity index for the business sector and the rate of productivity growth, one can resolve whether, in fact, productivity is declining and, if so, for how long and by how much.[1] The index of productivity also provides insights into both recent as well as historical trends in productivity.

The indicator used to measure productivity here is the index of output per hour worked in the business sector, which encompasses the farming, manufacturing, and service sectors and typically accounts for nearly 80 percent of gross domestic product (GDP). The manufacturing sector, by itself, accounts for over 20 percent of GDP. The farm sector accounts for 1–2 percent of GDP. This index is the inflation-adjusted, that is, constant dollar (1987 = 100), output in the total business sector divided by the number of hours worked in the sector. This productivity measure reflects, but does not distinguish between, the fundamental determinants of productivity. Usually cited among these fundamental determinants are technological change, research and development, and economic restructuring. Other factors that influence productivity are the joint effects of capital investment, level of output, utilization of capacity, energy and materials, the organization of production, managerial skill, and the characteristics and effort level of the workforce. The inflation-adjusted data series is provided by the Bureau of

Labor Statistics, Productivity Research Division and is presented in Figure 7.1 for 1947–93 for the entire business sector.

GROWTH IN THE COMPENSATION INDEX

The compensation index is selected in tandem with the productivity index to examine how compensation and productivity behave with respect to each other. This juxtaposition helps to show whether, on average, the workforce is rewarded for productivity gains or penalized for lack thereof. In addition, the question has been raised as to whether compensation has also trended downward. Some politicians, for example, have alleged that in recent years "people have been working harder for less money." Although which "people" is not specified, the trends in compensation for the business sector as a whole can broadly confirm or refute this belief.

The compensation index measures the growth in hourly wages adjusted for inflation, that is, real wages. The index is applied to the same sectors and uses the same base year as the productivity index. Compensation includes wages and salaries and contributions of employers to Social Security and private health and pension funds but excludes "perks" such as company cars, expense accounts, free parking, and so on. The data series for compensation is also provided by the Bureau of Labor Statistics, Productivity Research Division.

OVERVIEW OF TRENDS IN THE LONG RUN, 1947–93

The indexes of real productivity and compensation are available back to 1947 and are depicted in Figures 7.1 and 7.2, respectively, and give a good representation of the long-run trends in these two variables. Growth rates of these indicators might also have been chosen, but they fluctuate such that they would not have illustrated as clearly the trends in productivity and compensation. However, average growth rates are the primary basis for the presidential rankings.

Productivity

Figure 7.1 shows that business productivity has been on a more or less steady rise throughout the entire time period. The exceptions have been single year drops in 1974 (recession) and 1989 and a two-year drop during 1979–80. Thus, contrary to what many might believe, the United States has not experienced overall long-term declines in productivity since World War II. Some economic sectors, such as textiles and steel, have become less internationally competitive, but that has not translated into a productivity decline for the nation as a whole.

The continuous rise in productivity has occurred at different rates, with alternating fast and moderate-to-slow growth periods. Over the

FIGURE 7.1
Productivity Growth — All Business Sector, 1947–93
(Index of Output/Hour — Adjusted for Inflation)

Index 1987=100

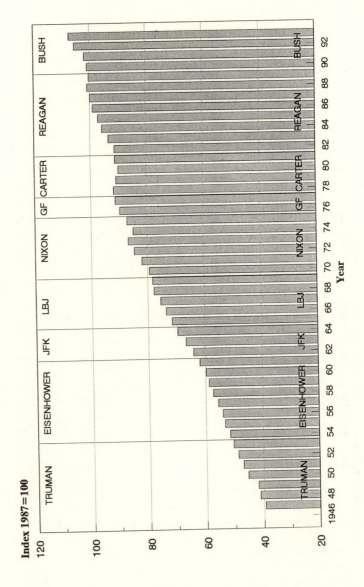

Source: U.S. Bureau of Labor Statistics.

FIGURE 7.2
Compensation Growth — All Business Sector, 1947-93
(Index of Compensation/Hour — Adjusted for Inflation)

Index 1987=100

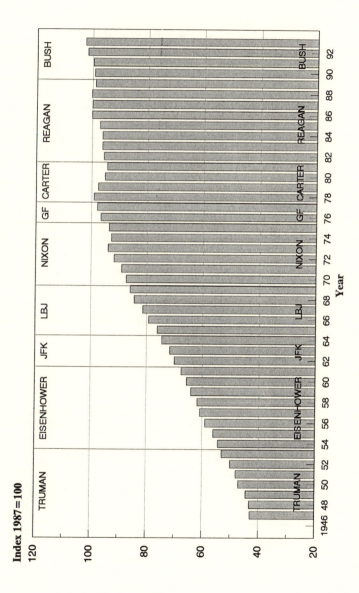

Source: U.S. Bureau of Labor Statistics.

entire period, the growth of productivity averaged 2.2 percent. As would be expected, productivity growth was strongest in the late 1940s and early 1950s, with an annual average in the 4.0 percent range, including a very high growth rate of 8.5 percent in 1950. The establishment of peacetime industry and gearing productive capacity to domestic consumer demand and industrial demand abroad contributed to the high rate of productivity growth. Korean War needs also maintained a substantial demand for military goods. For the rest of the 1950s, productivity growth moderated to the 1.5–3.5 percent range. Growth surged again in the first half of the 1960s (3.5–4.0 percent), moderated in the second half, and continued to slow down throughout the 1970s and early 1980s. Productivity growth picked up during 1983–86 but was soon back to low levels in the late 1980s through 1991. Productivity jumped to 3.3 percent in 1992 and settled back to 1.8 percent in 1993.

Compensation

Figure 7.2 depicts the path of compensation that more or less shadowed the upward trend of productivity until 1973, then followed the brief dip and recovery in productivity during 1974–78. Compensation, however, began to lag behind productivity by 1979. In fact, for three successive years, 1979–81, real compensation dropped, whereas the drop in productivity lasted only two years and was not as severe. From 1982 through 1993, real compensation began to grow, albeit at a snail's pace, averaging 0.5 percent per year with some minor fluctuations during the 12-year period.

PRESIDENTIAL RANKINGS

Growth rates are selected as the basis for presidential rankings rather than the values of the indexes because of the clearly time-dependent nature of these indexes. Specifically, there is a clear upward trend in the productivity and compensation indexes from Truman through Ford; like real GDP, real productivity and compensation simply rise over time. Therefore, for those six presidents, the ranking would be just a reverse chronological listing of presidents, with Truman in last place. The use of growth rates, as in the case of GDP, reduces (although does not eliminate) the time dependency of these indexes and establishes a better relative measure of improvement of U.S. productivity and compensation.

The choice of average growth rates as the primary basis for ranking dictates that the indicator of trend change is the change in growth rates. However, the high volatility of these growth rates means that the changes in growth rates are also volatile, making the latter a less valuable measure of performance. Had the average *values* of the indexes of productivity and compensation been chosen as the primary basis for ranking, the value of the trend change indicator would be the change in the indexes from the beginning to the end of the presidential administrations and would have been a more valuable performance measure.

Productivity

As mentioned, productivity growth rates are the basis for the rankings, and are presented in Table 7.1 along with the trend change indicator. For the six years recorded under Truman, productivity grew at its most rapid rate, an average of 4.1 percent annually. Kennedy is second with a 3.9 percent average productivity growth but, of course, sustained over only three years. Under Eisenhower, the post–World War II boom had moderated, and productivity growth cruised along at 2.6 percent for his eight years in office. Ford matches Johnson at 2.3 percent average growth, but, again, Ford took over during recovery years and reigned for only two years and five months. Johnson also lowered productivity growth by more than any other president by far, 3.7 percentage points, reflecting the productivity slowdown, while Ford decreased the rate by 0.7 of a percentage point. Nixon follows with an average productivity growth rate of 1.8 percent; Bush, 1.7 percent; Reagan, 1.2 percent; and Carter at the bottom with zero (actually slightly negative growth.

TABLE 7.1
Productivity Growth — All Business Sector

Productivity Index — Average Growth Rate			Change in Growth Rate — Trend	
President	Term	Percent	President	Percentage Points
Truman	1945–53	4.1	Bush	2.5
Kennedy	1961–63	3.9	Nixon	1.8
Eisenhower	1953–61	2.6	Eisenhower	0.6
Ford	1974–77	2.3	Kennedy	0.5
Johnson	1963–69	2.3	Carter	−0.4
Nixon	1969–74	1.8	Ford	−0.7
Bush	1989–93	1.7	Truman	−1.3
Reagan	1981–89	1.2	Reagan	−2.0
Carter	1977–81	0.0	Johnson	−3.7
Average, 1948–93		2.2		

It was observed earlier that productivity increased with every administration until Carter's. It is also true that the growth of productivity slowed down from Truman through Carter, with the exception of Kennedy and Ford. However, these are the presidents with the shortest tenures, and if the average of Ford is combined with that of Nixon, then, with the exception of the Kennedy years, average productivity growth rates slowed continuously and chronologically by presidential administration from Truman through Carter. Thereafter, with Carter recording no productivity growth and as productivity rebounded under Reagan and Bush, the long productivity growth slowdown was reversed.

Compensation

The presidential rankings of compensation growth are shown in Table 7.2. The first three presidents recorded the fastest growth in compensation, with Truman first at a 3.5 percent annual average, Kennedy second at 3.2 percent, and Eisenhower third at 3.0 percent. Truman also left office with a compensation growth rate of 6.0 percent, which resulted in the highest trend improvement, 5.5 percentage points. Eisenhower had the largest drop in the compensation growth rate, 3.1 percentage points, and Kennedy improved the trend 1.0 percentage point. Johnson, Ford, and Nixon, next in line chronologically, occupy the fourth, fifth, and sixth positions, with averages of 2.8, 2.3, and 1.4 percent, respectively. Ford improved the trend slightly, consistent with the recovering economy. Johnson recorded a substantial decline, and Nixon, a moderate decline.

TABLE 7.2
Compensation Growth — All Business Sector

Average Compensation Index Growth Rate		Change in Growth Rate — Trend	
President	Percent	President	Percentage Points
Truman	3.5	Truman	5.5
Kennedy	3.2	Bush	2.1
Eisenhower	3.0	Kennedy	1.0
Johnson	2.8	Ford	0.6
Ford	2.3	Reagan	–0.5
Nixon	1.4	Nixon	–0.9
Bush	0.9	Johnson	–2.2
Reagan	0.6	Carter	–2.2
Carter	–0.9	Eisenhower	–3.1
Average, 1948–93	1.9		

Bush, Reagan, and Carter constitute the bottom third, with growth rates of 0.9, 0.6, and –0.9 percent, respectively. They are also the most recent chronologically, supporting the thesis of a gradual, although not continuous, slowdown over time. Carter had a 2.2 percentage point drop in compensation growth, Reagan had a 0.5 percentage point drop, and Bush improved the trend by 2.1 percentage points, the second highest.

SELECTED ISSUES

Productivity is a key to higher living standard; the more productive a worker, the more valuable is his labor and the higher the compensation he can claim. Although productivity has increased through almost the entire 1948–93 period, the increases have become progressively smaller, with the first slowdown occurring in the mid-1960s and the second by the mid- to late-1970s. Despite considerable effort by policy makers (both helpful and counterproductive), productivity growth has not recovered to the rates of earlier periods. Perhaps one explanation is in the indicator itself. The productivity measure does not take fully into account the quality improvements that have occurred over this 46-year period. For example, consumer products such as cars and stereos have a far superior performance now compared with their counterparts of the late 1940s. Although these products have higher prices today, after adjusting for inflation, current prices may not fully reflect improved quality. Hence, the consumer's living standard has improved without a commensurate increase in *measured* productivity. Another example is health care, which, although much more expensive, even in real terms, for some of the same procedures, has undeniably better outcomes than 45 years ago. In some respects, therefore, the productivity slowdown may not be as pronounced as the data would suggest.

As far as attributing changes in the productivity index to presidential administrations with a one-year lag goes, caution is advised. Some analysts have pointed out that it can be a very slow process to increase productivity. Years of training and education, research and development, and assimilation of technological change are required before related productivity increases are realized. It is difficult to place the right lag period (e.g., one year, two years, or more) on indicators of productivity during presidential administrations that accurately anticipate the effect of their policies' impact on productivity, especially because various inputs, for example, training and research and development, take different lengths of time to increase productivity. Moreover, productivity and compensation tend to follow economic cycles that are, themselves, irregular and usually do not coincide with presidential administrations. Hence, it is stressed that the one-year lag applied to the productivity index may not be particularly accurate in measuring a president's true contribution toward improving productivity but is more appropriately characterized as a measure of what essentially happened on the president's watch with some breathing room left for the initial policy effects on productivity to be felt.

There is also an important conceptual weakness in the productivity index. In assessing productivity performance, it should be understood that growth in the productivity index may not always be indicative of a good performance. Productivity, as measured by the productivity index, is equal to the ratio of GDP in a sector to the hours worked in a sector. Thus, a productivity increase is recorded if either production increases at a faster rate than hours worked or if the number of hours worked in the sector falls faster than production. In the latter case, the productivity increase does not indicate a desirable economic trend. Reduction in the number of hours worked often is caused by a reduction in employment. This reduction, for example, was one source of the Bush average productivity growth of 1.7 percent. Carter demonstrated the opposite case. Only under Carter did productivity decline, but a good deal of employment was created, at least during the first two years of the Carter administration. Yet, 0 percent productivity growth is still 0 percent productivity growth. Both examples attest to the need for a broader range of indicators, in this case, employment indicators, such as those presented in Chapter 3, in assessing presidential economic performance.

In spite of these limitations on the productivity index, it can still shed some light on historical trends and recent controversies. For example, the controversial statement that "people are working harder for less money" can be tested. This controversy deserves examination because it has been a frequently expressed concern in the political arena and it impinges on workers' standard of living. The compensation indicator provides a good measure of the validity of this statement in its broadest sense because it is adjusted for inflation and is based on hours worked, not just the number employed. When the compensation index rises, living standards rise. The phrase "working harder for less money" is a rather vague concept, because it is not specified how much "harder" and how much "less." For the sake of argument, it is assumed that "working harder for less money" has virtually the same meaning as "working harder for the same money" and may be fairly interpreted as meaning that there has been a drop in compensation per hour worked. For example, if working harder means working 10 percent more hours in a year and if the same salary is earned, then there is an effective drop of 10 percent in wages and a drop in standard of living as workers have less leisure time.

The "working harder for less money" charge is usually made by those who view it as a trend which began in the Reagan administration. Actual compensation trends suggest that, to the extent that this concern is valid for the business sector as a whole, it preceded the Reagan administration. Like productivity, compensation growth rates fell slowly, but fairly steadily after 1946. However, compensation growth actually bottomed out during 1979–81, in which there were three successive years of declines in compensation. Under Reagan, although real compensation per hour worked did fall two out of eight years, on average it *grew* (0.9 percent), albeit at a slower rate than that of all other presidents except Carter. Compensation increased faster under Bush but still was the third slowest of the nine presidents. Thus, across the business sector as a whole, the rise in the compensation index (stressing again that it represents hourly wages, adjusted for inflation) meant that people were getting *more* money for the *same* hours worked. The only time that, in a broad sense, people were working harder for less money over an extended period of time was during 1979–81. The concern may be valid in other years for certain subsectors of the economy, such as portions of manufacturing because of economic restructuring, but not for the economy as a whole.

SUGGESTIONS FOR FURTHER READING

Baumol, William J., Blackman, Sue Anne Batey, and Wolf, Edward N., *Productivity and American Leadership: The Long View*. Cambridge, Mass.: MIT Press, 1989. Points out that there are long and variable time lags between implementing productivity improving measures and actual productivity increases.

Baumol, William J., and McLennan, Kenneth, eds., *Productivity Growth and U.S. Competitiveness*. New York: Oxford University Press, 1985. Describes slowdowns in productivity growth in the mid-1960s and the mid-1970s, provides comparison with Japan, and charts similar productivity growth slowdowns in other countries.

Black, Stanley W., ed., *Productivity Growth and the Competitiveness of the U.S. Economy*. Boston: Kluwer Academic Publishers, 1989. Includes analysis of U.S. productivity during 1950–86 and by subperiods, with comparisons of 11 other industrialized nations.

Denison, Edward F., *Accounting for Slower Economic Growth: The United States in the 1970s*. Washington, D.C.: The Brookings Institution, 1979. Explains productivity trends and causes in the post-war era to the mid-1970s.

Kendrick, John, *International Comparisons of Productivity and Causes of the Slowdown*. Cambridge, Mass.: Ballinger, 1984. The cyclical nature of labor productivity and labor compensation is demonstrated in the chapter on leading indicators.

Lipsey, Richard G., Steiner, Peter O., and Purvis, Douglas D., *Economics*. New York: Harper & Row, 1984. Chapter 13 provides a basic introduction to productivity and its measures. Later editions are also available.

NOTE

1. Clearly, the question of international competitiveness depends on comparisons of productivity growth in other countries as well, which is not part of this analysis.

8

Population below the
Poverty Line

The indicators described so far deal with measures of the whole "economic pie" and the inputs for increasing that pie. The poverty line statistic deals with a more social aspect of economic performance, in particular the controversial question of income distribution. Here, income distribution is examined through the percent of the population below the poverty line, a commonly cited indicator that measures the share of "have-nots" in the population. Changes in the poverty line indicator show the percentage of the population that, over time, slipped into poverty or shared in the benefits of economic growth sufficiently to emerge from poverty and whether, as a general trend over a longer time frame, the growth achieved by the U.S. economy in recent history led to less poverty. In addition, it may shed some light on the validity of such theories as "trickle-down" economics and "a rising tide lifts all boats."

The poverty line indicator was conceived in 1964, and the series was estimated back to 1959. Therefore, Truman is not included in the rankings, and only three of Eisenhower's eight years are available for this indicator. The poverty line measure is based on the level of income needed to purchase the goods and services, mostly food, clothing, shelter, and medical care, required for "basic human" needs. This income level is known as the poverty threshold, and its calculation is based on the most economical of four nutritionally adequate food plans designed by the Department of Agriculture and a 1955 survey by the Department of Agriculture that found that families of three or more spent about one-third of their income on food. Therefore, the poverty level was set at three times the cost of the least expensive food plan. Adjustments were made for families of one or two persons in order to make up for the higher fixed costs of rent, utilities, and so on. Modifications in 1969 changed the inflator of the poverty threshold for nonfarm families from the price index of the economy food plan to the consumer price index and raised the farm threshold from 70 to 85 percent of the nonfarm thresholds. These changes resulted in an increase of 360,000 families and 1.6

million individuals counted as poor in 1967. Further changes in 1980 were that separate thresholds for farm families were eliminated, thresholds for female household heads and "all other families" were averaged, and the poverty matrix was extended to families of nine or more.

Because the smallest economic units are families (of one or more people), thresholds are calculated specific to family size. The poverty threshold is compared to the family's total money income, for example, earnings, interest income, Social Security, public assistance payments, unemployment and workmen's compensation, and all pensions. The estimate of family income excludes nonmonetary transfers such as food stamps, subsidized school lunches, subsidized housing, medicaid, and medicare. Families whose income falls below the threshold are considered poor. Thus, there is a poverty threshold for each family size, and, of course, that threshold increases as family size increases. If, for example, a family of nine fell below the poverty threshold of $27,942 (1991 level), then all nine members of that family were said to be below the poverty line.

The percentage of the population belonging to families below the poverty line is depicted in Figure 8.1. Changes to the poverty threshold are made annually according to the inflation rate (CPI). For example, the 1990 poverty threshold for a family of four was $13,359 and in 1991 it increased to $13,924. Table 8.1 shows the poverty thresholds during 1959–93 for a family of four. The yearly percent below the poverty line figure is slightly different from the other indicators in that the data are collected in March of the following year but pertain to the recently ended calendar year. For example, for 1992, poverty line data are collected in March 1993 but cover calendar year 1992. Further details about this indicator are provided in Appendix A.

TABLE 8.1
Poverty Thresholds for a Family of Four, Selected Years, 1959–93

Year	Amount ($)	Year	Amount ($)
1959	2,973	1979	7,412
1964	3,169	1984	10,609
1969	3,743	1989	12,674
1974	5,038	1993	14,763

Source: *Poverty in the United States: 1992* (Washington, D.C.: Bureau of the Census, 1993), p. A-6.

The merits of the exclusion of nonmonetary benefits have been debated for years. Whether or not it is advisable to include noncash benefits depends on whether the aim is to evaluate how many poor people

FIGURE 8.1
Percent of Population below the Poverty Line, 1959-93
(Eisenhower to Bush)

Percent of Population

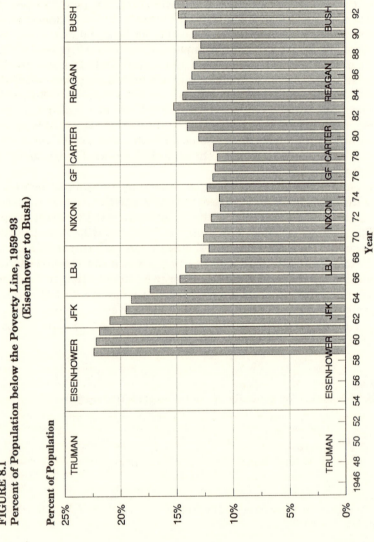

Source: U.S. Census Bureau.

still need to be rescued from poverty or to assess the need for the economy to provide more and better wage jobs to low income people so they can rise from poverty on their own. In the former case, the social program policy maker must determine who, after all poverty-alleviating inputs are accounted for, including income and social programs, is *still* poor. This goal argues for the inclusion of noncash benefits in families' total income. In this way, the social program policy maker can estimate the magnitude of unaddressed poverty. In the second case, the economic policy maker (and the taxpayer) wants to know the full need for jobs and wage increases for poor and borderline poor so that they no longer require economic assistance. Thus, to include noncash benefits would be to mask the true degree of poverty in the United States, because noncash benefits artificially lift people out of the poor category, which understates the problem of poverty from an economic point of view. A strong case also could be made that all government transfers, noncash and cash (other than pensions and most Social Security, to which beneficiaries have already contributed), be excluded from the calculation of income.

An important weakness of the poverty line indicator from both an economic and a social point of view is that it is based on pretax income. Thus, tax breaks for the poor are not directly reflected in the poverty line data. There is also a tendency for respondents to underreport their income. Probably the main reason for underreporting is that many of the programs of which the respondents are beneficiaries are means-tested programs, and they obviously do not want to disqualify themselves.

OVERVIEW OF TRENDS IN THE LONG RUN, 1959–93

Unlike many other indicators, the percent of the population below the poverty line did not fluctuate sharply on a yearly basis during 1959–93 but, rather, moved in fairly smooth waves over long time spans, as Figure 8.1 shows. This pattern is partly because this indicator is measured as a level in Figure 8.1 rather than a growth rate.

The trend in poverty was first estimated for 1959 at a rate of 22.4 percent. The percent below the poverty line declined for the next 15 years, which included the last three years of the Eisenhower administration, the Kennedy and Johnson years, and the first five years of Nixon's administration. It was interrupted by only a minor upsurge during 1970–71 and recorded the lowest level of the period in 1974 at a level of 11.1 percent. The decline in the poverty share ended in 1975, when it rose to 12.3 percent, but it then fell again for the next three years, the two years under Ford and the first year of Carter, to 11.4 percent by 1978. For the next five years, three under Carter and the first two under Reagan, the percent of the population under the poverty line increased, reaching 15.2 percent in 1983, as the poverty impact of the recession peaked. This level was the highest since 1965. For the next six years, all under Reagan, the percent below the poverty line decreased, dropping to 12.8 percent in 1989. Finally, when Bush took office, the percent below the poverty line increased during 1990–93, reaching 15.1 percent. It should be noted that poverty estimates for 1992 and 1993 are updated using the 1990 census information, which results in estimates of poverty that are higher than those based on the previous census.

PRESIDENTIAL RANKINGS

For the purposes of ranking, it is assumed that, for a given level of economic growth, the lower the percentage of the population below the poverty line, the better.[1] In other words, the lower the percentage of poverty, the better the performance and the higher the ranking (Table 8.2). Taking into account, however, that the world of the 1950s inherently had a much higher level of poverty than the world of, say, the 1970s, it is probably more important in ranking presidents to look at the rate at which the administrations reduced poverty during 1959–70, rather than just the average level for each administration. The trend change indicator is, therefore, very important with respect to the percent below the poverty line, because it measures the overall reduction/increase in the percent below the poverty line. A more refined trend indicator is the improvement in poverty reduction per year and is also provided in Table 8.2. This annual average improvement compensates for the different durations of the various administrations.

TABLE 8.2
Percent of Population below the Poverty Line

Average Percent Below Poverty Line			Reduction in Percent Below Poverty Line — Trend		
President	Term	Percent	President	Percentage Points	Per Year
Ford	1974–77	11.7	Johnson	–6.9	–1.4
Nixon	1969–74	11.9	Kennedy	–2.9	–1.0
Carter	1977–81	12.5	Reagan	–1.2	–0.2
Reagan	1989–93	13.9	Ford	–0.7	–0.4
Johnson	1963–69	14.2	Eisenhower	–0.5	–0.1
Bush	1981–89	14.4	Nixon	0.2	0.0
Kennedy	1961–63	19.8	Bush	2.3	0.6 (0.58)
Eisenhower	1953–61	22.1*	Carter	2.5	0.6 (0.63)
Truman	1945–53	na*	Truman	na	na
Average, 1959–93		14.6			

*No data are available for Truman and only three years for Eisenhower.

After 1970, as poverty sank to a level at which it became more difficult to eradicate at the margin, administration averages gain in importance as indicators of performance. For example, although it was first
under Nixon that the percent under the poverty line increased slightly
(and for only one year), it was at its lowest under Nixon, and the uptick
in poverty does not cancel out the fact that the poverty line was maintained at a low level in his administration. After 1979, the behavior of
the poverty line indicator changed significantly, rising as high as 15.1
percent in 1993 and falling to as low as 12.8 percent in 1989. Thus, the
post-1979 low was still 1.7 percentage points higher than the low of the
entire period of 11.1 percent (in 1973). Realistic goals for policy makers
in the 1980s and 1990s, then, appeared to be modest reductions in the
percent below the poverty line in nonrecessionary times, modest
increases in recessions, and a general and sustained return to an average of below 13 percent, near the levels of the early 1970s.

Ford and Nixon had the lowest average percent below the poverty
line for their administrations, having benefited from coming at the end
of the long downward trend as well as from high levels of social spending. Ford recorded a modest decrease of 0.7 percentage point in the
poverty trend, while Nixon recorded a modest increase of 0.2 percentage
point. Carter is third with a 12.5 percent average but recorded the
largest increase in poverty of 2.5 percentage points as well as the highest annual increase. Reagan's average ranked fourth at 13.9 percent but
with a reduction in poverty during his administration of 1.2 percentage
points, 0.2 percentage point annually.

Johnson recorded an average of 15 percent but had the greatest percentage reduction in poverty of 6.9 percentage points, the best per year
reduction of 1.4 percentage points, and, thus, the best record overall.
Bush is sixth with a 14.4 percent average and the second highest total
and annual increases of 2.3 and 0.6 percentage points, respectively.
Kennedy averaged 20.3 percent below the poverty line, a sizeable reduction of 2.9 percentage points and the second best per year reduction.
Although only three years of data for Eisenhower are available, they are
revealing in that they show the beginning of the long-term downward
trend in the population below the poverty line. Eisenhower, coming at
the beginning of the period for which data are available, understandably had the highest average at 22.1 percent but reduced the poverty
rate by 0.5 percentage point in three years. In general, the per year
average reduction in poverty indicators results in nearly the same
ranking for the presidents as the ranking according to total poverty
reduction. The only difference in the rankings is that Reagan and Ford
switch third and fourth places. Thus, the two indicators are mutually
reinforcing.

SELECTED ISSUES

The relationship between movements in the percent below the poverty line and overall economic conditions provides insights into how poverty has been reduced in the past. A comparison of the long-term gross domestic product growth from Chapter 2, Figure 2.1, and the population below the poverty line shows a strong correspondence between economic cycles and changes in the share of poor people in the economy. Periods of economic growth coincide with declines in the percentage below the poverty line, and recessions coincide with upswings or less rapid reductions in the share of the population below the poverty line. The empirical evidence that the fortunes of the poor are closely tied to overall economic growth supports the hypothesis that "a rising tide raises all boats." This hypothesis, although not inconsistent with, still is different from the trickle-down theory, which contends that it is the increase of resources (e.g., through tax breaks) specifically in the hands of the relatively wealthy that will result in greater savings and investment in the economy that will achieve increased economic growth that will then raise the wealth of the poor (largely through employment creation). The observed link between economic growth and a lower share of poor in the population supports a pillar of the trickle-down theory. Inasmuch as trickle-down policies were actually implemented by the Reagan administration, the fact that poverty shares declined at least partially supports the theory. For some policy makers, however, even if it is true that giving incentives to the better-off in society is an important source of the economic growth that later translates to a lessening of poverty, the time required for the "trickle" may not be acceptable from a social policy point of view.

In addition to improvement in overall economic conditions, social programs also apparently contributed to poverty reduction. It is observed that the Great Society measures of Johnson coincided with a rapid downward trend in poverty, far ahead of the rates achieved by Kennedy, Eisenhower, Reagan, or Ford. This decline is expected because of the creation and expansion of social programs and because the monetary transfer payments of these programs are included in the estimation of the incomes of the recipients for comparison with the poverty threshold. Some analysts argue, however, that such transfer payments result only in a short-term reduction in poverty but foster long-run dependency on the social programs, which may actually result in higher levels of poverty in the future. The perennial debates on welfare reform are driven by this concern. This thesis also may be supported by the fact that although Nixon and Ford continued increasing social spending (see Part II), there was not a commensurate reduction in the percent below the poverty line, although low poverty levels *were* maintained. The difficulty or inability to reduce poverty below relatively low levels is discussed separately below. Increasing progressivity of the tax structure through lowering the effective rates on the poor also would have a poverty-reducing impact but, unfortunately, is not captured by the poverty line indicator, which is based on pretax income.

The difficulty Nixon and Ford found in trying to reduce poverty further through high levels of social spending was probably because the share of poor in the population dropped to historically low levels, 11–12 percent of the population. The poor who remained probably were those, at the margin, for whom it was the most challenging to elevate out of poverty. In historical terms, it undoubtedly would be a major accomplishment in the future to lower the percent of poverty below 10 percent for a sustained period, assuming that the poverty threshold value is preserved. Such a goal likely would be reached only if prosperous economic times prevailed for a substantial period of time, educational levels of the poor were raised, and, at least initially, efficiently targeted antipoverty programs were maintained.

Although the relationship between poverty reduction and economic growth is empirically clear, some may still be surprised that under the Reagan administration, poverty was actually reduced. The antipoverty effects of economic growth under Reagan apparently overcame the effects, real or perceived (see Part II), of the cuts in social spending that occurred during his administration. The initial surge in the share of poverty under Reagan occurred during the deep 1982 recession, when unemployment topped 10 percent and real gross domestic product dropped by more than 2 percent. Once the recession had ended, the share of the population below the poverty line decreased from 15.2 percent in 1983 to 12.8 percent at the close of his administration.

SUGGESTIONS FOR FURTHER READING

Burton, C. Emory, *The Poverty Debate — Politics and the Poor in America*. Westport, Conn.: Greenwood Press, 1992. Deals with definition and measurement issues but concentrates on sociological aspects of poverty.

Poverty in the United States: 1992. Current Population Reports, Consumer Income, Series P-60, No. 185. Washington, D.C.: U.S. Department of Commerce, Economics and Statistics Administration, Bureau of the Census, September 1993. Fully explains the poverty line indicator and recent trends and disaggregates poverty statistics by race, gender, age, geographical area, and so on.

NOTE

1.   This assumption does not mean that policies that would accelerate income redistribution are advocated here.

9

Growth of the Stock Market — The Dow Jones Industrials Average

The stock market is regarded as a barometer of the economy. The public, through the stock market,[1] registers its optimism or pessimism about the future performance of companies through the quantities of stock it supplies and demands. Of course, an increasing demand for a stock drives up its price. The higher the share price, the more investment dollars a company can secure by selling a given share of the company. In other words, the higher the stock market index, the lower the average cost of investment to the companies comprising that index and, therefore, the more investment they can afford.

Although it is only one of many stock market indexes and may not be the most indicative of the performance of the overall stock market, the Dow Jones Industrials Average (DJIA) is reported more often than any other index. In this sense, the selection of the DJIA as the stock market indicator is a positive rather than a normative selection. The DJIA is reported throughout the day and after the close of the market. Other well-known stock indexes include Standard and Poor's (S & P 500),[2] Barron's 50-stock average, and the Wilshire 5000. The DJIA has been compiled since the late nineteenth century, first appearing on a daily basis in 1896, which was also the first year the index was composed entirely of industrial stocks. These "industrial" stocks also included companies in commodities such as sugar, leather, cotton oil, and tobacco. An early precursor to the DJIA, which began in 1884, contained 11 stocks, 9 of which were railroads.

The composition and size of the DJIA necessarily has changed over time as companies have started up, gone out of business, merged, and been taken over.[3] For the entire 1946–93 period, the DJIA has been the unweighted,[4] total dollar value of the stocks of 30 leading U.S. companies divided by the number of companies in the index and adjusted for stock splits and dividends. Because of the many stock splits and stock dividends during this period, the DJIA, in order to preserve comparability of stock market performance over time, has changed the formula for calculating its index. Specifically, it has recalculated the divisor to account for stock splits and stock dividends. To illustrate by numerical example, assume that the index is composed of two stocks, one worth $50 per share and the other worth $100 per share. The index is worth ($50 + $100) / 2 = $75. Now assume that the $100 stock splits two for one and is now worth $50 per share. Without adjusting the index's divisor, the index value would be ($50 + $50) / 2 = $50, implying a 33 percent drop in the index, when, in fact, there was really no drop in the total value of stock on the market. To account for the stock split, the DJIA changes the divisor, which is calculated as follows: $PV / PD = NV / ND$, where PV is the index's previous value, PD is the previous divisor, NV is the new value of the index after the split, and ND is the new divisor. Using the above example, the new divisor can be calculated: $150 / 2 = $100 / ND$, which yields $ND = 1.33$. Every time there is a stock split or stock dividend, there is a reduction in the index's divisor.[5,6]

A good illustration of the change in composition that the DJIA sometimes undergoes is the change that occurred in 1985 (the previous change in the DJIA had taken place in 1977). In 1985, IBM, American Express, Merck, McDonald's, and Philip-Morris were added to the DJIA, while Johns-Manville, Esmark, Chrysler, American Brands, and General Foods were deleted. The DJIA are presented as real (adjusted for inflation as measured by the consumer price index) values as well as nominal (not adjusted for inflation) values, and, like most other indicators, the averages and trends for each administration are lagged one year.

OVERVIEW OF TRENDS IN THE LONG RUN, 1946–93

Figure 9.1 illustrates the stock market index adjusted for inflation (consumer price index), and Figure 9.2 depicts the stock market not adjusted for inflation. Both figures are based on year-end (not year-average) DJIA data. Although there is a great deal of year-to-year fluctuation, the pattern of Figure 9.1 shows four distinct trends: eight years of small fluctuations under Truman, a long upward trend from 1954 to 1965, followed by a long decline during 1966–81, followed by another long upward trend from 1982 continuing through 1993. Prior to the initial long-term upward trend, the stock market hovered around the 1,000 mark for the first five years under Truman. There were moderate increases during 1949–52 as the DJIA approached the 1,250 level and dropped to 1,193 in Truman's last year, 1953. The average annual real growth rate for the 1946–93 period was 2.2 percent.

The stock market began to take off under Eisenhower in the second period, albeit with sharp fluctuations. In 1954, the market soared 512 points to 1,706 (in real terms). The next year saw another large increase of 363 points. The DJIA rose a small amount in 1956 but dropped

FIGURE 9.1
Stock Market (Real), 1946–93
(Dow Jones Industrial Averages)

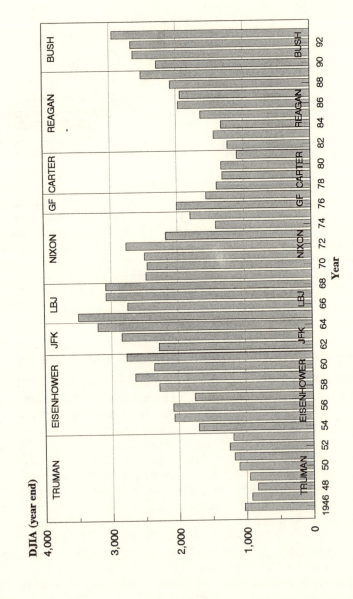

Source: Dow Jones Averages 1885–1990; *Wall Steet Journal,* 1991–93.

FIGURE 9.2
Stock Market (Nominal), 1946–93
(Dow Jones Industrial Averages)

DJIA (year end)

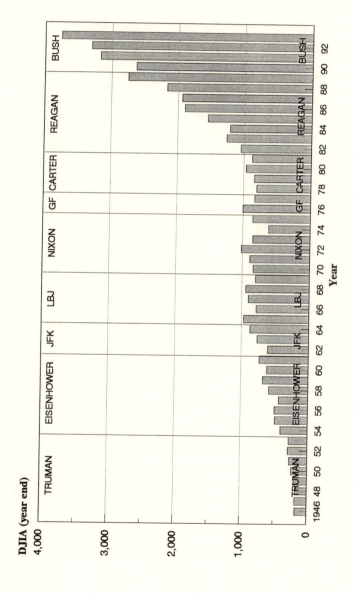

Source: Dow Jones Averages, 1885–1990; *Wall Street Journal,* 1991–93.

sharply in 1957 by 325 points. The following two years, the market soared again, rising 538 points in 1958 and 357 points in 1959. It dropped 287 points in 1960 but closed out the Eisenhower administration with a 414 point gain in 1961, almost reaching the 2,800 level. Stock market growth continued through Kennedy, although also in a seesaw fashion. In 1962 the DJIA dropped 486 points, increased 557 points the next year, and increased a further 355 points in 1964. The DJIA reached its peak in 1965, Johnson's first year, with another 293 point gain, almost achieving the 3,500 mark. The fluctuation during this period is shown by the tally of plus and minus years. Of the 20 years of the first two periods, there were ten increases (seven over 300 points), five declines of over 100 points, and 5 years in which there was less than a 100 point change either way.

Then began the third long trend, a 16-year stock market decline, as the real value of the stock market fell to below 1,100 by 1981, the lowest real value since 1949. The downswing began inauspiciously with the second worst year for the stock market as the DJIA fell 740 points in 1966. It recovered 323 points in 1967 and remained near the 3,075 level before dropping precipitously again, by 604 points in 1969. The DJIA held at the 2,450–2,500 level during 1970–71 before increasing 270 points in 1972. Then came another bad stretch for the DJIA as the market plummeted 1,351 points to 1,420 (the lowest level since 1953) during 1973–74, the Watergate period, with 1974 recording the largest drop of the entire period, 757 points. The years 1975 and 1976 were good years as the market rose 586 points to 2,006. However, the final tumble to the period low began immediately afterward in 1977, as stocks dropped 448 points. The changes during 1978–81 in order of occurrence were a 155 point loss, a 90 point loss, a 10 point gain, and a 236 point loss. The Dow bottomed out at 1,094 (875 in nominal terms) in 1981. In summary, during this 16-year downswing, there were four drops of 500 or more points, three drops of 100–500 points, four gains of 200 or more points, and 5 years of changes less than 100 points.

The second long-run upswing began in 1982 and was not characterized by the seesawing of previous periods, as most years recorded substantial increases. The second upward trend began with a 138 point increase from 1,094 to 1,232, followed by a 204 point gain in 1983. Jumps of over 300 points were achieved in 1985 and 1986. The DJIA did not change much in 1987 but rose 150 points in 1988 and 440 points in 1989. There was a 233 point drop in 1990, a 354 point increase in 1991, no significant change in 1992, and a 278 point increase in 1993, as the DJIA closed the year at 2,953. In the 12 years of the second upswing, there were 8 years of gains of 150 points or more, two declines of 100 points or more, and two even years.

Juxtaposing the nominal (not adjusted for inflation) DJIA (Figure 9.2) with the real (inflation-adjusted) DJIA graph (Figure 9.1) serves two purposes. The first is that the DJIA is never quoted to the public in real terms. As a point of reference, then, the stock market index should also be presented with the actual values that have been reported in the news, that is, non-inflation-adjusted values. Gross domestic product, in contrast, is almost always quoted as a real growth rate (relative to the previous year) but never as a level, except, perhaps, in references such as "our 6 trillion dollar economy." The second purpose of presenting the nominal DJIA index in Figure 9.2 is that it demonstrates the importance of adjusting for inflation. In the case of the DJIA, the nominal index values contain highly inflated stock prices, which, if not adjusted for inflation, conceal the measurement of *real* movements in the stock market. The result is that stock market increments and decrements in recent years swamp those in previous years such that the latter are underrepresented and the former are overrepresented. Figure 9.2 shows clearly the effect of not adjusting for inflation, as the sharp rise in real terms (in Figure 9.1) during 1954–65 dissolves into a very gradual rise in nominal terms. In addition, the steep drop in real terms during 1966–81 virtually disappears on the nominal DJIA graph, and the second upward trend from 1981 through 1993 becomes exaggerated in Figure 9.2. Adjusting for inflation restores the ability of the DJIA index to illustrate real relative year-to-year changes. Another way of illustrating stock market trends is by a graph of real growth rates. Real growth rates would go even further in depicting relative performance year to year, but because of the nature of this indicator, that is, its strong volatility, it would not present as coherent a picture of stock market performance over the longer term.

PRESIDENTIAL RANKINGS

Two likely bases for ranking the presidents' stock market performance are the average real DJIA level of each administration and the average annual real DJIA growth rate. Although a graph of the yearly DJIA growth rates does not present a clear picture of stock market behavior, the average annual growth rate of the DJIA is preferred to the average level as the primary basis for ranking. The average growth rate provides a better relative measure of performance in that it is less dependent on the historical time period in which a president governed. Thus, as in the cases of productivity and compensation, although the index is depicted in the graph, it is the growth rate by which the presidents are ranked.

As pointed out previously, the choice of the primary basis for ranking also determines the choice of the trend change variable. The choice of the growth rate of the stock market dictates that the trend change is the change in the growth rate. In this case, because stock market growth rates fluctuate sharply from year to year, the trend change has limited meaning. If, on the other hand, the average level of the DJIA were selected, then the trend change would be the real increase/decrease in the DJIA during the administration, which is a much more meaningful indicator. The objective is, wherever possible, to ensure that the primary basis for ranking is of primary importance and that the trend indicator is of secondary importance.

The presidential rankings for growth of the DJIA are presented in Table 9.1. Eisenhower and Reagan stand out with by far the best performances with respect to the DJIA, with average annual growth rates of 10.6 and 10.4 percent, respectively. These growth rates are especially impressive because each occurred over full, two-term administrations. The next performance tier is occupied by Kennedy, Bush, and Truman with moderate to small, positive growth rates of 4.8, 3.9, and 2.1 percent, respectively. The last group consists of Johnson, Nixon, Ford, and Carter, who presided over moderate declines in the stock market. Johnson had negative growth of 5.2 percent, and Nixon, almost the same, had a decline of 5.3 percent. The stock market declined at a somewhat faster rate under Ford, 7.2 percent, and Carter, 8.8 percent. It is interesting to note that the four presidents with the lowest growth rates were in office in succession at exactly the same time as the long-run stock market decline of 1965–81.

TABLE 9.1
Growth of the Dow Jones Industrials Average

Average Real Growth of DJIA			Trend Change in DJIA Growth	
President	Term	Percent	President	Percentage Points
Eisenhower	1953–61	10.6	Nixon	46.4
Reagan	1981–89	10.4	Reagan	38.9
Kennedy	1961–63	4.8	Eisenhower	22.1
Bush	1989–93	3.9	Truman	10.7
Truman	1945–53	2.1	Carter	4.6
Johnson	1963–69	–5.2	Kennedy	–5.1
Nixon	1969–74	–5.3	Bush	–10.7
Ford	1974–77	–7.2	Johnson	–32.1
Carter	1977–81	–8.8	Ford	–49.1
Average, 1946–93		2.2		

SELECTED ISSUES

The pattern of the real DJIA may be quite surprising to some in that, although the stock market rose rapidly and more or less steadily during 1982–93, in real terms, its level at the end of this period was still 17 percent below that of the peak year of 1965. However, as was shown in

Figure 9.1, real stock market growth during 1966–81 was sharply negative such that over the last 12 years of the 1946–93 period, the stock market could recuperate only partially from the erosion of real stock market value during the previous 16 years. It is possible that a different pattern would emerge during the 1946–93 period if another stock market index were used. However, it is difficult to find data on other stock indexes that are consistent over this period. In any case, regardless of the trend in the stock market during the long-run, investors can make or lose fortunes. Furthermore, it is the nominal, not the real, DJIA on which money is made and lost.

Another interesting example of stock market behavior was the stock market crash of October 19, 1987 (Black Monday), and its subsequent recovery (Table 9.2). The stock market crash of 1987, which is usually measured in terms of the associated loss in the DJIA, was the largest one-day loss in the history of the DJIA, 508 points, or 22.6 percent of total DJIA value. A five-day schedule leading up to the crash is presented below, which shows that there were three large declines leading up to the 508 point drop, such that the total point drop was 769.42 points. Apparently, investors took note of the rapid stock market decline during these five days, and their fears accumulated during the weekend prior to Black Monday, when this fear was unleashed. The famous crash of 1929, in contrast, transpired over a protracted period rather than in one sudden collapse, beginning after September 3, 1929, with the DJIA

TABLE 9.2
Stock Market Behavior Surrounding the 1987 Crash

Date	DJIA Close	Change	Percent Change
Leading to the Crash			
October 13	2508.16	—	—
October 14	2412.70	–95.46	–3.8
October 15	2355.09	–57.61	–2.4
October 16	2246.74	–108.35	–4.6
October 19	1738.74	–508.00	–22.6
Aftermath of the Crash			
October 20	1841.01	+102.27	+5.9
October 21	2027.85	+186.84	+10.1
October 22	1950.43	–77.42	–3.8
October 23	1950.76	+0.33	+0.0
October 26	1793.93	–156.83	–8.0
October 27	1846.49	+52.56	+2.9
October 28	1846.82	+0.33	+0.0
October 29	1938.33	+91.51	+5.0
October 30	1993.53	+55.20	+2.8

Source: Pierce, Phyllis, ed., *Dow Jones Averages 1885–1990* (Homewood, Ill.: Irwin, 1991).

at 381.17 (in nominal terms) and continuing until July 8, 1932, reaching a low of 41.22.

Analysts blame the magnitude of the Black Monday crash, in part, on programmed trading, like-thinking MBAs who engineered the transactions, and other factors. What appeared to precipitate the crash was news that foreign investors in U.S. debt were selling off their holdings. After the crash, dire predictions were made by market analysts about the stock market and the economy in general; large budget deficits and the fact that the United States had become a debtor nation were to blame. In all likelihood, these two factors did contribute to the decision of foreign investors to sell their U.S. debt (further discussion of this topic is found in Part II). Fortunately, the Federal Reserve assuaged fears of a national liquidity crisis by offering to play the role of lender of last resort. New trading rules were established in the stock market in order to combat future occurrences of the snowballing effect witnessed in October 1987 and the stock market began to recover. The remainder of October, after the crash, was marked by very sharp fluctuations, with the net result being a recovery of almost 255 of the 769 points lost during October 14–19, as Table 9.2 shows. During the two days after the crash, the stock market recorded its largest two-day gain ever, 289 points. The continued recovery from the crash was fairly steady and rapid. The market, in nominal terms, proceeded to rise 72.5 percent by mid-July 1990, regaining its full, precrash value. In contrast, after the crash of 1929, the stock market did not regain its height (again in nominal terms) for 25 years, that is, not until 1954.

SUGGESTIONS FOR FURTHER READING

Barro, Robert J., et al., eds., *Black Monday and the Future of Financial Markets.* Homewood, Ill.: Dow-Jones Irwin and Mid-America Insititute, 1989. Assesses the impact and lessons learned from the October 1987 stock market crash.

Stillman, Richard J., *Dow Jones Industrial Average.* Homewood, Ill.: Dow Jones-Irwin, 1984. Gives a brief overview of the major events in the history of the DJIA and provides in-depth discussion of the strengths and weaknesses of the DJIA as a stock market indicator.

Teweles, Richard J., and Bradley, Edward S., *The Stock Market.* New York: John Wiley and Sons, 1987. A comprehensive primer on the stock market that explains basic concepts and gives information on the stock exchanges, securities houses, regulations, and other aspects of the stock market.

NOTES

1. This stock market is also referred to as the secondary stock market simply because it consists of stocks that are being resold, rather than new stock issues. The latter are sold on the primary stock market.

2. Actually, the S & P 500 is more comprehensive and probably better conceived than the DJIA. It includes 400 industrials, 20 transportations, 40 utilities, and 40 financial institutions, compared with the DJIA's 30 industrials. The S & P 500 is also

weighted according to the total value of all the stock on the market for each company, whereas the DJIA weights stocks equally. The DJIA also omits several important economic sectors, including banking, transportation (for which there is a separate Dow-Jones Index), hotels, entertainment, and the media. Yet, the DJIA is still the most popular index, if frequency of reporting in the media is the main criterion.

3.   A detailed summary of changes in the composition of the DJIA over time can be found in Phyllis Pierce, ed., *Dow Jones Industrials Averages 1885–1990*. Homewood, Ill.: Irwin, 1991.

4.   That the DJIA is unweighted means that the higher-priced stocks have more importance than lower-priced stocks and that the market value of a company plays no role in the DJIA.

5.   Because of so many stock splits, the divisor has shrunk and is now close to one, even though there are still 30 stocks. The result is that small increases in stock prices result in large increases in the DJIA. It has been suggested that the DJIA should account for stock splits by specifically weighting the stock that splits, for example, a stock that splits two for one would receive a double weight. In this way, the divisor would be remain constant, and an increase in the price of a stock would not result in an exaggerated increase in the index.

6.   There are a couple of other biases in the DJIA as well. First, because of the way in which the DJIA is computed, the same percentage change in a higher-priced stock in the DJIA will have a much larger effect on the index than that of a lower-priced stock, regardless of the total value of the outstanding shares of either stock on the market. For example, Stock A is worth $100 per share, with 1 million outstanding shares, and Stock B is worth $10 per share, with 10 million outstanding shares; thus, the total value of all shares on the market of each stock is $100 million. If Stock A increases by 10 percent and Stock B decreases by 10 percent, then the DJIA will rise by (0.1 X $100 − 0.1 X $10) / (DJIA divisor) or $9 / (DJIA divisor). Thus, the DJIA increases, even though there was no change in the total market value of the stocks in the index. Second, the DJIA does not consider *stock* (as opposed to *cash*) dividends of less than 10 percent. Hence, the DJIA underrepresents gains in the stock market to the extent that companies declare relatively small stock dividends.

II
THE FEDERAL GOVERNMENT

Part II deals primarily with the federal budget and taxation. These variables clearly are far more under the control of the president and Congress than the indicators of Part I, which are largely determined in the private economy. Part II begins with the total federal budget, its growth, and its share of gross domestic product, which can be viewed as the size of the public sector relative to the total economy. The trends in budget deficits and the national debt follow, which puts current levels into some historical perspective. Next is the composition of the budget, which reflects the president's (and Congress's) spending priorities. The trends in Social Security, both revenues and outlays, are presented, showing this category's growing importance. Concerns about funding and financial integrity for this program in the future also are examined. It is important to note that Social Security, although an "off-budget" item, is, nevertheless, usually meant to be included in references to the federal budget. Taxation, the revenue side of government, charts total individual and corporate tax contributions over time. Data for Part II are mainly from the U.S. Office of Management and Budget, the Internal Revenue Service, and the Social Security Administration.

10

Federal Budget Growth and Share of Gross Domestic Product

The share of the federal budget in gross domestic product (GDP) and the real growth rate of the federal budget provide two ways to view the changing size of the government sector.[1] The budget growth rate takes into account how much additional resources are added to the government sector on an annual basis, showing, for example, that by 1993, GDP had grown to almost five times its 1947 level in real terms. The share of the government budget in GDP, on the other hand, shows the size of the public sector relative to the overall economy for each year. Both indicators are derived from absolute budget expenditures. It is also informative to compare government budget growth with GDP growth to chart whether government growth outpaced or lagged behind overall economic growth. The share of the budget in GDP provides another way to verify whether, in a given year, the government budget became a more or less important component of the economy as a whole. Shares are calculated by dividing current dollar amounts for the total federal budget by the current dollar GDP for the same year.[2] All budget data are published by the U.S. Office of Management and Budget and refer to the government fiscal year.[3]

Social Security outlays *are* included here as part of the total federal budget, even though 98 percent of these outlays are officially designated as "off-budget." However, when the media, the president, or the Congress refers to the federal budget and, notably, the deficit (see Chapter 11) in public, they are usually lumping in Social Security, which typically accounted for about 20 percent of total (on- and off-budget) outlays in the latter years of the 1946–93 period. (Chapter 13 discusses Social Security in detail.) A distinction is also made between government outlays and government purchases. The former is the subject of this chapter. The latter refers to government outlays minus transfer payments such as welfare and unemployment compensation. Government purchases is the same as G in the equation, $C + I + G + (X–M) = GDP$. As stated in Chapter 2, transfer payments, subsidies, and so on, do not constitute production and, as such, are not included in the calculation of GDP. Transfer payments constitute the bulk of total federal outlays, amounting to over 70 percent in 1993.

OVERVIEW OF TRENDS IN THE LONG RUN, 1946–93

Federal Budget Outlays as Share of Gross Domestic Product

The percent of GDP accounted for by the federal government is depicted in Figure 10.1. For the time period as a whole, the average share of government outlays to GDP was 20.2 percent. No distinct subperiods emerge, though it is observed that each successive president increased the percent of GDP accounted for by the government, with the exception of Bush. Looking at four subperiods, chosen arbitrarily, the progression of increasing shares of government in GDP is evident: 1946–60 — 17.8 percent, 1961–70 — 19.3 percent, 1971–81 — 21.0 percent, and 1982–93 — 23.1 percent.

The early post-war drop in the federal budget's share of GDP reflects the dramatic demilitarization after 1945. After the 43.7 percent share in 1945, the budget dropped to 26.0 and 14.8 percent in 1946 and 1947, respectively. By 1948, the downsizing was complete, as the share fell to 12.1 percent, the lowest share recorded during the period. However, the budget's share rose rapidly for the rest of the Truman administration to the 14.8–16.0 percent range for 1949–51. The Korean War expenditures in fiscal 1952 helped push the budget to 19.9 percent of GDP. Truman closed out with 20.9 percent in 1953, a level unsurpassed until 1968.

Under Eisenhower, the share dropped for the first three years a total of 3.9 percentage points to 17.0 percent by 1956. Over the five-year remainder of the Eisenhower administration, the share climbed 1.9 share points of GDP to 18.9 percent. Under Kennedy, the budget share remained near the 19.0 level with little variation, closing at 19.0 in 1964.

Lyndon Johnson's first budget saw the share drop to 17.6 percent of GDP (1965), perhaps because of the need to keep expenditures down to compensate for the large tax cut that was implemented during 1964–65. However, the costs of the Great Society programs and the Viet Nam War began to raise the share of the budget, which reached 21.0 percent in 1968 before settling in the range of 19.8–20.1 percent from 1969 to 1972, that is, the last two Johnson budgets and the first two Nixon budgets. In 1973 and 1974, the Nixon budgets dropped as a share of GDP to 19.3 and 19.2 percent, respectively. The fiscal 1975 budget jumped 2.8 percentage points to 22.0 percent of GDP. Under the two years of Ford, shares were 22.1 and 21.3 percent. Carter's first budget, 1978, remained at 21.3 percent, then dropped to 20.7 percent in 1979. However, in the recession of 1980, Carter's budget reached 22.3 percent of GDP and rose further to 22.9 percent in 1981. In the early Reagan

FIGURE 10.1
Federal Outlays Percent of Gross Domestic Product, 1946-93
(Based on Current Values)

Percent of GDP

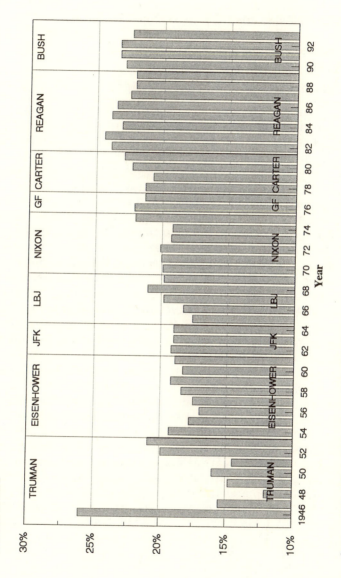

Source: U.S. Office of Management and Budget.

years, shares continued to rise, reaching 23.9 percent in 1982 and 24.4 percent in 1983, the highest since 1946. In 1984, the share dropped to 23.1 percent as GDP growth soared. In 1985 and 1986, shares were higher, at 23.8 and 23.5 percent, respectively, before dropping to 22.5 percent and closing out the administration with a share of 22.1 percent for both 1988 and 1989. During a sluggish economy in 1990, the budget share rose to 22.9 and then to the 23.3 percent level for 1991–92. In 1993, the share was 22.4 percent of GDP.

Growth Rate of the Federal Budget

The real growth rates of the federal budget offer another angle from which to view a president's spending record. The average growth for the 1946–93 period was 1.9 percent, but as Figure 10.2 shows, the fluctuations in government growth rates were very sharp. For scaling purposes, the graph does not measure the full magnitude of five of the first seven years' growth rates (1946–52), all of which were under Truman. However, the calculated averages and trends take into account the full magnitude of these growth rates. In the first three years following World War II (1946–48), the government budget declined by 43.0, 50.2, and 16.3 percent, respectively. These declines are very understandable, because at the peak of wartime spending, 1944, the federal government accounted for 45.3 percent of GDP. However, no sooner had the budget begun to fall to pre-war levels, than budget growth soared to 27.3 percent in 1949. It moderated in 1950 to 6.1 percent and rose rapidly again in 1951 and 1952 at 9.8 and 45.5 percent, respectively. These budget surges of the latter two years were mainly a result of defense expenditures required for the Korean War.[4] When the war was over, the government sector dropped substantially in real terms during 1954–56, at rates of 9.7, 5.3, and 2.5 percent, respectively. After the three-year decline, the budget rose moderately for three years and fell again in 1960 by 4.2 percent. From 1957 onward, the real government budget declined five times and only twice after 1969. Growth was positive for all of the Kennedy years, including a rapid growth rate of 7.4 percent in 1962. Johnson's five years as president consisted of three large increases (10.4, 13.7, and 8.7 percent) during 1966–68, flanked by two small decreases in 1965 and 1969 of 2.3 and 2.4 percent, respectively.

Nixon's presidency consisted of rather small increases during 1970–74, with a big jump in 1975 of 11.7 percent. Ford's budget growth was 4.4 and 1.6 percent in 1976 and 1977, respectively. Carter presided over increases in the budget for all four years. His administration opened with 4.5 percent growth, which dropped to 1.0 percent in 1979, increased to 6.4 percent in 1980, and closed with 4.3 percent the next year. Under Reagan, budget growth was of a smaller magnitude. With the exception of 1983 and 1985, when the budget grew at 3.4 and 7.3 percent, respectively, growth rates of all other budgets were below

FIGURE 10.2
Growth of Federal Budget, 1946–93

(Adjusted for Inflation)

Real Growth Rate

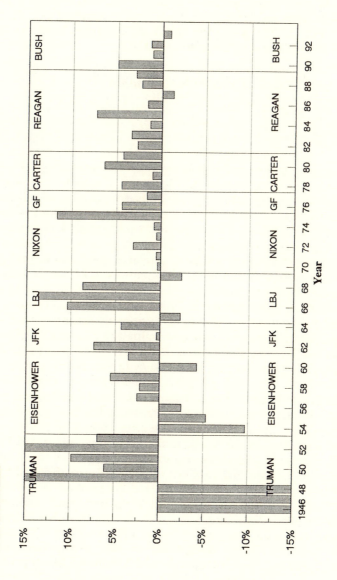

Source: U.S. Office of Management and Budget.

3 percent. In 1987, one of only two *decreases* in the budget since 1969 was recorded at –1.3 percent. Under Bush, the budget grew at 5 percent in 1990 but at only 1.1 and 1.3 percent in 1991 and 1992. In 1993, the budget declined 0.8 percent in real terms, which was only the second decline since 1969.

PRESIDENTIAL RANKINGS

Ranking presidents is somewhat problematic in that it is not known what is the proper share or growth rate for the budget. The "right" share of government depends on a subjective judgment as to what the role of the government should be. In addition to a president's or Congress's particular priorities, which may emphasize national security, social needs, or something else, government spending also may be dictated by unexpected exigencies. It is almost impossible to translate prevailing conditions into an optimal government share and, thus, to rank presidential shares. Given the set of conditions when Nixon governed, for example, it may have made perfect sense for his average to be 20.1 percent, which also happened to be the median among the presidents' average shares. A share of 17.5 percent (the lowest presidential average) might have been below the optimum and 23.2 percent (the highest presidential average) might have been above the optimum for the circumstances. Although the budget level on which he and Congress agreed may have been optimal, it would require an in-depth evaluation of every situation that Nixon faced to prove it.

As for trends over the entire time period, it may have been preferable that government shares declined if it were the case that real resources to perform government's "proper" role did not need to increase as fast as GDP. In addition, the complementary role of state and local governments in terms of both the resources they commanded and the functions they served vis-à-vis the federal government during the time period must be considered in order to better determine what the federal government share should have been. A cursory examination of the trends in state and local government outlays during 1946–93 reveals that their share of total government outlays increased. This growth in state and local outlays may have obviated otherwise larger increases in the federal government outlays.

For the purpose of rankings, it is assumed that the lower the share of GDP and the lower the growth rate of the government budget, the better. This convention is supported primarily from the standpoint that it is rather easy to pump up the economy in the short run simply by increasing government spending, but this choice may lead to financing problems such as are posed by the currently large budget deficits. The uncertainty of *how much better* is a lower government share of GDP is considered when weighting this indicator in the overall economic performance of the presidents (Chapter 15).

TABLE 10.1
Share of Federal Budget in Gross Domestic Product

Average Share of GDP			Change in Share of GDP	
President	Term	Percent	President	Percentage Points
Truman	1945–53	17.5	Truman	−5.1
Eisenhower	1953–61	18.3	Eisenhower	−2.0
Kennedy	1961–63	19.1	Reagan	−0.8
Johnson	1963–69	19.3	Ford	−0.7
Nixon	1969–74	20.1	Kennedy	0.1
Ford	1974–77	21.7	Bush	0.3
Carter	1977–81	21.8	Johnson	0.8
Bush	1989–93	23.0	Carter	1.6
Reagan	1981–89	23.2	Nixon	2.2
Average, 1946–93		20.2		

Share of Gross Domestic Product

The presidential rankings of the share of the federal budget in GDP are shown in Table 10.1. As for many indicators, Truman's averages and trends present difficulties stemming from the transition from war to a peacetime economy. The tremendous budget share declines that are part of his averages are evidence of this characteristic. The trend indicator captures this phenomenon but, when it comes to measuring his economic performance, should be weighed in light of the extraordinary circumstances that he faced. The trend change, of course, captures the budget share movements of other presidents as well. For instance, although Reagan had the highest average share in his last year in office he did reduce the share to a level below that of the last year of his predecessor. Nixon's increase of 2.2 percentage points is significant because he left office with a share increase higher than the other presidents', although, typically, the share of government spending jumps up in recession years. Eisenhower's drop of 2.0 percentage points is also interesting and somewhat unexpected, especially because he followed Truman. The decline in Eisenhower's trend reflects that, in spite of the fact that Truman's average was lower than Eisenhower's, Truman left office with a budget share of nearly 21 percent, which was quite high for the time and not reflective of Truman's overall, lower average.

As mentioned, there was a progression of increasing government shares of GDP starting with Truman's 17.5 percent average share and continuing to Reagan at 23.2 percent but halted under Bush. Thus, the belief that the federal government has been taking up an ever-larger portion of GDP is essentially true. To determine whether government as a whole occupied a greater share of the economy, the size of the state and local government's shares must be added to the federal government total over time. Because state and local government outlays constituted a generally rising, although fluctuating, share of GDP and of total government outlays during the 1947–93 period, it is clear that total government increased as a share of GDP during the period (see Appendix B). The combined federal, state, and local increase in outlays as a percent of GDP during the period was nearly 13 percentage points, from 20.4 percent in 1947 to 33.3 percent in 1993, including a high of 34.2 percent in 1992.

Growth of the Federal Budget

The presidential rankings of the growth of the federal budget are shown in Table 10.2. Eisenhower recorded the lowest growth rate at –1.1 percent, with Truman second at –0.6 percent (measuring from the budget level at year-end 1946).[5] The statistical quirk as to why Eisenhower recorded negative average annual growth but had a government share of GDP higher than his predecessor's is examined in detail in the Selected Issues section below.

TABLE 10.2
Growth of the Federal Budget

Average Growth of Federal Budget		*Change in Growth Rate of Federal Budget*	
President	*Percent*	*President*	*Percentage Points*
Eisenhower	–1.1	Ford	–10.1
Truman	–0.6	Johnson	–6.8
Bush	1.6	Bush	–3.8
Reagan	2.5	Eisenhower	–3.3
Nixon	2.7	Reagan	–1.3
Ford	2.9	Kennedy	0.8
Carter	3.9	Carter	2.7
Kennedy	3.9	Nixon	14.1
Johnson	5.3	Truman	49.9
Average, 1946–93	1.9		
1947–93	3.4		

Bush, who halted the increasing trend, had the third lowest growth rate, 1.6 percent, which still exceeded his GDP growth rate of 1.4 percent. Reagan is fourth at 2.5 percent. Nixon and Ford follow at 2.7 and 2.9 percent, respectively. Ford's budget growth rate was below his GDP growth rate, while Nixon's budget growth rate exceeded his GDP growth rate. Carter, Kennedy, and Johnson recorded the highest budget growth rates of 3.9, 3.9, and 5.3 percent, respectively.

The trend change in budget growth rates is of minimal value because of the high degree of fluctuation in budget growth rates. The volatility is particularly evident with Truman, with a 49.9 percentage point increase in the government budget growth rate. Although in recent years the volatility has declined, the year-to-year percentage changes on which the trend changes are based generally did not represent significant turning points in government spending and do not offer a strong basis for presidential comparison.

SELECTED ISSUES

Calculation Issues

Even though the calculations of averages and trends are rather simple and straightforward, they can be puzzling at times. As a rule, delving into the minutae of data calculations is appropriately left for the technical notes; however, further exploration into the comparison of real GDP and government budget growth and budget shares is useful to clear up some confusion surrounding these indicators. For example, if a president's real GDP growth rate exceeds his real budget growth rate, then, intuitively, the budget share of GDP should fall during his presidency. Given that all presidents had successively higher government shares of GDP, with the exception of Truman, whose predecessor's (Roosevelt's) average predates the period of analysis here, and Bush, who halted a seven-president trend of increasing budget shares, it is puzzling how any president could have recorded a negative average budget growth rate. In addition, there were several presidents whose budget share of GDP increased even though their average GDP growth exceeded their real budget growth. Moreover, recalling that the average annual GDP growth rate for 1946–93 was 3.0 while real average annual budget growth for the same period was 1.9 percent, that is, GDP growth outpaced budget growth by 1.1 percent per annum in real terms during 1946–93, the question arises of why the government budget gained rather than lost in share points of GDP throughout most of the period.

The solution to most of these puzzles is that growth rates are calculated based on the endpoints of a period, whether over the entire 1946–93 period or over one presidential administration. The 1.9 percent real average annual budget growth rate for the whole period began in 1946, when demobilization was not complete and the budget share of GDP was still 26.0 percent, which was higher than that of 1993 (22.4 percent).[6] Hence, the fact that the GDP growth rate was higher than the budget growth rate for the period is consistent with the falling budget share (from 26.0 to 22.4 percent).

Although this analysis does seek to capture the entire post-war era, it is, nevertheless, more representative of the trend in government spending to calculate the growth rate from the end of 1947, when demilitarization of the government budget was more or less complete. Table 10.3 shows the sensitivity of growth rates to various starting points. From this table, it can be observed that only when starting from year-end 1947 or later (and extending through 1993) does the government growth rate exceed the GDP growth rate. This observation is consistent with the gain in share points of the government sector during 1947–93.

TABLE 10.3
Comparisons of Gross Domestic Product and Budget Growth Rates

	1945–93	1946–93	1947–93	1948–93
GDP growth rate	2.4	3.0	3.1	3.1
Budget growth rate	0.7	1.9	3.4	3.9
Current budget share beginning of period	43.7	26.0	15.5	12.1
Current budget share end of period	22.4	22.4	22.4	22.4
Increase/(decrease) in share points	(21.3)	(3.6)	6.9	12.3

The case of Eisenhower's negative budget growth is an anomaly and is explained simply by the fact that Truman closed his adminstration with an atypically high government share of GDP. Truman's closing level of government outlays was actually higher in real terms than Eisenhower's closing level of government outlays, hence, the negative real growth rate for Eisenhower. However, there were enough years between the Eisenhower administration's endpoints in which the share of GDP was sufficiently high to raise his overall average above that of Truman (see Appendix B for detailed year-to-year data).

Another factor that influences the relationship between the shares and growth rates, though much less strongly than changes in endpoints, is a bit more complicated and centers on the fact that separate deflators are used for government outlays and for GDP. During 1946–93, prices of the goods and services that comprise GDP increased more slowly than those that comprise the government sector. The respective deflators reflect the different price changes (the indexes increased from 16.7 to 124.2 for GDP versus 11.9 to 125.0 for government), and when the GDP and government data are converted from current to constant series using these deflators, their relation to each other, that is, the share of government in GDP, is altered in accordance with the difference between the two deflators. Specifically, because prices rose more slowly for GDP over the period, the constant GDP value for 1946 (in 1987 dollars) will need to be inflated less than the 1946 value for government budget. Thus, the constant dollar share of the government of

GDP is higher than the current dollar share for that year. Because the growth rates are based on constant, or real, government and GDP values and the shares are based on current data, the data in constant terms imply higher government shares than do current data before the base year (1987) and lower shares after the base year. For the period as a whole, constant dollar shares suggest a higher percentage point increase in government share between 1946 and 1993 than do current shares.

Weaknesses in Official Federal
Budget Growth and Share Data

With regard to attributing performance rankings with respect to public sector categories on the basis of official government data, a couple of dissenting views on their value should be mentioned. One view states that deficit spending per se is irrelevant with respect to resource allocation because consumers and taxpayers recognize that lowering taxes today implies higher taxes tomorrow. What matters is the use to which the tax revenue is put. Does the revenue purchase goods from the private sector, or is it wasted? This view is called "Ricardian equivalence" and is articulated by Robert Barro (1989).

Another view, propounded by Robert Eisner (1994), focuses, among other things, on government accounting itself, which has implications for conventional measures of debts and deficits (dealt with in Chapter 11). First, government accounting does not distinguish between capital and current accounts. Thus, investments in durable capital goods, infrastructure, airplanes, and so on, are treated like current expenses. Revenues from sales of mineral rights are treated the same way as income tax revenue, although the former is merely the transformation of wealth from one form to another (e.g., oil in the ground into cash). Government accounting also does not include liquid financial assets of the federal government. For example, the Federal Reserve holds substantial U.S. Treasury obligations, while the Treasury has held enormous quantities of gold reserves at various times. Government assets also are not valued at market prices. For example, the gold in Fort Knox should be valued at market prices and not at the arbitrary value of $35 per ounce.

Eisner also argues that an evaluation of government fiscal policy should take into account the condition of the macroeconomy. Revenues fall during a recession because of a shrinking tax base. Therefore, deficits may arise. To the extent that recessions are beyond the control of presidential administrations, recession-induced deficits should not be considered part of the performance record of the administration. However, the purpose of this book is, first, to show, through the basic data, what happened on the president's watch and, second, to convey caveats about conclusions with respect to actual performance. Eisner also supports the view, similar to Ricardian equivalence, that higher deficits are no more undesirable than higher taxes or lower spending, both of which ultimately may lead to higher unemployment.

Finally, government accounting is deficient in that the government is not considered as a "creative entity." Because the value of government output (e.g., services) is so difficult to measure, its portion of GDP is priced at cost, or the value of inputs (e.g., wages). Hence, in most cases, the value that is added to the inputs by government is omitted from the national accounts, which, therefore, systematically underestimates the value of the public sector. In contrast, the other main components of GDP, private consumption and investment, reflect the prices paid by the final consumers, households, and firms, respectively, and, therefore, their *full* value inclusive of value added.

SUGGESTIONS FOR FURTHER READING

Collender, Stanley E., *The Guide to the Federal Budget — Fiscal 1994*. Washington, D.C.: Urban Institute Press, 1993. Provides a good primer on the way the budget process works. There are 11 previous editions.

Pechman, Joseph A., ed., *Setting National Priorities*. Washington, D.C.: The Brookings Institution. A publication with annual editions from 1971 to 1994 describing policy aspects of the federal budget by year.

NOTES

1. State and local budgets are not considered in detail here. However, it should be noted that state and local shares have increased somewhat over the 48-year time period. Although in the early 1930s, they accounted for twice the total of the federal government, in the late 1940s and 1950s, their outlays were about 40–45 percent of federal outlays and, by the 1990s, close to 50 percent.

2. Current shares are used rather than constant shares to avoid distortions introduced when separate GDP and government price deflators are used to compute the constant series for the federal budget and for the GDP. If the appropriate GDP deflator is used to deflate GDP and the appropriate government deflator is used to deflate current dollar government levels, then the constant and current budget shares of GDP diverge to the extent that the two deflators diverge. This divergence is appreciable.

3. In 1976, the government changed its fiscal year from July 1–June 30 to October 1–September 30. This move resulted in a hiatus or "transition quarter" in 1976. This quarter's statistics are not represented in either 1976 or 1977, because fiscal year 1976 ended on June 30, 1976, but fiscal year 1977 did not begin until October 1, 1976. Thus, the period July 1–September 30, 1976, is omitted from annual government statistics but is, rather, quoted as a separate "transitional quarter" in government publications. For simplicity in calculating averages and trends, this transition quarter is ignored, which may have some minor impact on President Ford's statistics.

4. The causes of changes in Part II (budget) indicators can be traced much more definitively than for Part I indicators, because Part I indicators result mainly from the interplay of market forces, while Part II indicators are dependent on the choices of the president and Congress.

5.   Again, to soften the distortion caused by post–World War II demobilization, growth is calculated from the end of 1946, that is, growth during the year 1946 is omitted.

6.   Recall that the actual post-1946 peak government share of GDP was 24.4 percent, occurring in 1983.

11

Federal Budget Deficits and the National Debt

Were it not for the historically recent ballooning of federal debt and deficits, a separate chapter devoted to these indicators might not have been justified. However, U.S. economic history has shown that even when deficits were *not large* by today's standards, there was substantial concern over deficits, causing the government to overreact and harm the economy further through ill-advised policies. Such was the case leading up to the Great Depression. The rapid growth of the real debt level in the 1980s and 1990s led to renewed concern about its effects. Even if serious consequences were not felt in the macroeconomy, the situation arose in which the size of the discretionary budget, defined here as federal budget outlays minus mandatory interest payments,[1] fell significantly relative to gross domestic product (GDP). Hence, although government outlays as a whole increased, a smaller portion of the budget was available for government activities and goals. One of the purposes of this chapter is, as in other chapters, to put the indicators (deficits and debts) into historical perspective.

Many do not understand the distinction between budget deficits and the national debt. Deficits result when government outlays exceed government receipts. They pertain to a specific budget of a specific year and represent a change in the amount of debt. Thus, deficits may be classified in economics and accounting as a "flow". The national debt (in nominal terms), on the other hand, is the *accumulation* of past deficits (in nominal terms). Because the national debt is an accumulation of past deficits, it can be viewed as a "stock," that is, the amount of something on hand.

When the yearly national debt level is converted from nominal into real terms, as is required to calculate real growth rates, a discrepancy arises between a stock indicator and a sum of flow indicators. An explanation is given here to stave off some of the confusion this discrepancy might cause when comparisons are made between the deficit and increments in the debt. When deficits are converted to real terms and are summed, they do not equal the total national debt in real terms, because when the deficits are deflated, each deficit is deflated for a specific year. For example, to convert the deficit for 1957 into real terms, it has to be greatly inflated to reflect all of the inflation that occurred between 1957 and the base year, 1987. However, when that deficit is accounted for in the calculation of the real debt, the value assigned to that 1957 deficit *as part of the overall debt* depends entirely on the year for which the real debt level is calculated. Thus, the real debt level calculated for 1980 reflects only the inflation between 1980 and 1987, even though this 1980 debt level contains deficits from the 1940s, 1950s, 1960s, and 1970s.

Budget deficits can be measured in terms of their share either of the total budget or of GDP. Here, the share of the budget is selected mainly to illustrate the degree of adjustment needed to bring the budget into balance. Deficits as a share of GDP are found in the statistical appendix. In contrast to debt, deficit growth rates are not particularly informative of performance, because of their degree of annual fluctuation over the 48-year period. The national debt also can be measured in a variety of ways, including by its real growth rate, its ratio to GDP,[2] and its real level. Both the real level of national debt and its ratio to GDP are selected for illustration because they capture the indicator's behavior quite clearly and are mutually reinforcing in their portrayal of trends in the national debt. In converting the national debt from nominal to real terms, required to calculate the real level and the real growth rate (the latter is used for the presidential rankings), the nominal debt levels are deflated using the government budget deflator series for 1946–93.

There is another possible approach for presenting the national debt that is strictly from a financial viewpoint. If, for example, a $25 billion deficit is incurred and added to the debt in 1968, then, assuming that only annual interest payments were made to service that $25 billion, in 1993 that debt increment would still be $25 billion and could be repaid in inflated 1993 dollars. Thus, from a financial viewpoint, the question arises, why convert the debt into real terms when it is the nominal debt that has to be repaid? The problem with this financial approach is that it does not provide for a realistic intertemporal comparison of performance. Obviously, the $25 billion increment to the debt in 1968 was far more significant than a $25 billion increment in 1993, and this fact should be reflected in measures of performance.

OVERVIEW OF TRENDS IN THE LONG RUN, 1946–93

Deficits

Figure 11.1 displays federal budget deficits as a percent of total outlays for fiscal years 1946–93. Because the graph also depicts surpluses,

FIGURE 11.1
Deficits Share of Budget, 1946–93

(Based on Current Values)

Percent of Budget

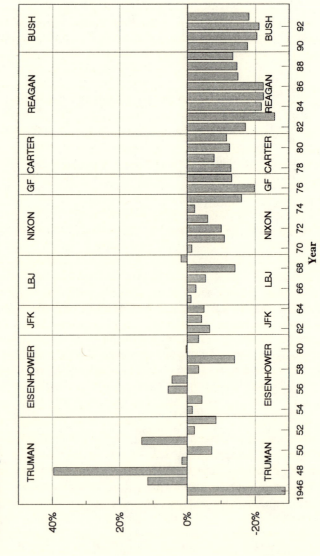

Source: U.S. Office of Management and Budget.

which are positive numbers, deficits are represented as negative percentages of the budget, which represent the vast majority of the fiscal years. There appear to be three distinct periods of deficit behavior: the volatile Truman years (1946–51) oscillating between first large and then small surpluses and deficits; the period 1952–74, which was marked by small to moderate deficits in all but four years, in which there were small surpluses; and the high deficit period of 1975–93, with all years but one falling in the range of 11.6 to 25.7 percent of the budget and with the larger deficits occurring under Reagan and Bush.

The deficit in 1946 was the last in a succession of huge wartime and pre-wartime deficits from 1940 to 1946. These deficits ranged from 28.9 to 69.4 percent of the budget. The 1946 deficit, from Truman's first budget, was 28.9 percent. In the next three years, Truman achieved four of the eight budget surpluses of the post-war period. The budget recorded a surplus of 11.6 percent in 1947, 39.6 percent in 1948, and 1.5 percent in 1949. There was a deficit in 1950 of 7.3 percent, and, in 1951, another surplus was achieved, amounting to 13.4 percent. Over the next four years, there were moderate deficits of 2.2, 8.5, 1.6, and 4.4 percent, Truman's last two budgets and Eisenhower's first two. Eisenhower recorded the fifth and sixth of the eight surpluses of the period at 5.6 and 4.5 percent in 1956 and 1957, respectively. These surpluses were followed by two deficits of 3.4 and 14.0 percent, a small surplus in 1960, and a deficit of 3.4 percent in 1961. In the first 15 years after World War II, there were seven surpluses, three by Eisenhower and four by Truman. There was only one more surplus during the next 32 years.

Kennedy had moderate deficits, ranging from 4.3 to 6.7 percent during 1962–64. Johnson recorded small deficits in his first two years of 1.2 and 2.7 percent, which increased to 5.5 percent in 1967 and 14.1 percent in 1968, but in 1969, he had the last recorded budget surplus of 1.8 percent. Nixon began with a small deficit of 1.5 percent in 1970, which then increased to 11.0 and 10.1 percent in 1971–72. The deficits fell to lower levels for the next two years but rose again to the highest levels since 1946, reaching 16.0 percent in 1975. Under Ford, the deficit climbed to 19.8 percent and dropped to 13.1 percent in 1976 and 1977, respectively. Carter's deficits began at 12.9 percent, then dropped to 8.0 percent in 1979 before rising again to 12.5 and 11.6 percent during 1980–81. Under Reagan, deficits jumped immediately to 17.2 percent and then to the highest level since 1946, 25.7 percent in 1983. Deficits as percent of the budget remained in the 21.8–22.4 percent range for 1984–86. In 1987, the deficit dropped 7.4 percentage points to 14.9 percent and continued to drop through 1989 to 13.3 percent. The Bush administration saw an increase in deficits' share in all four years, first jumping to 17.7 percent in 1990 and continuing up to 20.4, 21.0, and 22.2 percent during 1991–93.

Debt

Real Level of Debt

The debt levels illustrated in Figure 11.2 are adjusted for inflation using government budget deflators. As with the deficits, movements in the real national debt also show three distinct periods but at different intervals. The first period runs from 1947 to 1961, which is characterized by small declines in the real level of national debt. The second period runs from 1962 to 1981, in which the debt remained virtually constant. The third period, from 1982 through 1993, experienced uninterrupted and rapid increases in the national debt.

Truman began in 1946 with an outstanding debt of $2.3 trillion in 1987 dollars, $271 billion in nominal terms. The real debt level dropped to $1.7 trillion in 1947 and then settled down and began the first long-run subperiod, which was dominated by small declines in the real debt level. The declines in the debt level were interrupted in 1951, when there was a slight increase in the debt that coincided with the heavy outlays and large deficit incurred for the Korean War. Truman closed his presidency with a debt of $1.5 trillion. In every year of the Eisenhower administration, the national debt outstanding declined in real terms. This performance is consistent with his favorable deficit performance. His deficits were small in all years except one, and he recorded three surpluses. In the one year in which his deficit was sizeable, 1959, the real debt level still decreased because, although the nominal debt rose 2.8 percent in 1959, the deflator rose 6.1 percent. After Eisenhower, the second period began and continued for 20 years. Throughout the Kennedy, Johnson, Nixon, Ford, and Carter administrations, the real debt level remained in a very narrow range of $1.2–1.3 trillion, with the low occurring under Nixon in 1974 and the high under Carter in 1978. In 1982, Reagan's first year and the recession year, the national debt started a steep ascent, jumping to $1.4 trillion in 1982 and climbing to $3.5 trillion by 1993. During the 12-year period, the national debt essentially tripled in real terms.

Debt as a Percent of Gross Domestic Product

Debt as a percent of GDP goes a step beyond real debt levels in measuring the burden of the national debt on the U.S. economy. The real level of the debt captures the degree to which the government has been accumulating debt (through the real value of the debt) but leaves out the fact that the overall economy has been growing. Debt measured as a percent of GDP compares the level of debt in each year with the level of output in the economy for that year. The behavior of the indicator, debt as a percent of GDP (i.e., current debt divided by current GDP), as shown in Figure 11.3, follows a similar pattern to that of the real debt level in Figure 11.2 but with a more pronounced decline in the first part

FIGURE 11.2
Federal National Debt, 1946–93

(Adjusted for Inflation)

Real National Debt Level ($ billions)

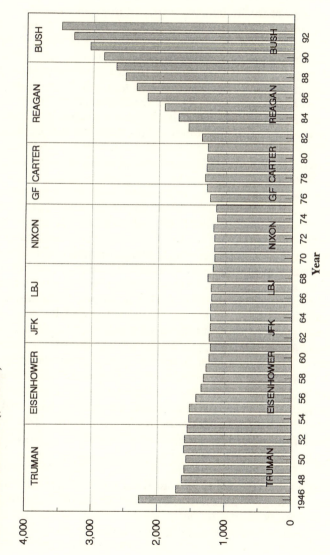

Source: U.S. Office of Management and Budget.

of the period and a less pronounced increase in the second part of the period. In addition, the pattern of debt as a percent of GDP is composed of two, rather than three, subperiods, that is, there is only a long-term decline and a long-term increase with no real flat period between. The reason for the difference between the two figures is that GDP (the denominator of the indicator illustrated in Figure 11.3) was rising faster throughout the period than the debt deflator (the denominator of the indicator illustrated in Figure 11.2) resulting in steeper declines and flatter increases in debt as a percent of GDP.

Figure 11.3 shows that, during the first subperiod, the federal debt as a percent of GDP steadily dropped to a low of 33.5 percent in 1981. This trend was interrupted only six times by small upticks in 1950, 1954, 1958, 1968, 1971, and 1975–76. In the second subperiod, from 1982 until 1993, the debt percentage increased every year, surpassing the 1955 level. The first subperiod began with astronomical, but rapidly shrinking, debt percentages, starting at 127.5 percent in 1946, then dropping to 115.3 percent in 1947, 102.1 percent in 1948, and 96.2 percent in 1949. There was a slight increase to 96.7 percent in 1950, but the rapid decline resumed in 1951, when the share fell to 81.4 percent and continued down to 73.1 percent by 1953. Thus, since the beginning of the period, the debt percent had fallen 54.6 percentage points. Except for the slight increases in 1954, 1958, 1968, and 1971, the debt percentage fell throughout the administrations of Eisenhower, Kennedy, Johnson, and the first five years of Nixon to 34.5 percent, representing a further decline, from 1953 to 1974, of 38.6 percentage points. The recession of 1974–75 forced an increase in the debt to 37.3 percent of GDP by 1976, but the debt declined for the next three years to the 34.1 percent level in 1979. There was a small increase in the debt to 34.4 percent of GDP in 1980 before dropping to the period low of 33.5 percent in 1981. In all, the debt percent of GDP had fallen 94.0 percentage points since 1946.

In 1982 and 1983, because of a deep recession as well as tax cuts without sufficient accompanying spending cuts, the debt began to grow rapidly in relation to GDP, reaching 36.4 and 41.3 percent, respectively, thus, inaugurating the second of the two subperiods. In the high GDP growth year of 1984 (6.2 percent), the debt percentage still rose, albeit by only 1.0 percentage point. However, as GDP growth moderated, the debt percentage grew more rapidly, 3.5 percentage points in 1985 and 4.4 percentage points in 1986. The debt percentage climbed more gradually over the next three years, reaching 55.4 percent by 1989. As economic growth slowed, debt percentages grew more rapidly again, increasing by 3.1, 4.9, and 4.2 percentage points during 1990, 1991, and 1992, respectively. In 1993, as the economy further recovered, the increase in debt's percent of GDP was 1.9 percentage points, closing the period at 69.5 percent of GDP. Since the upswing began in 1982, debt as a percent of GDP climbed 36.0 percentage points.

FIGURE 11.3
Federal Debt as a Percent of Gross Domestic Product, 1946–93
(Based on Current Shares)

Percent of GDP

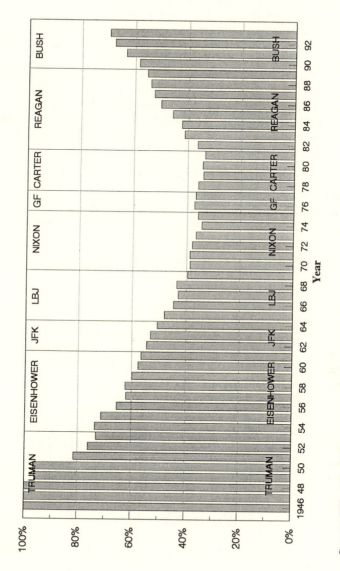

Source: U.S. Office of Management and Budget.

PRESIDENTIAL RANKINGS

Deficits

In spite of the controversies surrounding government accounting (Chapter 10) in general and debts and deficits (see Selected Issues below) specifically, all other things being equal, the position is taken here that the lower the deficit, the better the performance, and the presidents are ranked accordingly (Table 11.1). For the trend change, clearly the greater the reduction in the deficit share the better, although this indicator is rather volatile and, therefore, of limited value. Truman, Eisenhower, and Johnson had the best records regarding the deficit. Truman actually *averaged* a surplus budget (2.4 percent), four surpluses in all, even including 1947, in which the military had not finished building down from World War II. However, Truman's trend change benefits from the World War II build-down, because he is credited with reducing the share of the deficit in GDP from 28.9 to 8.5 percent (20.4 percentage points). Eisenhower, as mentioned, recorded three of the eight budget surpluses of the period within his administration alone and had the second lowest average deficit share of the total budget. He also reduced the deficit share by 5.1 percentage points below that of Truman's last year. Johnson was third with an average of 4.4 percent and a 6.8 percentage point improvement in the trend.

TABLE 11.1
Deficit Shares

Average Deficit Share of Budget			Deficit Share — Trend Change	
President	Term	Percent	President	Percentage Points
Truman	1945–53	−2.4*	Truman	−20.3
Eisenhower	1953–61	2.0	Johnson	−6.8
Johnson	1963–69	4.4	Eisenhower	−5.1
Kennedy	1961–63	5.3	Ford	−2.9
Nixon	1969–74	7.8	Carter	−1.5
Carter	1977–81	11.3	Kennedy	1.6
Ford	1974–77	16.5	Reagan	1.7
Reagan	1981–89	19.0	Bush	4.7
Bush	1989–93	19.3	Nixon	17.8
Average, 1946–93		8.1		

*Surplus

Kennedy, Nixon, and Carter are in the middle of average deficit shares at 5.3, 7.8, and 11.3 percent, respectively. Carter lowered the deficit share slightly, Kennedy increased it slightly, and Nixon raised the share by far more than any other president, from a surplus of 1.8 percent to a deficit of 16.0 percent. Ford, Reagan, and Bush had the highest average deficit shares at 16.5, 19.0, and 19.3 percent, respectively. However, Ford improved the trend by 2.9 percentage points, while Reagan and Bush increased the deficit share by 1.7 and 4.7 percentage points, respectively.

Growth of Federal Debt

With respect to the growth of the federal debt, the lower the growth, the better the presidential performance (Table 11.2). The trend change is of modest value, because the debt growth rate is rather volatile and its changes, as a rule, did not signal important changes in debt behavior. Truman, Eisenhower, and Johnson were, once again, first, second, and third in performance with respect to average real debt growth, all of whose growth rates were negative. Truman achieved an average real reduction in the debt of 5.4 percent and a reduction in the growth rate of 2.1 percentage points. Eisenhower reduced the debt by an annual average of 3.1 percent but slightly increased the debt growth rate. Johnson had an average debt growth of –0.6 percent and reduced the growth rate by 5.9 percentage points, the most among presidents. Nixon's average debt reduction was the same as Johnson's, but the tie is broken in that he left office with a debt growth rate 7.5 percentage points higher than that of Johnson's last year.

Carter's record on the debt was respectable as well, because he recorded a slightly negative average growth and reduced the growth

TABLE 11.2
Federal Debt Growth Rates

Average Debt Growth		Change in Debt Growth Rate	
President	*Percent*	*President*	*Percentage Points*
Truman	–5.4	Johnson	–5.9
Eisenhower	–3.1	Carter	–4.2
Johnson	–0.6	Truman	–2.1
Nixon	–0.6	Bush	0.0
Carter	–0.1	Eisenhower	0.8
Kennedy	0.1	Kennedy	1.4
Ford	5.8	Ford	2.3
Bush	6.8	Reagan	6.2
Reagan	9.2	Nixon	7.5
Average, 1946–93	0.9		

rate 4.2 percentage points. Kennedy did not affect the outstanding debt very much, because his growth averaged only 0.1 percent. Ford, Bush, and Reagan, however, increased the debt substantially at average growth rates of 5.8, 6.8, and 9.2 percent, respectively. Bush did not increase the debt growth rate, but Ford and Reagan did, at 2.3 and 6.2 percentage points, respectively.

Debt as a Percent of Gross Domestic Product

For debt as a percent of GDP, presidents are ranked in ascending order for both averages and trends, because the lower the debt, the better is the performance (Table 11.3). The trend change and the average are of comparable importance in indicating presidential economic performance. Carter, Nixon, and Ford recorded the lowest debt ratios of 34.5, 37.1, and 37.1 percent, respectively. Nixon lowered the debt the most of the three, by 3.6 percentage points, Carter followed with a 3.3 percentage point reduction, while Ford slightly increased the debt ratio by 1.0 percentage point. Thus, Nixon and Carter are close competitors for the best record on debt as a percent of GDP. Johnson, Reagan, and Kennedy had debt ratios of 43.7, 47.3, and 52.7 percent, respectively, but with decidedly different effects on the trend. Johnson and Kennedy lowered the debt ratio by 11.0 and 6.0 percentage points, respectively, while Reagan increased the debt ratio by more than any other president, 21.9 percentage points. The highest debt ratios were recorded by Eisenhower, Bush, and Truman, at 63.6, 64.7, and 96.1 percent, respectively. However, under Truman, the debt percent fell by 54.4 percentage points, far more than under any other president, and under Eisenhower,

TABLE 11.3
Federal Debt as a Percent of Gross Domestic Product

Average Debt Share of GDP		Change in Debt Percent of GDP	
President	Percent	President	Percentage Points
Carter	34.5	Truman	−54.4
Nixon	37.1	Eisenhower	−16.5
Ford	37.2	Johnson	−11.0
Johnson	43.7	Kennedy	−6.0
Reagan	47.3	Nixon	−3.6
Kennedy	52.7	Carter	−3.3
Eisenhower	63.6	Ford	1.0
Bush	64.7	Bush	14.1
Truman	96.1	Reagan	21.9
Average, 1946–93	56.8		

the debt percent fell another 16.5 percentage points. In contrast, Bush raised the debt ratio by the second most of any president, 14.1 percentage points. Truman's record was largely determined by the large debt incurred from World War II and the military build-down thereafter. Hence, Truman had a horrendously high debt ratio but an exaggerated reduction in the debt as well.

SELECTED ISSUES

The behavior of the national debt leading up to 1981 may be somewhat curious to most people. The large and steady increases after 1981 are, however, well-known to the public, given the attention paid by the media to the large deficits during those years. Although many Americans still cannot distinguish between the concepts of debt and deficit, U.S. debt levels have been presented in the news with sufficient regularity that most of the public has a sense of the growth of the national indebtedness. Prior to the early 1980s, the national debt was not a serious concern to policy makers nor a news-making economic issue, and, therefore, the public was probably not aware of the trends in the national debt. It would likely surprise the majority of Americans that the real value of debt actually declined significantly between 1946 (or even 1947 after most of the post–World War II demobilization) and 1981 and declined even more rapidly as a percent of GDP during this time. This fact is even more astounding in light of the fact that the United States ran budget deficits 28 out of the 36 years of that period.

The apparent contradiction between the high incidence of budget deficits and the decline in the national debt is explained by the fact that, as mentioned in the introduction to the chapter, when the debt is deflated, it is not the year-to-year debt increments because of the deficit that are deflated and then summed but, rather, the total debt outstanding is deflated. Although there are some problems with this approach, the deflation of the entire debt can be defended. If the government had decided to pay off the total debt during any one year in the time period, then the true burden of paying off the debt would be measured best by the real total amount of the debt *in that year*. Thus, the real value of the national debt (i.e., converted to constant 1987 dollars) provides a better intertemporal comparison of the burden of liquidating the national debt.

Although deficit-induced economic calamity, as predicted by some economic analysts, did not come to pass, there were some costly consequences. The first was that interest payments on the debt increased to over 14 percent of the budget, which reduced the percentage of government resources for descretionary spending, or spending on programs.[3] The impact on programs, however, was not felt fully, because Congress and the president responded by approving budgets with deficits of over 20 percent of the total budget.

Nevertheless, this practice resulted in a dependency on foreign investors to buy U.S. debt as U.S. investors became saturated with holdings of U.S. debt. In the sense that foreigners had an interest in seeing the United States do well (especially in the case of longer-term foreign direct investment in the United States), the increasing share of U.S. debt in foreign hands was not necessarily a bad trend. However, U.S. policy makers were restricted further in the range of economic policies they could pursue. For example, exchange rate changes with respect to the dollar had increasingly strong effects on the attractiveness to foreigners of U.S. debt instruments, which served to reduce flexibility in U.S. exchange rate policy. In addition, the fact that foreign financing increased by so much during the debt build-up points to the increasingly precarious position with respect to the supply of financing for the U.S. debt — that is, if conditions in those countries that are exporting capital to the United States were to worsen and dictate that these countries keep savings and investment at home, then they must curtail their financing of the U.S. deficit. The burden then would fall on domestic savings, which would be diverted from other productive investment and drive up interest rates.[4] The issue of foreign ownership of U.S. debt underscores the fact that it is not only the level but also the composition of the federal debt that is important to the well-being of the U.S. economy. A detailed review of the composition of the debt over time would yield further insights into the current debt position in which the United States finds itself.

Another concern with current debt/deficit trends is the phenomenon of "twin deficits," that is, budget deficits and international accounts deficits. The interrelationship of the two is important to U.S. economic strategy. The reliance of the United States on investors abroad to finance the government credits from the U.S. budget deficit (and housing and other investment) runs counter to the goal of reducing the trade deficit. The reason is that the higher interest rates that attract foreign capital[5] also increase the value of the dollar. When the value of the dollar increases, U.S. exports become more expensive to foreigners in terms of their own currency and, therefore, less competitive. Simultaneously, with a stronger dollar, imports become cheaper to U.S. consumers. The result is a worsening of the trade balance. The policy choice of the presidents and Congress during the latter part of the 1946–93 period was continued reliance on foreign saving to finance U.S. budget deficits, with the consequent continued large trade deficits.

The cumulative effect of this policy choice was a build-up of future charges against the current account of the balance of payments.[6] Paul Volcker's warning in 1984 that the United States was about to become a net debtor internationally and, in a few years, the largest came true. The compounding of the interest charges on U.S. international debt will pose serious and nagging problems for policy makers for many years.

SUGGESTIONS FOR FURTHER READING

Budget of the United States Government Fiscal Year 1995 — Analytical Perspectives. Washington, D.C.: U.S. Government Printing Office, 1994. Offers a detailed explanation of how deficits are calculated.

Fink, Richard H., and High, Jack C., *A Nation in Debt.* Frederick, Md.: University Publication of America, 1987. An interesting collection of views of famous economists on public debt, from Adam Smith and Karl Marx to Herbert Stein and Alice Rivlin.

NOTES

1. Officially, "discretionary" has a more restrictive definition, which is not intended here. In U.S. federal budget parlance, "discretionary" is defined to distinguish between mandatory program spending and nonmandatory spending. The latter is considered discretionary.

2. "Ratio" is actually a better term than "share" (of GDP), because the national debt is not a component, per se, of GDP as is the federal budget or, more accurately, government purchases.

3. Discretionary spending is referring here to government expenditures that are not interest payments on the debt.

4. Of course, domestic savings, which is used to service the U.S. national debt, does not simply disappear into a black hole; through U.S. creditors, it recirculates in the economy in the form of further consumption and investment, however, it may not be just the type of consumption and investment, which are as beneficial as if these domestic savings did not have to pass through the filter of government debt service.

5. Some analysts contend that changed tax incentives were more responsible for the capital inflow into the United States than were interest rates. After the early 1980s, interest rates did fall, while foreigners continued to finance substantial percentages of U.S. deficits.

6. The current account consists mainly of exports minus imports but also of government grants and other transactions. If there is a deficit on the current account, then, for the balance of payments to equal zero (which, by definition, it must), there must be a surplus on the capital account. In recent years, the capital account surplus has taken the form largely of a net increase in foreign investments in the United States. When U.S. payments on that foreign investment exceeded the payments foreigners made on U.S. investment abroad in 1985, the United States became a debtor nation.

12

Composition of the Government Budget

The size of the federal budget and the deficits and debt discussed in the previous chapters showed the relative importance of the government to the economy as a whole and how it has changed over time, across and within administrations. However, it is of interest not only how much is spent but also on what it is spent, which is the subject of this chapter. The insights gained from this examination of the composition of the government budget may be more political than economic, yet, it is clear that spending on one budget category has quite different economic consequences than spending on another, for example, defense versus human resources. Those consequences are left to other analysts to determine.

Five areas of government expenditure are reviewed. In descending order of their shares of the budget at the end of the time period, they are human resources (which includes Social Security), defense, physical resources, interest payments on the debt, and other functions. Some of these categories contain quite different types of subcategories. The defense and interest categories are single purpose categories, while human resources contains items as disparate as Social Security, unemployment compensation, aid to families with dependent children, and veterans benefits. Foreign aid, for example, is located in the international affairs subcategory under other functions. Because of its importance, Social Security is discussed in greater detail in a separate chapter (Chapter 13) and as a major tax category in Chapter 14. In selected cases, behavior of the major subcategories is described.

The major subcategories for each category in descending order of most recent subcategory shares are as follows:

human resources — Social Security (on- and off-budget), income security, medicare, health, education, training, employment and social services, and veterans' benefits and services;
defense — no subcategories;

physical resources — transportation, commerce and housing credit (on- and off-budget), natural resources and the environment, community and regional development, and energy;

net interest (on- and off-budget) — no subcategories; and

other functions — agriculture, international affairs (which includes foreign aid), general science, space and technology, administration of justice, and general government.

There is also a category entitled "undistributed offsetting receipts" both on- and off-budget that consists of receipts collected by the government that are not attributed to any functional category. The current sources of these receipts are from employee retirement contributions, royalties from oil leases, proceeds from the sale of federal assets, and so on.

OVERVIEW OF TRENDS IN THE LONG RUN, 1946–93

Figure 12.1 depicts the composition of the federal budget during 1946–93. The categories depicted in this figure are defense, human resources, physical resources, interest payments, and other, whose contents have been defined above. The most striking change over time is the shift of resources out of defense and into human resources. Only during the Korean War and the Reagan administration was this resource shift interrupted. Another salient trend is the increase in interest payments as a share of the total budget, which rose from a 7.0 percent share in 1975 to 14.8 percent by 1989.

Human Resources

The trend in human resources shares showed strong swings before and after World War II. Shares of human resources were much higher before than during the war, accounting for 43.7 percent of the budget in 1940 and 30.5 percent in 1941, but plummeted during the war to a low of 2.0 percent by 1945. After the war, although human resources shares fluctuated on a year-to-year basis (as the trend changes in the presidential rankings show), *average* expenditures increased with every administration except Carter's and Reagan's, with the highest share occurring under Bush.

In 1946, when the bulk of demilitarization had yet to take place, human resources were only 9.9 percent of total outlays but quickly jumped to 28.7 and 33.2 percent in 1947 and 1948, respectively. These increases were accounted for mainly by the subcategory veterans' benefits and services. Shares fluctuated for the rest of Truman's administration, dropping 5.4 percentage points to 27.8 percent in 1949 and rising again to 33.4 percent the following year. The share dropped sharply again to 24.2 percent in 1951, 17.4 percent in 1952, and closed the administration at 15.6 percent in 1953. The reason for the decline

FIGURE 12.1
Composition of the Federal Budget, 1946–93
(Current Shares)

Percent Shares of Federal Budget

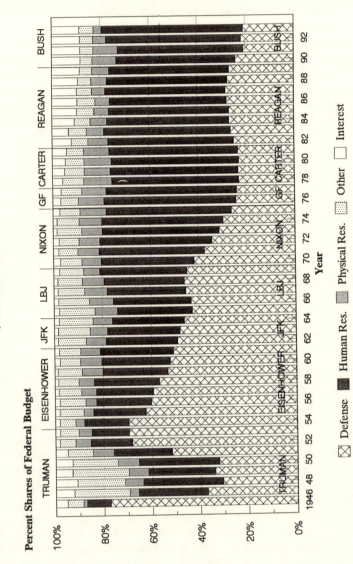

Defense   Human Res.   Physical Res.   Other   Interest

Source: U.S. Office of Management and Budget.

in share of human resources in the last couple of years of Truman's administration is not that absolute human resources spending went down but that overall government spending, mainly because of defense, increased rapidly from 14.5 percent of GDP in 1951 to 20.9 percent in 1953. Although Truman ended on a downward trend, the share of human resources, nevertheless, increased during his tenure by 5.7 percentage points (9.9 to 15.6 percent).

Under Eisenhower, human resource shares rose again, climbing 2.9 percentage points in his first budget to 18.5 percent in 1954, and continued upward gradually to 23.7 percent by 1957 before jumping to 27 percent in 1958. The share held at 27 percent in 1959 but continued to rise for the next two years and closed out Eisenhower at 30.5 percent in his 1961 budget, for an increase of 14.9 percentage points during his eight-year tenure. Eisenhower's trend in human resources was virtually the reverse of that of defense, which fell 18.8 percentage points. Under Kennedy, the share of human resources actually dropped by 0.7 percentage point, although his three-year average was higher than his predecessor's. During Johnson's administration, the share increase was steady, climbing 6.4 percentage points in five years from 29.8 percent in 1964 and reaching 36.2 percent in 1969.

Nixon witnessed another very large increase in the human resources share as in the six-year span from 1969 to 1975, the share rose 15.9 percentage points to 52.1 percent. Under Ford, the share continued to rise to 54.8 in 1976, the highest share up to that time, and he closed out his administration at 54.2 percent in 1977. After these massive increases, the share eased back slightly, 1.4 percentage points in Carter's first budget year, 1978, and remained in the 52.8–53.4 percent range during his administration. Carter closed out with an overall decline of 0.8 percentage point to 53.4 percent in 1981. Under Reagan, the human resources share immediately dropped 1.3 percentage points to 52.1 percent in 1982 and rose slightly to 52.7 percent before continuing back down to 50.7, 49.9, and 48.6 percent in 1984, 1985, and 1986, respectively. Thereafter, the human resources share hugged the 50 percent level during 1987–89. In the end, Reagan had managed to lower the human resources share by 3.7 percentage points to 49.7 percent. Under Bush, the share initially dropped to 49.4 percent in 1990 and then resumed an upward trend, rising to 52.1, 55.9, and 58.8 percent (the period high) in 1991, 1992, and 1993, respectively.

The shares of subcategories *within* human resources also changed substantially throughout the period. An examination of some of these changes provides insights into the continuous reshaping of the goals of government spending. In Table 12.1 which contains data from the beginning and end of the period and at ten-year intervals, very large share shifts are observed. It can be seen, for example, that the combined share of income security and veterans' benefits comprised over 88 percent of the human resources budget in 1946 but only 29 percent in 1993.

It is also observed that income security and Social Security were the most important subcategories after the first ten-year period, together accounting for 63.3 percent of the budget outlays in 1956, a peak of over 70 percent in 1966 and 61.2 percent at the close of the period in 1993. Although it constituted a very high share in the beginning of the time period, over 40 percent, income security was fairly steady, in the 22–30 percent range, from the 1950s onward. Social Security was still a new program in 1946 and comprised only 6.5 percent of budget outlays for human resources. At the ten-year intervals that followed, its share oscillated between 34 and 48 percent and closed the period at 36.3 percent. Medicare rapidly gained in importance, increasing from near 0 percent in 1966 (because it had just started) to 15.8 percent of human resources by 1993. Health, which is distinct from medicare, remained near the 6–8 percent range for much of the period but jumped to 12.5 percent by 1993. The total health and medicare share of human resources increased from 3.7 percent in 1946 to 6.0 percent in 1966 and to 28.3 percent in 1993. Education and training increased until 1966, then decreased and held at a little over 6 percent. Veterans' benefits were high after the war, accounting for almost half of the budget for human resources. As expected, veterans' benefits gradually declined and closed the period at only 4.2 percent.

TABLE 12.1
Percent of Human Resources Outlays by Subcategory

	1946	1956	1966	1976	1986	1993
Education, training, employment, and social services	1.5	3.7	10.1	9.3	6.4	6.3
Health	3.7	2.2	5.9	7.7	7.5	12.5
Medicare[a]	na[b]	na	0.1	7.8	14.6	15.8
Income security	43.4	29.5	22.3	29.9	24.9	24.9
Social Security	6.5	34.1	47.8	36.3	41.3	36.3
Veterans' benefits	44.9	30.5	13.7	9.1	5.5	4.2

[a]The first year for medicare outlays was 1966.
[b]na, not available.

Source: percentages are calculated based on data from Budget of the United States Government — Historical Tables, Washington, D.C.: Office of Management and Budget, 1994.

Defense

In 1945, at the end of World War II, the defense budget had reached 89.5 percent of the total budget. In 1946, the share dropped to 77.3 percent, and in 1947 the share dropped a whopping 40.2 percentage points to 37.1 percent. The early post-war defense share bottomed out at 30.6 percent in 1948. During 1949–50, the share edged up to the 32–34 percent range. However, no sooner had the defense budget resumed peacetime proportions than the Korean War began. In 1951, defense spending shot up 19.6 share points to more than half the total federal budget, 51.8 percent, and another 16.3 share points to 68.1 percent the next year and peaked in 1954 at 69.5 percent. It proved harder to get the defense budget down after the Korean War to peacetime levels than it was after World War II, most likely because of heightened cold war tensions. After a 7.1 percentage point drop in 1955, the year after the peak post–World War II defense share, defense shares declined rather gradually. Nine years of small declines of approximately 1–3 percentage points brought the defense share down to 46.2 percent by 1964. The share dropped a bit faster in fiscal 1965, 3.4 percentage points, to 42.8 percent, but, as the Viet Nam War escalated, the downward trend was reversed in 1966 as the share rose 0.4 percentage points, rose another 2.2 percentage points in 1967, and peaked in 1968 at 46.0 percent.

Under Nixon's "Vietnamization," defense expenditures resumed the downward trend, dropping 3.1 percentage points in 1970 to 41.8 percent and another 4.3 percentage points to 37.5 percent in 1971. This trend continued rapidly for the next five years, falling to 24.1 percent by 1976. During Carter, defense expenditures remained near the 23 percent level, with a slight drop, 0.6 percentage point, recorded during his administration. After six years in office, Reagan had increased the share by 4.9 percentage points to a peak of 28.1 percent in 1987. The defense share had not been this high since 1974, when it was 29.5 percent. The Reagan defense shares subsequently declined to 27.3 and 26.6 percent in 1988 and 1989, respectively, probably reflecting approaching victory in the cold war. The 26.6 percent defense share at the end of the Reagan years was also higher than any defense share, with the exception of Reagan's other budgets, since 1974.

The "peace dividend" from the ending of the cold war was clearly in evidence during the Bush administration. Defense shares fell a total of 5.9 percentage points to 20.7 percent by 1993, the lowest defense share since 1940. The defense share fell 2.7 and 3.3 share points in 1990 and 1991, respectively, in spite of the Gulf War. The defense share did increase 1 percentage point in 1992 but fell 0.9 percentage points in 1993. From the 1987 peak of defense spending to the end of the Bush administration, the defense share dropped a total of 8.5 percentage points.

Net Interest on Government Debt

At the outset of the 1946–93 period, the United States was emerging from a mountain of debt accumulated in order to finance World War II, during which budget deficits reached 25 percent of GDP. Net interest payments increased for the first three years after the war to 7.4, 12.2, and 14.6 percent of the budget. In 1949, the share fell to 11.6 percent, beginning a five-year decline in interest payments share to 6.8 percent in 1953, the end of the Truman years. From that point until 1978, a span of 26 years, interest payments remained within a narrow 6.2–8.0 range, with all presidents during this period recording remarkably similar percentages. Eisenhower's range was 6.3–7.5 percent; Kennedy's, 6.4–7.0 percent; Johnson's, 6.2–7.3 percent; Nixon's, 6.7–8.0 percent; and Ford's, 7.2–7.3 percent.

Under Carter, the share of interest payments began to rise, as his range climbed to 7.7–11.2 percent. His high share is explained more by the high interest rate level during his presidency than by increases in debt, because his average debt outstanding averaged the lowest as a percent of GDP (Chapter 11). Further explanation of this phenomenon is given below. Interest payment shares took off under Reagan, increasing to 11.4 percent in 1982, leveling off at 11.1 percent in 1983, but increasing again to 13.0 percent in 1984 and to 13.7 percent in 1985 and 1986. Shares continued to rise for three more years, reaching 14.8 percent in 1989, the high water mark for the period. Although deficits continued to rise under Bush, interest payments fell 0.7 percentage point during his tenure and were 14.1 percent in 1993.

Two factors are at play in determining the share of interest payments of the total budget: the size of the total federal debt outstanding and the prevailing interest rate or, more accurately, the structure of interest rates. The structure of interest rates refers to the various interest rates that prevail for financial instruments of different maturities, as is represented by the "yield curve" described in Chapter 5. Because the national debt is financed through instruments of different maturities, it is a structure of interest rates, rather than any one single rate, that determines interest payments on the debt. As was observed under Bush, even though budget deficits were at a historical high for the four-year period, interest payments share of the budget actually declined. This decline is explained by the fall in the interest rate, not by an improved national debt situation. Because much of the U.S. debt is short term and because the short-term interest rates were particularly low, interest payments were reduced accordingly. In the case of Carter, the opposite was true.

Physical Resources and Other Functions

As mentioned, physical resources contains subcategories as diverse as transportation, commerce and housing credits, natural resources and the environment, community and regional development, and energy. What the subcategories have in common is that they are related to the U.S. physical infrastructure in one way or another. Thus, there is a clear distinction from human resources. In the aggregate, of course, it is not clear what the behavior of the physical resources category means for government spending policy, but some inferences can be drawn from this aggregate behavior. The other functions category contains even more disparate subcategories, and only a discussion of the behavior of its subcategories is meaningful, one of which is briefly described.

Physical resources claimed a 1.5 percent share in 1946, and in 1993 the share stood at 3.3 percent. During the entire period, the shares ranged from 1.5 to 11.5 percent, with 77 percent of the shares (37 of 48 years) falling between 6 and 11 percent. After the low share start during 1946–47, moderate share levels of 6–8 percent characterized physical resources up to 1964. Physical resources accounted for higher shares of 8–11 percent during 1965–82 and generally lower levels of 5–7 percent for the rest of the period but with 1990–91 over 10 percent.

The other functions category began the period at 6.5 percent and ended it at 5.8 percent. Between 1946 and 1993, its share ranged between 5.4 and 23.3 percent, but in over 80 percent of the years, the shares were between 5 and 11 percent. Within other functions is a superfunction called international affairs, within which is a subfunction called international development and humanitarian assistance. This sub-subcategory comprises what is commonly known as foreign aid. This indicator is presented because, although insignificant to the overall budget and GDP, it is still a perennial hot topic and sheds some light on the posture of the United States with respect to grants and subsidized loans to developing countries.

Foreign aid is allocated largely through a government agency under the State Department called the U.S. Agency for International Development. The trends in foreign aid are reviewed from 1962 to 1993; thus, the Marshall Plan is not considered in the discussion. It is safe to say, however, that the share of foreign aid was much higher during the Marshall Plan than at any time during the 1962–93 period. In terms of the share of the total government budget, there was a steady downward trend in outlays for foreign aid. During 1962–66, the foreign aid share of the budget was at its high of 2.7–2.8 percent. From 1967 onward, with a few minor interruptions (as in 1974–75 and 1985, in which the foreign aid share increased), the foreign aid share slid from 2.6 percent to 0.4 percent of the budget. In fact, the share of the budget going to foreign aid was 0.4 percent for the last seven years of the period, 1987–93.

PRESIDENTIAL RANKINGS

As maintained at the outset, the composition of the budget probably provides more insights into policy makers' values and into the relative budgetary needs facing the government at the time than it does into economic performance. So it is with the ranking of presidents with respect to component shares of the budget (tables 12.2–12.5). The ranking depends on one's own values. Because the sum of the shares of all budget categories equals 100 percent, the gain in the share of one category of government expenditure means the loss in share of one or more of the remaining categories. Some may hold human resources expenditures more valuable than defense; others, the reverse. Assuming a best to worst ranking is to impose one's own preferences. The convention used here is to rank the presidents in descending order from highest to lowest share for *all* categories of the budget. The same convention holds for the trend change variable. Because the rankings in the case of budget composition do not really serve as performance measures, a narrative of the rankings would be of limited value. A discussion of issues surrounding the differences in shares between presidential administrations, however, is provided in the Selected Issues section.

TABLE 12.2
Human Resources Share of Federal Budget

Average Share			Change in Share	
President	Term	Percent	President	Percentage Points
Ford	1974–77	54.5	Nixon	15.9
Bush	1989–93	54.1	Eisenhower	14.9
Carter	1977–81	53.1	Bush	9.1
Reagan	1981–89	50.5	Johnson	6.4
Nixon	1969–74	46.6	Truman	5.7
Johnson	1963–69	33.0	Ford	2.1
Kennedy	1961–63	22.8	Kennedy	–0.7
Eisenhower	1953–61	25.0	Carter	–0.8
Truman	1945–53	23.8	Reagan	–3.7
Average, 1946–93		38.9		

TABLE 12.3
Defense Share of Federal Budget

Average Share		Change in Share	
President	Percent	President	Percentage Points
Eisenhower	58.1	Reagan	3.4
Truman	50.1	Carter	–0.6
Kennedy	47.7	Johnson	–1.3
Johnson	44.5	Ford	–2.2
Nixon	33.4	Kennedy	–4.6
Reagan	26.7	Bush	–5.9
Ford	24.0	Truman	–7.9
Carter	23.0	Eisenhower	–18.6
Bush	21.7	Nixon	–18.9
Average, 1946–93	39.0		

TABLE 12.4
Physical Resources Share of Federal Budget

Average Share		Change in Share	
President	Percent	President	Percentage Points
Carter	11.0	Nixon	4.2
Ford	10.3	Truman	3.8
Nixon	8.93	Eisenhower	2.6
Johnson	8.86	Carter	0.5
Kennedy	7.8	Kennedy	0.1
Reagan	6.6	Ford	−0.7
Eisenhower	6.18	Johnson	−1.5
Truman	6.16	Reagan	−3.4
Bush	7.2	Bush	−3.8
Average, 1946–93	7.6		

TABLE 12.5
Net Interest Payments Share of Federal Budget

Average Share		Change in Share	
President	Percent	President	Percentage Points
Bush	14.5	Reagan	4.7
Reagan	13.2	Carter	2.8
Truman	10.0	Ford	0.3
Carter	8.8	Eisenhower	0.1
Ford	7.3	Nixon	0.1
Nixon	7.2	Johnson	0.0
Eisenhower	7.0	Kennedy	0.0
Johnson	6.78	Truman	−0.6
Kennedy	6.77	Bush	−0.7
Average, 1946–93	9.3		

SELECTED ISSUES

As pointed out, the largest resource shift in the government budget during 1946–93 was out of defense and into human resources. Both categories averaged about 39 percent each over the entire time period, but at the end of the period, the defense share stood at 20.7 percent, while human resources was 58.8 percent. This resource shift is made more remarkable because mainly Republican presidents effected it. First of all, every president except Reagan reduced the share of the military budget, but it was the cold warriors Nixon and Eisenhower who reduced it the most. Truman, another cold warrior, and Bush also reduced the defense budget by substantial amounts. Given that both Eisenhower and Truman were building down from World War II and the Korean War, respectively, it would be expected that their defense shares would drop. Although Truman had to build up for the Korean War, World War II was of such a greater magnitude that Truman was still able to record a share decrease in defense expenditures. Eisenhower's build-down after the Korean War still did not bring defense shares to pre–Korean War levels, even though his defense share decreased by over 18 share points. Nixon and Bush, on the other hand, decreased defense shares substantially, 18.9 and 7.0 percentage points, respectively, when shares were already lower than they had been for years. Granted, Nixon's reduction in defense share was substantially attributable to the ending of the Viet Nam War, but his reductions went far below pre–Viet Nam War share levels, below any seen in the post-war era. Bush erased the Reagan build-up by twofold, that is, his four-year reduction amounted to twice the share points of Reagan's increase.

Not surprisingly, the two presidents who decreased defense the most, Nixon and Eisenhower, increased the share of human resources by more than the other presidents, by amounts comparable to their defense reductions. Bush raised human resources the third most by an amount almost identical to his defense reduction. Thus, it was three Republican presidents who increased the share spent on human resources the most. Their combined increase was 37.9 percentage points, comprising a large majority of the 1993 share of 58.8 percent. (Of course, the period began at a very low human resources share of only 9.9 percent.) With his Great Society initiatives, it would be expected that Johnson would have ranked higher than fourth in increasing the human resources share. The explanation is probably that he provided the mechanism by which social spending could balloon but was not in office long enough after the new programs were in place for the social spending to gain momentum. Nixon, who followed Johnson, was well-placed to rapidly increase social spending. The Johnson programs had been firmly established, and Nixon helped to expand them further into the middle class. With the addition of indexation of social programs to inflation, which was high in the 1970s, it was difficult to control spending, and the human resources shot up almost 16 share points in Nixon's six years.

The two presidents who stand out as raising the share of interest payments as a share of the total budget are Reagan, 4.7 percentage points (from a 10.1 to a 14.8 percent share) over eight years, and Carter, 2.8 percentage points (7.3 to 10.1 percent share) over four years. Truman's interest share increased rapidly at first but was brought down to near his starting level by the end of his administration. Bush, although averaging the highest interest payment share of the budget, actually lowered the share by 0.7 percentage point. For the other presidents, the national debt level and interest rates did not change much, which left the share of the budget going to interest payments virtually unchanged. As mentioned, in the case of Bush, interest payments would have been a lot higher had interest rates been higher. This concern is reflected in the measure of Bush's performance with respect to his deficit totals, but it is also reflected in his performance that interest rates were favorable.

On the subject of foreign aid, although it is a relatively unimportant economic category, it is an area of expenditure that has frequently been demagogued and has been a favorite target of politicians during tough times in the domestic economy. It was shown, however, that foreign aid, as measured by the line item international development and humanitarian assistance, which is nonmilitary, comprised only 0.4 percent of the budget in 1993 and had been declining since the mid-1960s. Nevertheless, many people still believe that significant budgetary resources can be saved from the U.S. foreign aid budget and used to reduce the deficit and address other needs at home. Eliminating the foreign aid budget, simply by virtue of its minuscule share, would have little effect on either. Without delving into the pros and cons of U.S. aid, it should also be recognized that the bulk of this aid is tied to the purchase of U.S. goods (equipment) and services (consultants) and, thus, is not simply a giveaway of taxpayer dollars.

SUGGESTIONS FOR FURTHER READING

Meyer, Annette E., *Evolution of United States Budgeting — Changing Fiscal and Financial Concepts*. Westport, Conn.: Greenwood Press, 1989. Reviews fiscal and financial institutions, the budgetary process, and trends in the composition of budget receipts and outlays.

Pechman, Joseph A., *Setting National Priorities*. Washington, D.C.: The Brookings Institution. Published annually since 1971, it examines major areas of the budget in the context of the priorities facing the United States.

13

Social Security

Although Social Security is only one of many government budget subcategories, it merits a separate chapter because it has risen faster and grown larger than any other component of the budget during the 1946–93 period. Social Security as measured here encompasses two main benefits categories: the Old Age and Survivors Insurance Trust Fund, initiated in 1935, and the Disability Insurance Trust Fund, resulting from amendments made in 1956. Together, these categories are referred to by the acronym OASDI (hereafter used interchangeably with Social Security). The trust fund expenditures include the payments made to beneficiaries and the expenses in administering the trust. Trust administration expenses during the period were typically 1–2 percent of total outlays, although in recent years, expenses have been kept below 1 percent. As an insurance fund, the purpose of Social Security is not to provide a defined contribution or benefit pension plan[1] to participants nor to ensure that every participant receives equal benefits but, rather, to protect Americans from the financial risks of disability, income shortfall during old age, or death of an income-earning parent (for family dependents).

The *Annual Statistical Supplement to the Social Security Bulletin, 1993* describes the OASDI program as follows:

The OASDI provides monthly benefits to retired and disabled workers and their dependents and to survivors of insured workers. Benefits are paid as a matter of earned right to workers who gain insured status and to their eligible spouses and children and survivors. Retirement benefits were provided by the original Social Security Act of 1935, benefits for dependents and survivors by the 1939 amendments, benefits for the disabled by the 1956 amendments, and benefits for the dependents of disabled workers by the 1958 amendments. In 1965, the Health Insurance program, generally known as Medicare, was enacted. Medicare is administered by the Health Care Financing Administration.

A person builds protection under the OASDI program through work in employment covered under Social Security. Coverage is in general compulsory. Taxes on wage and salary workers' earnings up to a statutory maximum taxable amount each year are withheld and matched by employers. Self employed persons pay taxes on their annual earnings up to the same maximum as employees but at the combined employer-employee rate.

President Roosevelt signed the Social Security Act in 1935, payroll taxes began in 1937, and old-age benefits were first paid in 1940. Initially, the act covered workers in commerce and industry, comprising about 60 percent of the total labor force. In the 1950s, legislation brought most of the previously excluded workers, such as farm and domestic workers, the self-employed, state and local government employees (on an elective basis), and members of the armed forces, under the Social Security umbrella. In addition, in 1983, federal government civilian employees hired from 1984 onward were covered. By 1993, more than 130 million Americans paid Social Security taxes and over 40 million received benefits, constituting virtually universal coverage. Three-fourths of the beneficiaries were elderly, and the remaining primarily were disabled workers and their spouses, children under 18, disabled who never could work, and widows caring for children. Outlays for Social Security in 1993 topped $300 billion, while receipts were more than $350 billion. Over 90 percent of receipts came from Social Security taxes on income, borne equally by individuals and employers (except in the case of the self-employed, who bear the entire tax), and the rest from interest on trust funds and taxes on Social Security benefits. Medicare, which had 35 million beneficiaries, added another $150 billion in outlays. The sheer size of Social Security also has made it an important antipoverty program. The Census Bureau has reported that Social Security does more to reduce poverty and income inequality than welfare or even the progressivity of the U.S. tax system.[2] Understandably, Social Security is probably the most politically sensitive item in the budget. Any efforts to tamper with it, especially attempts to curtail benefits, are invariably met with a firestorm of political reaction.

In keeping with Social Security's high importance to the budget, it appears not only in this chapter but also in two other chapters in the book. In Chapter 12 Social Security as a share of the human resources budget component is given over ten-year intervals in Table 12.1 and in Chapter 14 Social Security tax and other social insurance (mainly medicare) receipts as a percent of total receipts are presented in Figure 14.1. As seen in Chapter 14, social insurance receipts has also been the fastest growing component of tax receipts.

In theory, the U.S. Social Security system is a pay-as-you-go system, that is, the revenues from Social Security are paid out in benefits on a year-by-year basis, with the trust fund serving as only a contingency fund. However, there were also periods in which substantial reserves accumulated, as well as years of fund depletion. The trust fund gained in nominal asset value every year through 1958 (fiscal years), reaching $23.9 billion, experienced a combination of moderate reductions and small gains through 1966, when the fund stood at $21.7 billion, and then recorded nine straight years of increases, reaching $48.4 billion by the end of fiscal 1975 (although the increases during 1973–75 lagged behind the inflation rates, thus, constituting moderate real declines in the trust). For the next seven years, mainly because of excessive benefits increases in the 1972 act (which contained a large current benefits increase and indexing benefits to inflation to begin in 1975), the fund's value declined, slipping to $20.9 billion by the end of fiscal 1982.

In the midst of this decline, policy makers felt that the trust had become dangerously depleted. To avert insolvency of the program, Congress and the president acted in 1977, mainly through a payroll tax — FICA — increase and a less generous benefits formula,[3] but ignoring longer-run financing issues. Moreover, the assumptions on which the actions were based, primarily on inflation, declining birth rates, and rising real wages, turned out to be overly optimistic. By 1983, it was clear that the actions taken six years earlier were insufficient to restore trust value to an actuarially sound level. Among the elements of the 1983 reform that enhanced trust fund levels were the taxation of benefits introduced for higher income individuals, two increases in the retirement age after the year 2000, ending preferential treatment for the self-employed so that their Social Security taxes equaled the combined rates paid by employers and employees, moving up of already scheduled payroll taxes, and the delay of cost of living adjustments.

By 1985, the effect of these changes was clear, as the fund began to increase rapidly in value. The nominal value of the trust exceeded $365 billion by the end of fiscal 1993, up from $20.9 billion in 1982. Thus, although Social Security is supposedly a pay-as-you-go system, the trust fund, by the design of policy makers, was built up in order to provide benefits in the distant future. The demographic trends of increased life expectancies and lower fertility rates translate into an expanding base of beneficiaries and a shrinking base of contributors, both of which make necessary a Social Security reserve in order to meet its future obligations. As will be seen later, however, the OASDI trust fund does not constitute a $365 billion portfolio of private assets but, rather, exists only on paper.

Social Security data are maintained by the Social Security Administration (SSA) of the Department of Health and Human Services. However, the Office of Management and Budget also presents Social Security data in its *Budget of the United States Government — Historical Tables*. Data for Figures 13.1 and 13.2 are from the Office of Management and Budget *Historical Tables* and for Figure 13.3 are directly from the SSA. All data presented here are on a fiscal year basis, although the SSA also reports Social Security statistics based on calendar years.

OVERVIEW OF TRENDS IN THE LONG RUN, 1946–93

The Social Security category is described by more statistics than any other category or indicator in this book. Three indicators are used to illustrate Social Security trends (five if the measures in Chapters 12 and 14 are counted), the real value of Social Security outlays, Social Security outlays as a percent of the total budget, and the growth of the OASDI trust fund. Social Security outlays are converted to real terms using the consumer price index (CPI) rather than the government budget deflator. The intent here is to measure the real outlays and real trust fund levels from the beneficiaries' and contributors' points of view. Because Social Security outlays are basically transfer payments that typically are used to purchase consumer items, they should be converted into real terms using the CPI. The government price deflator is geared to government purchases, which consist of both wholesale and retail items, and not exclusively to consumer items. The growth in Social Security outlays is also captured through its increasing share of the total budget. The share of Social Security outlays is based on current (non-inflation adjusted) levels of Social Security outlays divided by current levels of the total federal budget.

Social Security Outlays

The clear message of Figure 13.1 is that real Social Security outlays increased throughout the period — in fact, the upward rise in real Social Security outlays was uninterrupted except for a very slight decline in 1979. Increases in the early part of the period are difficult to discern because of the small increments at low levels of outlays, also making it difficult to distinguish between the relative growth rates of spending in the early administrations. Yet, it is clear that under Truman, Eisenhower, Kennedy, and Johnson, the level of Social Security spending steadily increased. Figure 13.1 displays particularly steep absolute increases under Nixon, Ford, and Bush, while there was a relative leveling off under Carter and a more gradual rise under Reagan.

In terms of both nominal and real spending levels by decade, increases were very rapid. Because the program was still new, outlays were quite low in the period following the war, at a little over $2 billion ($267 million in nominal terms) in 1946 and rising to $3.1 billion ($657 nominal) by the end of the 1940s. The 1950s saw real levels climb from $3.7 billion to $38.0 billion ($9.7 billion nominal), and by the end of the 1960s real outlays rose to $84.4 billion ($27.3 billion nominal). Increases continued through the end of the 1970s, and at the end of the

FIGURE 13.1
Social Security Outlays, 1946-93 (Adjusted for Inflation)

Real Level ($ billions)

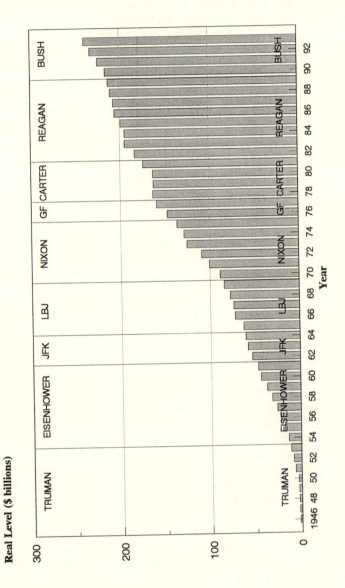

Source: U.S. Office of Management and Budget.

decade, outlays had reached $162.9 billion ($104.1 billion nominal). The 1980s began with a modest increase to $163.5 billion ($118.5 billion nominal) and finished the decade at $213.2 billion ($232.5 billion nominal).[4] By the end of fiscal 1993, Social Security outlays had reached $239.6 billion in real terms ($304.6 billion nominal).

Rates of Social Security growth, one of the bases for ranking the presidents, were in double digits from 1946 to 1960, with only four double-digit growth years coming thereafter. However, during these years, the program was relatively new, and growth rates are calculated on very small bases, at least until the late 1950s, when Social Security surpassed 10 percent of the total budget. From 1984 onward, the growth in real outlays never exceeded 3.8 percent. Average growth for the 1946–93 period was 10.1 percent.

Social Security Share of Budget Outlays

Figure 13.2 illustrates another side to the growth of Social Security: its share, or percent, of the federal budget. In comparing Figure 13.2 with Figure 14.2, Composition of Taxes, the reader may notice the contrast between the leveling off of Social Security budget shares from the mid-1970s onward and the continually rising share of tax receipts accounted for by social insurance taxes. The two phenomena which account for this contrast are that the Social Security program was not operated on a pure pay-as-you-go basis and there was no balanced federal budget from the mid-1970s onward.[5] Rather, Social Security began to realize large surpluses after the early 1980s (violating the pay-as-you-go principle), which were a result of Social Security tax receipts exceeding outlays by a wide margin and, for the federal budget as a whole, total tax receipts did not increase as rapidly as did total federal outlays, mainly during the 1980s (violating the balanced budget principle). Both effects served simultaneously to increase Social Security tax receipts relative to total tax receipts and to lower Social Security outlays relative to total federal outlays after the mid-1970s.

In 1946, Social Security outlays were only 0.6 percent of the budget. Seven years later, at the end of the Truman administration in 1953, in spite of small share losses in 1949 and 1952, its share had reached 3.6 percent. During the eight Eisenhower years, the share of Social Security in the budget increased every year and reached 12.8 percent in 1961. In 1957, disability insurance was added, prior to which Social Security consisted only of old-age and survivors' insurance. After Eisenhower and until 1970, share increases continued, albeit at a slower rate. Under Kennedy, the share increased to 14.0 percent and under Johnson to 14.9 percent but included two successive declines during 1967–68, a sharp decline in 1967 of 1.6 percentage points and a smaller decline of 0.4 percentage point the following year.

FIGURE 13.2
Social Security Outlays — Share of Total Budget, 1946–93

Percent of Total Budget

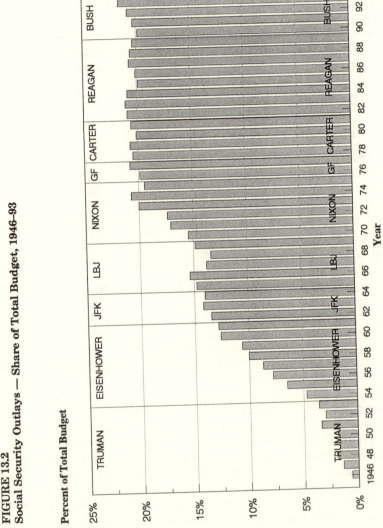

Source: U.S. Office of Management and Budget.

With the Nixon administration, share growth accelerated and reached 19.5 percent in 1975, which included a peak of 20.7 percent in 1974. The Social Security share further increased under Ford to 20.8 percent in 1977, which was, up to that point, the period high. Under Carter, the share of Social Security was fairly constant, and his administration closed with a slight decline at 20.6 percent. Social Security share trends under Reagan also were flat, with a slight decline to 20.3 percent by 1989. The Social Security share under Bush initially decreased to 19.8 percent in 1990 but then increased for the rest of his administration, reaching 21.6 percent in 1993, the all-time high for the 1946–93 period.

Real Social Security Trust Fund

Although the Social Security program is officially a pay-as-you-go program, nevertheless, the real dollar level (deflated by the CPI) of the Social Security trust fund varied widely during the 1946–93 period. As Figure 13.3 shows, the real trust fund levels followed a pattern that can be divided into five distinct trends:

1946–57, in which the Social Security trust fund grew moderately in real terms (annual average growth equaled 7.0 percent), although from a small base (that is, low trust fund level);

1958–66, when the fund declined somewhat (average growth was –2.4 percent);

1967–72, during which the fund increased at about the same rate as in the first period (average growth of 7.8 percent);

1973–84, when the fund declined rapidly (average growth for the period was –12.7 percent), leaving a very small base; and

1985–93, when the fund increased very rapidly (an annual average of 32.2 percent), although the first two or three years' high percentage growth rates were from a, once again, small base.

The average growth rate of the fund for the entire period was 4.0 percent.

In the first three years of the first subperiod, 1946–57, trust fund growth rates were moderate but jumped to more rapid growth rates for five of the six years during 1949–54. Fund growth rates reached 13.9 percent in 1949 and 12.5 percent in 1950, dropped to 5.9 percent in 1951, but accelerated again to 10.6, 9.8, and 8.4 percent during 1952–54. Growth rates tapered off over the next three years to 5.9 and 5.3 and closed the first subperiod at 0.1 percent in 1957. During the first subperiod, the trust fund had grown from $41.7 billion in real terms at fiscal year-end 1945 to $94.4 billion by 1957. In 1958, the second subperiod began with three straight declines. There was a modest increase in 1961, but four of the next five years saw small to moderate declines,

FIGURE 13.3
Social Security Trust Fund, 1946–93
(Adjusted for Inflation)

Real Level ($ billions)

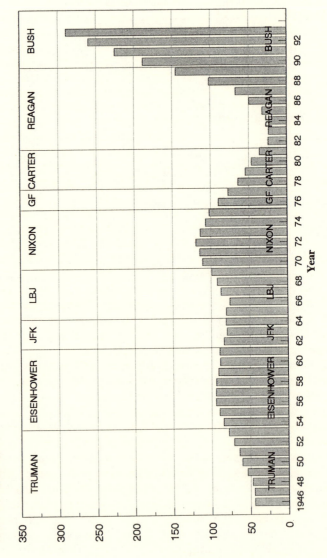

Source: Social Security Administration.

and the real trust value fell to $76.0 billion by 1966. Growth rates turned positive in 1967 with a large increase of 14.8 percent, inaugurating the third subperiod, which for four of the next five years (1968–72) had moderate growth rates and a rapid growth rate of 11.9 percent in 1970. At the end of the third subperiod in 1972, the fund stood at $119.6 billion in real terms (1987 dollars).

Toward the end of the Nixon administration, the fourth subperiod (1973–84) began and was characterized by a long-term erosion of trust fund value, occasioned by generous benefits increases enacted by Congress in 1972. The subperiod started with three years of moderate declines during 1973–75. Through the Ford and Carter administrations and the beginning of the Reagan administration, the real declines accelerated, reaching double digits for the next seven years, 1976–82. The magnitudes of the declines ranged from a *low* of −11.8 percent in 1976 to a *high* of −31.7 percent in 1982, albeit on a rapidly shrinking base. The period ended with small declines of −2.1 and −2.9 percent in 1983 and 1984, respectively. Until the mid- to late-1970s, there had been no serious concern about the Social Security program running out of money. However, with the 12-year real decline beginning in 1973, Congress and the president acted, as previously discussed, in 1977 and 1983 to remedy the chronic excess of outlays over receipts (occurring for all 12 years in real terms and seven of the 12 years in nominal terms) and the impending bankruptcy of the program. The changes to the program aimed at shoring up the Social Security trust fund in the short run and increasing the fund over the succeeding 30 or so years. In this way, the burden on the active workforce of Social Security funding, caused by past underfunding and current demographic trends, especially the aging of the U.S. population, could be spread out, and the funding of Social Security would be easier to manage in the future.

In response, the fifth period began in 1985 with a rapid restoration of trust fund value through an increase of 38.7 percent in real terms. The following year, the fund's value increased by 51.5 percent, followed by increases of 36.3, 51.6, and 42.7 percent in 1987–89, reaching $145.1 billion and eclipsing the previous high in the trust's real value of $119.6 billion in 1972. Trust value continued to climb at rates in double digits and closed the period at $289.2 billion in 1993, more than 12 times in real terms the trust fund level of only nine years earlier. Unfortunately, as discussed in the Selected Issues section, the trust fund that had been built up for these nine years was not set aside for future claims against the Social Security program.

PRESIDENTIAL RANKINGS

As mentioned, three measures are used for ranking — the real average growth rate of outlays, the percent share of Social Security of total budget outlays (in current shares), and the real growth of the Social

Security trust fund. In the case of the growth of outlays and the share of outlays, because it is a value judgment as to whether higher or lower is better, the convention is adopted to rank the presidents in descending order according to the value of both averages and trends. In the case of the growth in the trust fund, higher is viewed as better, because trust fund growth represents a form of saving (even though the program is supposed to be a pay-as-you-go system). Thus, presidents are ranked in descending order, not out of convention, but as indicative of performance.

In the case of Social Security outlays, because the growth rates are volatile, the trend change as measured by the change in the growth rate between administrations' end points is not very informative about sustained trends. An alternative concept of the trend change is, therefore, calculated, which is not based on end points but, rather, as the difference in average growth rates between the following and preceding administrations. This method serves to reduce the volatility of the indicator and increase its informational value. Because Truman's predecessor's averages are not calculated here, Truman is not assigned a trend change value.

Real Growth of Social Security Outlays

The time dependency of growth rates of Social Security outlays is clear, because presidential rankings are almost a chronological listing of presidents, with only Johnson, Bush, and Carter out of order (Table 13.1). The higher average growth rates occurred in the earlier

TABLE 13.1
Real Growth Rates of Social Security Outlays

Average Growth Rate			Change in Average Growth Rate	
President	Term	Percent	President	Percentage Points
Truman	1945–53	24.4	Nixon	1.5
Eisenhower	1953–61	17.7	Bush	0.4
Kennedy	1961–63	8.4	Reagan	0.2
Nixon	1969–74	8.0	Ford	−0.3
Ford	1974–77	7.7	Johnson	−1.9
Johnson	1963–69	6.5	Carter	−4.4
Bush	1989–93	2.9	Eisenhower	−6.7
Reagan	1981–89	2.5	Kennedy	−9.3
Carter	1977–81	2.3	Truman	na*
Average, 1946–93		10.1		

*na, not applicable.

administrations, when the trust fund bases were small and small increases in the trust resulted in high growth rates. Truman had, by far, the highest growth rate at 24.4 percent, with Eisenhower at 17.7 percent, Kennedy at 8.4 percent, Johnson at 6.5 percent, and Nixon, somewhat bucking the trend, at 8.0 percent. Ford dropped slightly to a 7.7 percent average, and then Bush, Reagan, and Carter were all fairly close together at 2.9, 2.5, and 2.3 percent, respectively. Thus, only three presidents averaged higher Social Security growth than their predecessors, two of which were very slight increases. Nixon stands out as significantly raising the average Social Security growth rate above that of Johnson, by 1.5 percentage points, while Bush and Reagan's average growth rates were only slightly higher than their predecessors. Kennedy and Eisenhower recorded the largest drop-offs in average growth rates at 6.7 and 9.7 percentage points, respectively, which would be expected as the rapid growth in outlays in the 1940s and 1950s subsided.

Nixon's record on expanding Social Security is consistent with the notion that Nixon aggressively increased social programs for the middle class; yet, there is more to this story. In the 1971–73 budgets, real Social Security outlays did grow very rapidly, at rates of 13.5, 8.5, and 15.1 percent, respectively. The 1972 act called for a 20 percent *nominal* increase in benefits in one year alone. In reality, these rapid increases were sought by Congress and in excess of what President Nixon wanted. Congress actually overrode Nixon's veto in order to pass the large benefits increases. Some interpreted Congress's zeal for the benefits expansion as a desire to make up for past inflation and to the efforts of Wilbur Mills, then head of the powerful House Ways and Means Committee and the top congressional expert on the workings of Social Security, who was considering challenging Nixon for the presidency in 1972.

Social Security Share of Budget

The ranking according to the share of the total budget conforms *exactly* to a reverse chronological listing of the presidents, although the differences in shares between the last four presidents, Ford, Carter, Reagan, and Bush, were very slight (Table 13.2). The trend change based on administration end points does complement and probably surpasses the average shares in value as a measure of relative presidential spending priorities (not necessarily performance). In average share, the top four presidents are bunched together between 20.3 and 20.7 percent of the total budget. The first real difference between presidents in the rankings occurs with the share recorded by Nixon in fifth place at 18.4 percent, 1.9 percentage points below Ford. Johnson is four share points lower than Nixon at a 14.4 percent average and is followed by Kennedy at 13.9 percent. There are two more significant share drops, to

TABLE 13.2
Social Security Outlays as a Share of the Total Budget

Average Share		Change in Share	
President	Percent	President	Percentage Points
Bush	20.7	Eisenhower	9.2
Reagan	20.6	Nixon	4.6
Carter	20.4	Truman	2.9
Ford	20.3	Ford	1.3
Nixon	18.4	Kennedy	1.3
Johnson	14.4	Bush	1.3
Kennedy	13.9	Johnson	0.8
Eisenhower	9.2	Reagan	−0.2
Truman	2.2	Carter	−0.2
Average, 1946–93	14.3		

Eisenhower at 9.2 percent and to Truman at only 2.2 percent of the budget.

Eisenhower recorded the greatest increase in the share of the budget going to Social Security, 9.2 percentage points, with Nixon second at 4.6 percentage points. Truman's share increased by 2.9 percentage points, and Ford, Kennedy, and Bush each increased the share by 1.3 percentage points, although over the different lengths of administration of two, three, and four years, respectively. Johnson increased the share 0.8 percentage point, while Carter and Reagan reduced the share by 0.2 percentage point.

Real Growth of Social Security Trust Fund

With respect to the trust fund, the presidents are ranked according to their average annual real growth rates for their administrations (Table 13.3). As growth rates are volatile on a year-to-year basis, the trend change is based on the change of a president's *average* growth rate compared with the *average* growth rate of his predecessor. Naturally, the higher the growth rate of the trust fund, which is a form of saving, the better the presidential performance, and the presidents are ranked accordingly. As shown below, an administration's ranking displays no systematic relationship to the time period in which it occurred. The lack of time dependency of trust fund growth rates is because the trust fund was at low levels several times during the 1946–93 period, providing low bases for growth rate calculations and each time resulting in somewhat "exaggerated" growth rates until the fund base was built up. Early in the period, the trust fund was low because it had begun receiving

TABLE 13.3
Social Security Trust Fund Growth Rates

Average Growth		Change in Average Growth Rate	
President	Percent	President	Percentage Points
Reagan	17.4	Reagan	36.5
Bush	17.2	Johnson	7.3
Truman	8.0	Bush	−0.2
Johnson	4.0	Nixon	−3.5
Eisenhower	1.7	Kennedy	−5.0
Nixon	0.5	Carter	−5.2
Kennedy	−3.3	Eisenhower	−6.3
Ford	−13.9	Ford	−14.4
Carter	−19.1	Truman	na*
Average, 1946–93	4.0		

*na, not applicable.

revenues only recently; in the second instance, the trust was drawn down in the early to mid-1960s; and in the third instance, the trust was drawn down from 1973 to 1982.

Unquestionably, the greatest improvement in the trust fund value occurred under Reagan, who had the highest real growth rate, 17.4 percent, and the greatest improvement in the average growth rate, 36.5 percentage points. In fact, Reagan's improvement was so sharp that the declines of all other presidents were more than counteracted by Reagan's improvement. This phenomenon is made all the more remarkable by the fact that during the first three years of the Reagan administration, the trust fund's value declined at very rapid rates. Bush's average is second at 17.2 percent. Yet, Bush's growth rate is also exceptionally high considering that the trust fund value left by Reagan was substantial, making it difficult to record such high growth rates. Bush recorded a slight decrease in the average growth rate, which is understandable given that he followed the large improvement under Reagan. Truman is third at an 8.0 percent average annual growth rate, but his trend change is not given because the average of his predecessor, Roosevelt, is not calculated. Roosevelt's average growth rate would, in any case, distort the analysis, because he started from a base of zero for the trust fund, and any growth above a base of zero is either undefined or infinity. Johnson ranks fourth with an average growth rate of 4.0 percent and an improvement in average growth of 7.3 percentage points, the only president other than Reagan to improve the real average trust fund growth rate over that of his predecessor.

Eisenhower and Nixon are fifth and sixth, with averages of 1.7 and 0.5 percent, respectively. Average growth under Nixon fell by 3.5

percentage points, while average growth fell 6.3 percentage points under Eisenhower. Kennedy's average trust fund growth was −3.3 percent, with a 5 percentage point drop in average growth compared with his predecessor. Ford and Carter round out the bottom with real rates of trust fund decline of −13.9 percent for Ford and −19.1 percent for Carter, the steepest decline of any president. Under Carter, average growth also fell by 5.2 percentage points, while under Ford, growth fell by far more than under the other presidents, 14.4 percentage points.

SUMMARY AND SELECTED ISSUES

When Social Security began with the signing of the Social Security Act in 1935, it was not intended to be fully funded, because the original legislation did not call for a substantial trust fund. It was not long afterward, however, in 1939, that the nature of the program was substantially altered. The beneficiaries base was expanded, the first payment date was moved up, and the scheduled payroll tax increases were postponed for three years. These changes served to convert the Social Security system to a pay-as-you-go system, with the reserve fund becoming a contingency fund. Reasons why the government may not have wanted to build up a large trust fund include the fear that the value of a large trust would be eroded by inflation, that the funds might not be spent for their intended purpose (which later came to be true), and that the government might have to make large private sector investments in order to realize a return on trust funds. In addition, because of the government's power to tax, however, a large trust fund also did not seem necessary.

In spite of the switch to pay-as-you-go financing in 1939, the Social Security trust fund generated surpluses until 1958, which substantially increased trust fund value (to $23 billion in nominal terms). This phenomenon is typical for the early stage of a contributory system, as eligibility requirements are set to keep benefit payments low in the early years, while contribution rates are generally set to cover long-term commitments. The 1971 Advisory Council recommended that contribution rates be set such that the trust fund maintained a contingency reserve equal to one year's outlays. As discussed, further changes were made in 1977 and 1983, with the expected result that contributions would exceed outlays until 2010, when the trust fund balance is projected to equal 20 percent of gross domestic product. This means that the baby boomers born in 1945–50 would begin to receive benefits just when the trust fund is peaking. It is also projected that the trust fund will be drawn down between 2010 and 2030.

Although, for the time being, Social Security appears to be on a sound footing, there are aspects to the system and controversies that cause concern among its participants. For example, although a Social Security trust fund is spoken of, it does not mean that Social Security taxes go into a special account to be tapped later for *each* individual's Social Security benefits. Rather, a record is kept of each individual's earnings that are subject to Social Security taxation, which later serves as the basis for determining eligibility and the size of benefits (recall the benefits formula cited earlier). Social Security tax receipts actually are accounted for in a large pool, the trust fund, against which all eligible beneficiaries can draw.

Another cause for concern is that in a world of persistently high budget deficits, members of Congress and, sometimes, the president look to modifications in the terms of the Social Security program that will afford budget relief. Commonly mentioned changes are reductions in cost of living adjustments and the raising of eligibility requirements. These changes effectively represent tax increases and/or benefit cuts and are usually met with fierce political opposition and, as a result, often do not get very far. However, sometimes the rules of the system are changed, which results in an effective cut in benefits. Two such examples were the adjustment of the benefit formula in 1977 and the taxation of Social Security benefits above a certain income level, begun in 1984, both of which reduced net benefits. Another often-debated effective benefit reduction is to increase the retirement age at which full benefits are received from 65 to 67. This increase in retirement age, in fact, is already scheduled to be phased in between 2003 and 2027, but there has been discussion in Congress of moving these dates up a few years.

However, political concerns about effects of Social Security outlays on budget levels would seem, on the surface, at odds with the historical trends of Social Security receipts and expenditures. The Social Security program has been in surplus since 1983, with large surpluses after 1984, including some in the $40–60 billion range, resulting in the trust fund increasing in nominal terms from $21 billion in fiscal year 1983 to $367 billion by fiscal 1993. Therefore, it is puzzling why Social Security is often represented as a budget-busting entitlement program. If the medicare trusts are added, the total combined trust reached $534 billion by the end of calendar year 1993. Moreover, Social Security is supposed to be a separate, off-budget program in which surplus receipts and interest income are held in trust for future Social Security needs. The surpluses are not intended for general budget purposes but are supposed to be held in trust in the form of special issues of the Treasury Department. The *Annual Statistical Supplement to the Social Security Bulletin, 1993*, describes the authorized inflows and outflows of the trust fund as follows:

All taxes are credited to the OASI and DI Trust Funds, which by law may be used only to meet the cost of: (1) Monthly benefits when the worker retires, dies, or becomes disabled; (2) lump-sum death payments to survivors;

(3) vocational rehabilitation services for disability beneficiaries; and (4) administrative expenses.

Benefits are financed principally through contributions from employers, employees, and the self-employed. The trust funds also receive income from: interest on investments of trust fund assets in securities issued or guaranteed by the U.S. Government.

However, Congress has apparently not confined the use of recent Social Security surpluses to the four items listed above. In the years when Social Security revenues exceeded outlays, the difference was not spent on the acquisition of real or financial private assets with which to finance subsequent shortfalls. Rather, Congress used these trust funds, in lieu of tax increases or expenditure cuts, to finance current expenditures in the general budget. The Treasury took the Social Security surpluses and issued "Special Treasury Issues" to the trust fund that guarantee the reimbursement of the fund. An interest return is earned on these Treasury issues that is tied to the Treasury bill rate. When the federal deficit is reported by the media and by Congress and the president, the off-budget Social Security surpluses are lumped together with the rest of the budget. In recent years, this practice has served to artificially reduce the quoted deficit by the amount of the Social Security surplus.[6] Thus, recent deficits have been underreported on the order of $40–60 billion.

How the Treasury will ultimately make good on these special Treasury issues as the trust begins to draw down in the next century is another subject for concern. The undeniable effect of this policy of incorporating Social Security receipts into general revenues is to shift the composition of taxes over time in which, in recent years, the relatively regressive Social Security payroll tax has been financing general government expenditures, while, in the future, the reverse will be true when general revenues will have to finance Social Security benefits payments.[7] Thus, although Social Security is actuarially sound through 2030[8] based on reported accounts (i.e., on paper), there will likely be very serious funding problems in Social Security for the Treasury Department early next century when the OASDI trust fund begins to cash in its special Treasury issues. In August 1994, Congress passed legislation making the SSA a separate agency (no longer under the Department of Health and Human Services). Under this legislation, the Treasury must actually issue debt instruments for the Social Security surpluses that they absorb. Whether this new independence will curb the practice of spending OASDI trust funds for general budget purposes is doubtful because the legislation appears to be aimed more at simply upgrading service delivery at SSA.

SUGGESTIONS FOR FURTHER READING

Bernstein, Merton C., *Social Security: The System that Works*. New York: Basic Books, 1988. Discusses past problems with the Social Security system and how they were solved; also looks at alternatives to Social Security.

Kingson, Eric R., and Berkowitz, Edward D., *Social Security and Medicare — A Policy Primer*. Westport, Conn.: Auburn House, 1993. Provides an overview of the history of Social Security and focuses primarily on policy issues, financial stability, intergenerational fairness, and so on.

Meyer, Charles W., and Wolf, Nancy, *Social Security and Individual Equity*. Westport, Conn.: Greenwood Press, 1993.

Meyers, Robert, *Social Security*. Bryn Mawr, Pa.: McCain-Foundation Series Books, 1990.

Nash, Gerald, Pugash, Noel H., and Thomasson, Richard F., eds., *Social Security — The First Half-Century*. Albuquerque: University of New Mexico Press, 1988. Overview of the Social Security program 1935–85 and future prospects.

NOTES

1. A defined contribution pension is one in which the employer and sometimes the employee set aside funds at a specified rate and the employee's pension benefit is determined by the accumulation of these contributions plus any investment earnings on the contributions. The defined benefit is a plan in which the employer and sometimes the employee contribute to a fund from which benefits are determined by the employee's length of service, compensation, or both.

2. From Kingson, Eric, and Berkowitz, Edward, *Social Security and Medicare*. Westport, Conn.: Auburn House, 1993.

3. The benefits formula is based on average indexed monthly earnings (AIME). The AIME is divided into three income intervals to which percentages are applied to arrive at monthly benefit levels. For example, in 1987, the benefits formula was 90 percent of the first $310 of AIME plus 32 percent of AIME between $311 and $1,866 plus 15 percent of AIME above $1,866 up to a stipulated maximum monthly benefit payment.

4. Recall that because there was positive inflation for almost all of the 1946–93 period, in order to calculate real levels, nominal levels must be *inflated prior to the base year* (in this case, 1987) and *deflated after the base year*. Thus, nominal figures are lower than real figures before 1987 and higher after 1987. They are, of course, equal for 1987.

5. If there are budget deficits and if Social Security receipts and Social Security outlays maintain the same share of total budget receipts and outlays, respectively, then there will be a deficit with respect to Social Security as well, which violates the pay-as-you-go principle.

6. This adding of off-budget Social Security receipts and outlays to the overall budget was initiated by Johnson in 1966 with the purported motive of increasing the size of the reported total budget so that the expenditures on the Viet Nam War would appear as a smaller share of the overall government budget.

7. Munnell, Alicia, "American Lessons for Korean Pensions." Seoul: Korea Development Institute, September 1993.

8. The SSA applies the criterion of 75 years to achieve actuarial soundness.

14

Taxation

The main, although not exclusive, source of revenue for the general government budget and for Social Security is the taxation of individuals and corporations. The power to tax is one of the two most important economic powers of government, the other being the power to print money. Whether to change the tax structure and/or raise or lower existing tax rates are decisions constantly facing politicians, on both federal and state and local levels. Politicians are especially afraid of raising taxes or taking away deductions, because of voters' concern about how tax issues affect their pocketbook. Presented here are the total taxes as a percent of gross domestic product (GDP) and the breakdown of tax receipts from individuals, corporations, social insurance (most of which is split evenly between individuals and corporations), and other, including excise tax, as a percentage of total receipts. Social insurance is not limited to Social Security and Disability Insurance (OASDI) but also includes hospital insurance, railroad retirement, unemployment insurance, and other retirement. The tax contributions of individuals and corporations during 1946–93 show how the government shifted the tax burden back and forth over time. Once the growth rates and shares are established, one can begin to draw inferences as to the economic effects of taxation.

Because the tax systems during the period were a complicated mix of tax rates, income brackets, allowable deductions, and other rules, it is not possible in a single indicator to depict a consistent long-run trend by which the tax regimes of each administration can be compared. In order to properly compare the various tax regimes during 1946–93 and to summarize the trends in effective tax rates, nominal tax brackets must be converted to real dollars. In converting tax brackets to real dollars, the brackets lose their neat, regular, incremental nature. For example, in the early 1950s, tax brackets could be only $1,000 apart, whereas in the 1980s and 1990s, the number of tax brackets was drastically reduced and the smallest interval was around $15,000. It turns out that the changes in the effective tax rates of various tax regimes can be seen only at very many small, and sometimes irregular, dollar increments. Even then, it would be difficult to account for the changing composition of deductions and other tax rules. Unfortunately, the statistical task of developing a series of effective tax rates across income groups for 1946–93 has not been undertaken, and, here, only the tax share of GDP and the composition of tax receipts are examined.

Viewing the trends in taxation helps determine which presidents taxed the most, which presidents lowered taxes the most, and how the shares of tax receipts from individuals, corporations, Social Security contributors, and so on, changed. It should be noted that the tax burden at the state and local levels is not considered here, but would provide a valuable context in which to evaluate the federal levels of taxation.

OVERVIEW OF TRENDS IN THE LONG RUN, 1946–93

Total Tax Receipts as a Percent of
Gross Domestic Product

Figure 14.1 shows that, contrary to the belief of many, the share of GDP taken in taxes showed no steady rise over the post-war period. The relative stability is evidenced by the fact that most years' tax shares fell within fairly narrow ranges: all years (48) were within the 14.8–20.2 percent range, 85 percent (41 years) of tax shares fell between 16.0 and 19.5 percent of GDP, and 33 of the 48 years fell within the 17–19 percent range. The 19 percent level was reached only four times: during the Korean War (19.1–19.4 percent, 1952–53), the Viet Nam War (19.6–20.2 percent, 1969–70), during 1979–82 (19.1–20.2 percent), and during 1987–89 (19.2 percent — actually, the middle year was 18.9 percent) following the 1986 tax reform. The 1979–82 period reached its peak tax share of 20.2 percent at the culmination of five straight share increases, largely because of inflation-induced bracket creep. Low tax share years by decade were 1949–51 (14.8–16.5 percent), 1965–66 (17.4–17.8 percent), 1976 (17.7 percent), and 1983–84 (18.0–18.1 percent). The average tax share for the 1946–93 period was 18.2 percent, while the annual average growth rate was 2.4 percent.

Still rather high after the end of World War II, tax receipts were 18.5 percent of GDP in 1946 but then eased to 17.3, 16.8, and 15.0 and bottomed out at 14.8 percent (the historical low) during the next four years. In 1951, the tax share of GDP began to rise again, reaching 16.5 percent, then jumping to 19.4 percent in response to the needs for the Korean War, and remaining at that level two years. After the war, tax shares fluctuated between 17.0 and 18.9 percent. From 1956 to 1966 (11 years), tax shares varied only slightly, remaining between 17.4 and 18.3 percent except for 1959, when the share dipped to 16.5 percent. For the first five years of the 1960s, shares were especially stable, staying between 18.0 and 18.3 percent. Tax shares edged downward in 1964 (0.2

FIGURE 14.1
Taxes Percent of Gross Domestic Product, 1946-93
(Current Shares)

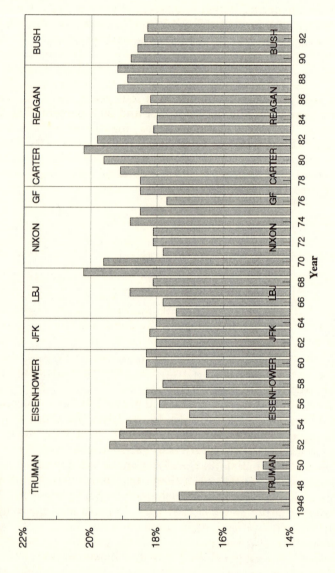

Source: U.S. Office of Management and Budget.

percentage point) and in 1965 (0.6 percentage point), decreases that were rather minor, considering that they coincided with the Kennedy-Johnson tax cuts.

Tax shares began to increase again in the latter part of the Johnson administration and reached 20.2 percent during his last year, 1969, the high for the period, which was later matched in 1981. Under Nixon, tax shares fell as a percent of GDP. In his first year, the share fell by 0.6 percentage point, by another 1.8 percentage points in 1971, stayed at the 17.8–18.1 level for three years, increased to 18.8 percent in 1974, and closed at 18.5 percent in 1975. The share initially dropped under Ford to 17.7 percent but rose the next year to 18.5 percent. After Carter's first year at 18.5 percent, the next four years, 1979–82, were high tax share years, ranging between 19.1 and 20.2 percent. The 20.2 percent share in 1981 matched the previously mentioned high of 1969. After the Reagan tax cut began to be phased in, tax shares dropped to the 18.0–18.5 percent range during 1983–86. Shares were higher for 1987–90, between 18.8 and 19.2 percent, perhaps reflecting the elimination of some income tax deductions with the 1986 tax reform act. The period ended with three small drops in tax shares to 18.6 percent in 1991, 18.4 percent in 1992, and 18.3 percent in 1993.

Composition of Tax Receipts

Figure 14.2 shows the composition of government tax revenue by source. There are essentially two sources, individuals and corporations. Three major trends are evident: relative stability of the share of government revenue coming from individuals, decline in the share of taxes paid by corporations, and increase in the share of revenue from social insurance taxes. The extremes of individuals' share of taxes were 39.5 in 1949 to 48.2 percent in 1982. The average individuals' share for the entire period was 44.5 percent.

Individuals' tax share was 41.0 percent in 1946 and jumped to 46.6 and 46.5 percent during 1947–48. In 1949, the share dropped to only 39.5 percent (the period low). Over the next four years, individuals' share increased to 42.8 percent by 1953, dropped slightly to 42.4 percent in Eisenhower's first year, and continued an upward zigzag to a 46.3 percent share in 1959. Individual tax shares fell during the last two years of Eisenhower's administration to 43.8 percent by 1961. Under Kennedy, shares rose the first year, 1962, to 45.7 percent but fell the last two years of Kennedy's administration and the first year under Johnson to reach 41.8 percent by 1965, perhaps reflecting the relative benefit to *individuals* of the Kennedy-Johnson tax cut. Shares increased slightly in 1966 and then dropped to 41.3 percent in 1967, a 17-year low and a level not seen again. Rates immediately jumped to 44.9 percent in 1968 and closed out Johnson at 46.7 percent. Nixon opened at 46.9 percent, but individuals' share was steadily lowered to 43.9 percent by

FIGURE 14.2
Composition of Taxes, 1946–93   **(Current Shares)**

Percent Shares of Federal Taxes

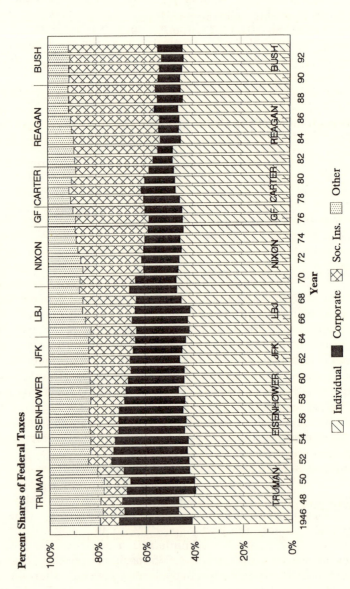

Source: U.S. Office of Management and Budget.

1975. Individuals' share increased for the next seven years (two years under Ford, four years under Carter, and the first year under Reagan), hitting new heights, reaching 48.2 percent in 1982, the period high. In 1983, individual shares, having reached the historical high, started down, to 48.1 percent, coinciding with the Reagan three-year phased-in personal tax cut, dropped 3.4 percentage points to 44.8 percent in 1984, and remained in the 43.7–46.0 percent range through 1993. Over the entire period, individual taxes paid grew an average of 2.4 percent per year in real terms.

In the early part of the period and continuing through 1958, corporate tax receipts were usually over a quarter of total receipts. By 1959 and through much of the 1960s, however, the share of receipts from corporations was headed downward, dropping from 23.2 percent in 1960 to 17.0 percent by 1970, although shares did climb to the 21.8–23.0 percent range during 1965–67. In the 1970s, the corporate tax share continued to decline and, by 1980, accounted for only 12.5 percent of total government receipts. Corporate shares recorded a precipitous drop of 6.3 percentage points between 1980 and 1983 as the corporate share hit its historical low of 6.2 percent. The following year, the corporate share was up to 8.5 percent, remained over 8 percent for two more years, and reached 9.8 percent in 1987. During 1988–89, the share increased to 10.4 percent and, for the next four years (through 1993), remained within the 9.1–10.2 percent range.[1] On an average annual basis, corporate taxes paid were virtually constant in real terms during 1946–93, with an annual average decline of –0.1 percent.

Throughout the period, social insurance receipts were on a rapid rise in terms of real growth and percentage share. Recall again that social insurance includes not only Social Security (or OASDI, the subject of Chapter 13) but also hospital insurance, unemployment insurance, and so on. Social insurance taxes and contributions accounted for 7.6 percent of total tax receipts in 1946, 15.9 percent by 1960, 23.0 percent by 1970, 30.5 percent by 1980, and 37.1 percent by 1993. The average real growth rate was 5.5 percent for the entire period, which was far more rapid than either the individual or corporate categories.

PRESIDENTIAL RANKINGS

Total Receipts as a Share of Gross Domestic Product

Ranking presidents from best to worst with respect to tax shares as a percent of GDP depends on some economic judgments. It may be that the president and Congress believe that bigger government is better or that each successive Congress and president had a conscious or unconscious desire to control a greater share of the economy, but these considerations are not relevant to economic performance.

On the one hand, it is generally believed by economists, a priori, that limiting the tax share and, therefore, leaving a greater share of resources in the competitive, private sector will ensure greater efficiency in the use of those resources and that the economy will perform better overall. In addition, if the government is collecting a smaller percentage of the GDP in taxes, it would, supposedly, impose stricter discipline on the part of the president and Congress regarding government spending and they would scrutinize expenditures more carefully. Both support the view that lower tax shares are better.

On the other hand, it could also be argued that taxes as a share of GDP may be too time dependent to serve as a meaningful performance measure. If the share of GDP taken in taxes tended to increase over time because circumstances dictated that the government needed to be bigger, then tax shares would not measure presidential performance so much as they would represent the changing demands on government and the corresponding taxation to pay for it. As in the case of the productivity index, ranking according to such a time-dependent indicator would resemble a list of presidents in chronological order. In actuality, the time dependency of tax shares was not very strong, and the presidents' tax shares are close together (the difference between second and eighth place is only 0.8 percentage point). Thus, presidents are ranked from lowest to highest average tax share of GDP (best to worst) and lowest to highest increase in the tax share for the trend change in Table 14.1. The degree to which tax shares as measured by the trend change provide some indication of how well the president held the line on taxes during his term.

TABLE 14.1
Tax Receipts as a Share of Gross Domestic Product

Average Share			Trend Change	
President	Term	Percent	President	Percentage Points
Truman	1945–53	17.2	Nixon	−1.7
Eisenhower	1953–61	17.9	Reagan	−1.0
Kennedy	1961–63	18.1	Bush	−0.9
Ford	1974–77	18.1	Eisenhower	−0.8
Nixon	1969–74	18.5	Kennedy	−0.3
Bush	1989–93	18.5	Ford	0.0
Johnson	1963–69	18.5	Truman	0.6
Reagan	1981–89	18.7	Carter	1.7
Carter	1977–81	19.4	Johnson	2.2
Average, 1946–93		18.2		

As expected, Truman and Eisenhower rank first and second, respectively, with respect to average tax shares. However, Eisenhower's performance was better, because he reduced tax shares by 0.8 percentage point while Truman raised tax shares by 0.6 percentage point. Kennedy and Ford are third and fourth in lowest average, both at 18.1 percent. Kennedy reduced the tax share level by 0.3 percentage point, and Ford left it unchanged. There is a three-way tie in average share between Nixon, Bush, and Johnson at 18.5 percent, but Nixon had the greatest reduction in tax shares of 1.7 percentage points and Johnson had the largest increase in tax shares at 2.2 percentage points. Bush reduced the tax share by 0.8 percentage point. Bush's declining tax share trend runs counterintuitive, because the combination of his slow GDP growth (lowering the denominator of the tax share of GDP) and the tax increase (increasing the numerator) of the 1990 budget agreement should have resulted in increasing tax shares. Reagan is eighth in tax share at 18.7 percent, but he reduced the tax share by the second largest margin, 1.0 percentage point. Carter was the highest at 19.4 percent and a 1.7 percentage points share increase. Either Eisenhower, by virtue of his low average tax share and reduction in the tax share, or Nixon, with the largest reduction in tax shares, probably showed the best performance. Either Carter or Johnson had the worst performance.

Composition of Tax Receipts

Presidential rankings according to the composition of tax receipts must be based at least partly on value judgments as to whether a greater share of taxes should be borne by individuals or by corporations and what the share of social insurance receipts should be. The total of all categories' shares of tax receipts must be 100 percent, which means that if one category's tax share goes down it must be compensated for by a rise in one of the other categories, that is, social insurance shares or corporate shares. Thus, a best-to-worst ranking is not implied here, but it is useful to know what the shares of tax sources were under each president. By convention, presidents are listed from lowest to highest share for each category (Table 14.2). Trend changes are in Table 14.3.

The individual tax share was highest under Carter with an average of 46.8 percent, who also increased the individual's share the second most, 3.4 percentage points. Yet, Carter's average was not much higher than the 44.5 percent period average, again attesting to the relative stability of individuals' share of total tax receipts. Reagan's average was the next highest at 45.9 percent, but he reduced individuals' share by 2.7 percentage points. The lowest individual shares were under Truman and Johnson, but they both increased the share paid by individuals. Corporate shares were especially low under Reagan and Bush, at 8.7 and 9.2 percent, respectively, although, surprisingly, from the beginning to the end of his administration, Reagan actually slightly increased the

TABLE 14.2
Composition of Tax Receipts — Average Shares

Individual	Percent	Corporate	Percent	Social Insurance	Percent
Truman	42.5	Reagan	8.7	Truman	9.6
Johnson	43.4	Bush	9.2	Eisenhower	13.7
Eisenhower	44.0	Carter	13.0	Kennedy	18.4
Ford	44.2	Ford	14.7	Johnson	20.7
Bush	44.4	Nixon	15.3	Nixon	26.6
Kennedy	44.5	Kennedy	20.6	Ford	30.2
Nixon	45.4	Johnson	21.2	Carter	30.3
Reagan	45.9	Eisenhower	25.6	Reagan	35.6
Carter	46.8	Truman	27.6	Bush	37.5
Average, 1946–93 44.5		18.2		23.4	

share paid by corporations; Bushonly slightly reduced it. The explanation is that by the end of the Carter administration, corporate tax shares were already extremely low, and they dipped further in the middle of the Reagan years and began to increase toward the end of his administration. Those under whom the corporate share fell the most were Eisenhower, 8.3 percentage points, Carter, 5.2 percentage points, and Nixon, 5.1 percentage points. The average corporate tax share for the entire period was 18.2 percent.

Presidential social insurance shares increased in exact chronological order from earliest to latest presidents. Truman had the lowest social insurance average share at 9.6 percent, and the shares increased rapidly through Bush at 37.5 percent. The largest increases in social insurance shares occurred under Nixon, 9.4 percentage points, Eisenhower, 7.6 percentage points, and Reagan, 5.8 percentage points. The average social insurance share of total receipts for all presidents was 23.4 percent.

TABLE 14.3
Composition of Tax Receipts — Trend Change

Individual	Percent	Corporate	Percent	Social Insurance	Percent
Nixon	−2.8	Eisenhower	−8.3	Ford	−0.3
Reagan	−2.7	Carter	−5.2	Carter	0.5
Kennedy	−0.6	Nixon	−5.1	Johnson	1.4
Bush	−0.5	Kennedy	−1.3	Bush	1.5
Ford	0.5	Johnson	−1.24	Truman	1.9
Eisenhower	1.0	Bush	−1.23	Kennedy	2.1
Truman	1.9	Reagan	0.2	Reagan	5.8
Carter	3.38	Truman	0.3	Eisenhower	7.6
Johnson	3.44	Ford	0.9	Nixon	9.4

SELECTED ISSUES

Throughout the post-war era, the debate has raged on about what the appropriate level of taxation should be. That level is driven by what the appropriate level of spending is, whether the spending should be paid for by current taxation, and what the effects on the economy are for a given level of taxation. The stridency of arguments on both sides of the tax debate would lead one to believe that the difference in tax shares of GDP would have differed widely among presidents and that the shares for individual taxpayers would also have varied a great deal more. The data from the 1946–93 time period, however, have shown that 85 percent of all annual average tax shares as a percent of GDP fell within a 3.5 percentage point range. It would appear, then, that regardless of all the puffery about radically different tax policies from administration to administration, the share of GDP taken by taxes has differed rather modestly. Still, it should be recognized that a difference of 2 or 3 percentage points of GDP can be significant in a $6 trillion-plus economy. Such a difference would amount to $120–180 billion. This sum is far greater than any spending cuts that Congress and the president have found to be politically feasible to make, in spite of $200–300 billion deficits. Thus, although tax shares did not differ as much as might have been expected from administration to administration, small differences may still have a substantial budgetary impact.

Although it might be predicted that Republicans (Nixon, Reagan, and Eisenhower) lowered the tax share of GDP by more than Democratic presidents, it might be less likely to be predicted that three of the top four reducers of individual tax shares were Republicans, because Republicans are said to favor corporations over individuals. In addition, the top three increasers of individual tax shares were Democrats (Truman, Carter, and Johnson). Finally, the fact that Republicans increased social insurance receipts by the most would also be unexpected, given that party's reputation for holding the line against imposing taxes for social programs.

Also somewhat puzzling are the trends in tax composition and how corporate shares went down so much, without being compensated for by increases in individuals' shares, while the U.S. budget continued to increase. The answer is that the shares of social insurance receipts increased substantially. Although these receipts were meant for specific purposes, not for the general budget (Chapter 13), nevertheless, surplus receipts for social insurance funds were used for general budget purposes, instead of being applied to the social insurance trust funds (OASDI, medicare, and so on) and, in this way, compensated for the decline in corporate tax shares. Thus, the U.S. budget deficits were higher than commonly reported by the amount of off-budget social insurance fund surpluses. This amount was substantial, exceeding $50 billion annually toward the end of the period. The result was lower current budget deficits but with strong prospects of severe funding problems for programs such as Social Security in the future. Funding the Social Security shortfalls in the future will, therefore, require funding out of general revenues, unless social insurance taxes are raised further.

SUGGESTIONS FOR FURTHER READING

Conlan, Timothy J., Beam, David R., and Wrightson, Margaret T., *Taxing Choices*. Washington, D.C.: Congressional Quarterly Press, 1990. Gives an overview of the basis for the U.S. tax system and a short history of its evolution.

Davies, David G., *United States Taxes and Tax Policy*. New York: Cambridge University Press, 1986. Discusses the foundations of U.S. tax policy and various types of taxation, including individual, corporate, capital gains, Social Security, value added, and state and local.

Steinmo, Sven, *Taxation and Democracy*. New Haven, Conn.: Yale University Press, 1993. Provides a summary of pre– and post–World War II U.S. tax policy, comparisons with Sweden and the United Kingdom, and a discussion of possible reforms.

NOTE

1. Receipts from corporations since 1987 include trust fund receipts for the hazardous substance Superfund. However, these amounts were relatively small, ranging from $196 to $607 million during 1987–93.

15

Overall Presidential Economic Performance: A Synthesis of the Indicators

As cautioned throughout this book, in many, if not most, instances, the president may not be responsible for what happened on his watch. The president's and Congress's policies are important, but business cycles and activities in the private sector dominate. Nevertheless, in order to ultimately evaluate and compare the presidents, the first order of business is to see what actually happened on their watches. This record has already been presented here. The purpose of this chapter is to bring the indicators together into one synthesized, composite indicator in an effort to evaluate overall economic performance during the various administrations.

As has been stressed also, presidential performance is limited, here, to economic performance; there is no consideration of performance in foreign policy or noneconomic domestic issues or the solution of any social problems. Neither has the degree to which a president was truly responsible for what occurred economically been thoroughly considered. However, a timeline of major events was provided so that the reader could compare and judge to what degree economic occurrences were under the control of the president.

This chapter provides a coalescing point to the broad survey of economic indicators over a long time frame in the form of an overall ranking. However, to consolidate the indicators into a single, rankable indicator necessitates a host of rather subjective judgments in assigning relative importance to the indicators (i.e., the weighting scheme) and in choosing indicators for measuring overall performance. Until this chapter, this set of judgments has been resisted in order to preserve objectivity in the presentation of indicators and, therefore, usefulness as a sourcebook. Thus, the judgments made from here on do not taint the basic, straightforward presentation of the official data in the previous chapters.

METHOD OF AGGREGATING THE INDICATORS

To boil the indicators down into one presidential ranking that identifies which president was "best," which was "worst," and who falls in between, the indicators cannot be simply summed and averaged, because the indicators are in different units, have different levels of volatility (variances), and differ in importance (weights) in measuring a president's performance. The difference in units is clear; some indicators are measured as growth rates (e.g., gross domestic product [GDP], inflation, productivity), some are percent shares (e.g., saving and investment rates, percent below poverty line), all trend changes are in percentage points, and the real interest rate is in a class by itself. Of course, it makes no sense to add together these dissimilar units. The second reason that indicators cannot be directly summed and averaged is that different indicators have different degrees of volatility, which, if not accounted for, would distort overall rankings. For example, presidential stock market growth trend changes range from 46.4 percentage points to –49.1 percentage points, compared with the poverty line trend changes, which range from 2.5 percentage points to –6.9 percentage points. It is typical for the stock trend to vary widely, but not for the poverty indicator. Not to account for this characteristic would be to over-reward the president who recorded the 49 percent trend improvement and to overpunish the president with the –49.1 percent trend decline while also undervaluing the importance of both the highs and lows of the poverty line indicator simply because its variance is relatively low. The third reason is that each indicator differs in importance in capturing economic performance, and an appropriate weight must be assigned to each indicator that is commensurate with this importance.

Statistical science offers standard and straightforward ways to combine these indicators to form one synthesized presidential ranking. The steps taken to combine the indicators are calculating the mean for each indicator's average and trend, normalizing the president's averages and trend values by converting them into standard deviations from the mean for that indicator, applying the appropriate weight to each normalized indicator for each president, and then summing the resulting values for all indicators for each president.

Normalizing the Indicators

The process of normalizing the indicators and accounting for their different volatilities is the main step that allows the indicators to be combined. The procedure follows from basic statistics, in which the average, or mean, presidential performance for each indicator first is calculated. The second step is to account for the volatility, or variance from the mean, of each indicator by calculating the standard deviation and then determining the number of standard deviations from the mean for each indicator for each president. The formula used to calculate the standard deviation is $[(X - \bar{X})^2/N]^{1/2} = \sigma$, where X is the president's average or trend for that indicator, $\bar{X}$ is the average, or mean, of all presidents for that indicator, N is the number of observations, in this case, the number of presidents compared for that indicator (nine for most indicators), and σ is the standard deviation.

Once the standard deviation has been calculated, the indicator value for each administration can be expressed as a quantity of standard deviations from the mean: $(X - \bar{X})/\sigma$, thus, unifying the indicators by converting them to the same unit,[1] and by accounting for their different degrees of volatility. A highly volatile indicator has a high standard deviation relative to a low volatility indicator. By dividing the standard deviation of a particular indicator into the specific deviation for each president for that indicator, the degree of variation for each president for each indicator is measured in terms of the volatility that has been calculated (the "standard" deviation) for that indicator. Thus, the indicator is normalized, and after being weighted, as discussed in the next section, it can be added to values for other indicators in order to produce the overall performance indicator.

Weights

The weighting scheme is driven by the degree of importance of indicators relative to each other in assessing economic performance. Weights for each indicator are shown in Table 15.1. The table includes the three essential elements for a composite ranking: the indicator average, or mean, for each president, the indicator's standard deviation from the mean, and the weight assigned to the indicator. These three parameters in combination allow all of the indicators for each president to be synthesized into one rankable number, or performance quotient.

There is no one right way to estimate the weights; even sophisticated mathematical approaches are still subjective. The weighting scheme followed here attempts to achieve reasonable proportions based on the considerations that are discussed below. However, any weighting scheme will give rise to questions and objections. For example, the weight for GDP growth, the bottom line of economic performance, arguably could be weighted much higher than, say, inflation. Yet, the weighting scheme must take into account that all of the other Part I indicators (with the exception of inflation and the real interest rate) are positively correlated with GDP,[2] and, therefore, the behavior of GDP is effectively weighted much more heavily than the specific weight assigned to it suggests. Inflation, on the other hand, is not closely correlated with any other indicator (although money supply is correlated with inflation, it is not included in the overall ranking). Similarly, the real interest rate is relatively uncorrelated with the other economic variables, although it is clear that if, for example, the other variables

TABLE 15.1
Indicator Averages, Trends, Standard Deviations, and Weights

Indicator	Average (A) or Trend (T)	Mean Value	Standard Deviation	Converted Weight	Total Indicator Weight	Percent of Total Weights	Part I, Part II Weights
GDP	A	3.1	1.2	.09	.2	16.3	
	T	0.5	3.2	.11			
Employment growth	A	1.8	0.8	.04	.05	4.1	
	T	-0.4	2.6	.01			
Unemployment rate	A	5.8	1.2	-.03	.07	5.7	
	T	0.3	2.5	-.04			
Inflation	A	4.5	2.6	-.09	.20	16.3	
	T	-0.6	3.9	-.11			
Real prime rate	A	2.2	2.3	-.06	.13	10.6	
	T	1.0	4.1	-.07			
Saving rate Personal	A	6.7	1.0	.04	.06	4.9	
	T	-0.4	2.2	.02			
Gross private	A	17.0	1.1	.02	.04	3.3	
	T	0.2	2.0	.02			
Investment rate — gross private	A	16.1	1.2	.04	.06	4.9	
	T	-0.1	1.8	.02			
Productivity	A	2.2	1.2	.05	.07	5.7	
	T	-0.3	1.8	.02			
Compensation	A	1.9	1.4	.009	.01	0.8	
	T	0.0	2.5	.001			
Percent below poverty line	A	16.1	4.6	-.035	.70	5.7	
	T	-0.9	2.6	-.035			
Stock market growth	A	0.6	7.0	.07	.08	6.5	
	T	2.8	29.4	.01			84.8

Budget growth	A	2.3	2.0	−.02	.021	1.7
	T	4.7	17.2	−.001		
Budget share of GDP	A	20.4	1.9	−.02	.04	3.3
	T	−0.4	2.1	−.02		
Deficit share of budget	A	9.2	7.3	−.02	.025	2.0
	T	−1.2	9.6	−.005		
Debt share of GDP	A	51.5	18.0	−.02	.04	3.3
	T	−6.6	20.7	−.02		
Growth of Social Security trust fund	A	1.4	11.7	.01	.02	1.6
	T	1.2	13.7	.01		
Taxes share of GDP	A	18.3	0.6	−.03	.04	<u>3.3</u>
	T	0.0	1.2	−.01		
					100.0	<u>15.2</u>
						100.0

Note: Money supply (M2) is not considered part of performance and is not factored into the overall performance ranking.

are unfavorable, then a higher real interest rate would reflect the pessimism in the economy.

A total of 18 indicators are combined and, for each indicator, the average and trend are considered, yielding a total of 36 statistics to be weighted. The averages and the trends of an indicator usually have different weights, reflecting their different values in capturing economic performance. The weighting scheme also is devised to ensure that the overall weight to the indicator (the average weight plus the trend weight) reflects its importance to overall economic performance. The absolute value of the sum of all the weights is greater than one, but that presents no problem, because the synthesized indicator, or "performance quotient," is used only to establish a relative ranking. The important point is that the weights reflect the relative importance of the indicators. Each indicator's weight as a percent of total indicator weight also is provided in Table 15.1.

The weights are based not so much on the president's degree of responsibility for that particular indicator as they are on the degree to which that indicator is or leads to a final economic performance goal. For example, investment underlies GDP growth (a final goal), and a lower real interest rate makes investment less costly. Because all three constitute or strongly contribute to growth, they deserve significant weights. There are also certain variables that work *against* good economic performance. These variables, such as inflation, percent below the poverty line, debts, deficits, and so on, must be subtracted from the rank score. Thus, a minus sign is placed in front of their weight value (yielding the converted weight), showing that they are negatively related to performance (also shown in Appendix B).

Part I Indicators — A Summary of the Weighting Scheme

Part I indicators are weighted much more heavily than Part II indicators, 85 percent versus 15 percent. This allocation of weights reflects the sum of the impacts of each category on the economy. This 15:85 percent ratio of Part II indicator weights to Part I indicator weights is, coincidentally, only a few percentage points below the size of the federal public sector relative to the private sector. Because government purchases are implicitly contained in some Part I indicators, the weighting for Part I and Part II indicators approximates the relative size of the public sector in the economy.

GDP growth is probably the most important indicator and does have the highest weight. However, its weight is the same as that of inflation at 0.09 for average and 0.11 for the trend change for a combined weight of 0.2, representing 16.3 percent of all indicator weights (Table 15.1). The trend change is judged more important than the average because it measures how much the GDP growth rate improved under an administration. There is a case for the weights on GDP growth to be higher, but because there are several other indicators closely correlated with GDP that indirectly give weight to GDP, its weight need not be higher.

Employment growth and the unemployment rate have a combined weight of 0.12. Although as important as inflation in measuring performance, both employment indicators are correlated with GDP and, thus, need not have as high a weight as inflation. Unemployment's combined weight, 0.07 (5.7 percent of all indicator weights), is greater than the employment growth weight, 0.05 (4.1 percent of total), because reducing the percentage of unemployed workers is a slightly more important performance measure than meeting an employment growth level, although the two obviously are related. The unemployment rate trend change is considered more important than the average because it matters more whether the president reduced unemployment than what he averaged. For employment growth, the average is much more important than the trend, simply because the growth rates are volatile from year to year and the resulting trend changes do not indicate significant shifts in the economy.

Inflation deserves a particularly high weight because it is very important to economic welfare and because it is not so closely correlated with the other economic indicators. Because it stands alone in accounting for one of the most serious economic problems, it is assigned a weight equal to that of GDP, 0.2 (16.3 percent of total weight). Conceivably, the weight on inflation could be even higher, because the combined weights on GDP and GDP-related indicators (including employment, saving and investment, productivity and compensation, and percent below the poverty line), which often move together with swings in the business cycle, amount to 0.63, or 51.3 percent of total weight. Inflation is different, tending to move more independently of the other indicators.

Real prime interest rate, like inflation, is also relatively uncorrelated with the other indicators; yet, it is an important determinant of economic growth and, therefore, deserves a substantial weight. Its combined weight is 0.13 (10.6 percent of total), with the trend slightly more important than the average. The trend is deemed important because, on a year-to-year basis, the real prime rate has, historically, not been particularly volatile, and it is probably more important in which direction a president "took" the real prime rate than what he actually averaged. For the purpose of ranking, it is assumed that a lower real prime rate is preferred.

Saving and investment are critical to growth and could be weighted as highly as GDP itself but it must be taken into account that other variables are correlated with saving and investment in measuring performance. Furthermore, if one of these correlated variables receives a higher weight, then the other correlated indicators should have proportionately lower weights. The weights on saving (both personal and gross private) and private investment are 0.1 (8.2 percent of total) and 0.06

(4.9 percent of total), respectively, totaling 0.16 (13.9 percent of total). It is true that investment drives growth and saving is needed for investment, and, perhaps, they should be weighted *more* highly than GDP or inflation or both. However, it should be recalled that the real interest rate is an important determinant of saving and investment, which already has a substantial weight. Furthermore, gross private saving and gross private investment are very similar concepts that, in many years, move quite closely together. Thus, a high weight devoted to each of them would ascribe too much importance to their value in capturing economic performance.

The personal saving rate is given a somewhat higher weight than gross private saving, because it captures the separate behavior of individuals and gross private saving overlaps significantly with the already-included gross private investment. In the case of the personal saving rate and the gross private investment rate, the average is considered more important than the trend change because rates change rather freely from year to year.

Productivity and compensation growth also contribute to economic performance, but productivity is decidedly more important. Productivity growth has a weight of 0.07 (5.7 percent of total), with 0.05 allocated to the average and 0.02 to the trend. Often, not even this much weight would be given to the trend of a growth rate, but because the rise in productivity was so steady during 1946–93, the growth rate was sufficiently stable for changes in the growth rate to have some value in measuring performance. Some might contend that productivity warrants a higher weight because output per hour worked is directly related to the standard of living and competitiveness. It is true that worker productivity supports the standard of living of a country, but, again, much of this performance measure is captured in GDP growth and the employment indicators. Recall that productivity is simply real output divided by the number of hours worked. In addition, as described in Chapter 7, the indicator has a weakness in that if employment falls but declines in production of the same magnitude do not follow, a productivity increase is recorded. It is, indeed, a productivity increase, but another adverse economic event has occurred, namely, a loss of employment.

Compensation is important from the standpoint that productivity increases are rewarded with increases in compensation. To some extent, it indicates that the economy, on average, is maintaining the incentives for further productivity increases. However, because the measure is very broad and encompasses many sectors, it does not show that compensation increases are proportionate to productivity increases in specific subsectors. Beyond this general indication that compensation is matched with productivity, there is little value as a performance measure, and the combined average and trend weight is only 0.01 (0.8 percent of total), with the average taking most of the weight.

Percent of the population below the poverty line, like GDP, is a final goal of economic policy. The reduction of people in poverty is not exclusively an income distribution problem but is also a growth problem (as shown in Chapter 8). Thus, a significant weight is assigned to this indicator. Both the trend and the average are weighted at 0.035 for a combined weight of 0.07 (5.7 percent of total). Even though movements in the percent below the poverty line are strongly correlated with economic cycles and GDP growth, the indicator represents two end goals of economic policy, namely growth and improved distribution. As discussed in Chapter 8, the relative importance of the trend and the average is problematic, because until the late 1960s, the trend change was more important, but in later years, the average became more important. The reason is that it was both necessary and possible to lower the percent below the poverty line in the earlier years, but once the percent in poverty reached 11–13 percent, it was difficult to reduce it further, and maintaining it at that level became a challenge. Thus, in spite of some obvious weaknesses in this approach, the trend and average are weighted equally.

Dow Jones Industrial Averages is only one of many stock indexes, but it is the most often reported. Because its changes indicate both the cost of investment to companies and return to stockholders and its real value is often unrelated to GDP, it has an important role in measuring economic performance and requires a significant weight. The average growth of the Dow Jones Industrial Average is weighted at 0.07 and the trend at 0.01 (together accounting for 6.5 percent of total indicator weight). The average is much more important than the trend, which is common when the average is a growth rate. In a sense, an average growth rate is already a trend. Hence, the trend becomes a trend of a trend, which reduces its informational value. More importantly, unlike the case of GDP and inflation, stock market growth rates are volatile, making the trend changes less indicative of significant market trends.

Part II Indicators

As mentioned, Part II, or federal government, indicators are weighted much less heavily than Part I indicators, roughly reflecting the share the federal government occupies in the U.S. economy. With federal government indicators, it is more difficult to state definitively what is a good or a bad movement in an indicator. For example, is a higher budget share of GDP necessarily bad, if circumstances, such as a war, called for it? Yet, all things being equal, it is probably better to hold the line on government spending. With respect to budget categories' shares of the total budget, it is virtually impossible to say what is bad and good without imposing a subjective set of values. Therefore, categories' shares are excluded from the overall presidential ranking.[3] Although the president and Congress have greater control over Part II compared with Part I indicators, suggesting that Part II indicators would be better measures at least of presidential responsibility if not of economic performance, the difficulty in establishing good versus bad with respect to federal government indicators calls for weighting them more lightly.

Federal budget growth and share have combined average and trend weights of 0.021 (1.7 percent of total) and 0.04 (3.3 percent of total), respectively. The average budget growth rate and budget share average and trend are each weighted at 0.02, while the budget growth trend is only 0.001, because of the volatility of budget growth. Budget share is given a higher total weight than budget growth because budget share measures the size of the federal government in the context of the size of the total economy, or GDP. The growth of the budget shows how rapidly the government increases its consumption of resources but does not incorporate the simultaneous increases in GDP growth rate in its measure of performance. Therefore, it gives no indication of the ability of the economy to pay for the growing government.

Debts and deficits can be more definitively labeled as undesirable than can other Part II indicators. Although some economists challenge their importance, they are indicative, at least, of poor matching of revenues and outlays and, at worst, of inferior economic performance in which resources that are needed for the future are spent in the present. The combined average and trend weights for debts and deficits are 0.04 and 0.025, respectively. The trend in the deficit share of GDP has a relatively low weight (0.005), because deficit shares fluctuate substantially. Debt shares, on the other hand, do not fluctuate as much, and debt share trend changes are weighted the same as the debt share averages. Because of the moderate combined weight assigned to debts and deficits, it might be feared that the recently large debts and deficits are underweighted. However, it should be recognized that this weight is multiplied by the number of standard deviations from the mean for each president, and because recent debt and deficit shares show large deviations from the mean, they are properly accounted for in the overall performance ranking.

Social Security poses a dilemma in evaluating a president's performance. For instance, the tremendous build-up of Social Security reserves that occurred under Reagan and Bush during 1985–93 was an impressive and positive trend. It represented a massive increase in saving and a substantial provision for future income security. Unfortunately, although the trust fund became actuarially sound, on paper, during those years, the trust fund itself was largely illusory. The surplus of outlays over receipts for those years was simply absorbed for general government expenditures and was not "tucked away" for the needs of future Social Security recipients. Moreover, the budget deficits that are popularly reported to the public combine on- and off-budget categories. Even though Social Security is an off-budget category, its substantial surpluses during 1985–93 were lumped into the overall budget funds and served to lower the "reported" deficit by the amount of the surplus. If the Social Security surpluses were considered to be totally separate from the rest of the budget, as they should have been, then the reported deficits would have been $40–50 billion higher.

Two solutions to this dilemma are to calculate and weight the deficit that existed without the benefit of Social Security surpluses and then give an appropriate weight to the improvements in the Social Security trust fund or to leave the deficits as they are, reported at their artificially low levels, and severely reduce the importance (weight) assigned to the build-up of the Social Security trust fund (because it is only a paper trust). It does not matter much to the overall ranking which solution is chosen, but it is simpler to do the latter. Thus, the reported overall (on- and off-budget) deficits are used along with a sharply reduced weight given to the changes in the trust fund. This weight reflects the importance of the "paper saving" represented by the Social Security trust fund. A president's score is helped, slightly, to the extent that he encouraged such saving. The total weight given to the average and trend of trust fund growth is 0.02, or 1.6 percent of total indicator weights.

Tax shares of GDP have a combined average and trend weight of 0.04, or 3.3 percent of total indicator weight. With all of the political debate revolving around taxes, a higher weight might be expected. However, as was pointed out in Chapter 14, tax receipt shares did not differ a great deal among administrations, and higher weighting would not materially affect the overall performance ranking. Furthermore, tax shares are, supposedly, driven by the size of the budget, which, in turn, should be driven by the government fulfilling its "appropriate" role. Thus, it is difficult to tag taxation as "bad" per se. In that respect, it may not be advisable to place any weight on taxation. However, as stated in Chapter 14, taxes do take resources out of the more efficient private sector, resulting in some economic loss. In the final analysis, although some economic loss is associated with higher taxes, taxes are necessary and, therefore, should not militate too strongly against a president's performance score. Because the size of the government is also captured in the budget share and growth indicators, only a moderate weight on tax shares is justified.

RESULTS

The resulting number, or score, has no particular meaning of its own in an absolute sense, but only insofar as it serves to rank the presidents and to establish the magnitudes of difference between their performances. Table 15.2 gives overall presidential rankings for the base case, which combines the indicators as presented in the previous chapters, including the one-year lag. The performance quotient has no absolute meaning; it is only the sum of the weighted standard deviations from the mean for all selected indicators for each president. An alternative 100 base scale is given that converts the top score to 100, and the remaining scores are relative to the 100 base, making margins between performances easier to understand.

Base Case

Truman ranks first in overall performance, significantly ahead of Kennedy, who is in second place, and Ford, in third (Table 15.2). There is a large drop-off to fourth, fifth, and sixth places for Eisenhower, Reagan, and Johnson. For seventh and eighth places, there is another large drop-off for Nixon and Bush. Finally, there is a precipitous drop to ninth place, held by Carter. In this base case, the 100-based scale displays a rather neat distribution of presidential scores, with top, middle, and bottom ranges. The underlying data to and the calculation of the composite ranking of all presidents with the one-year lag are found in Appendix B.

TABLE 15.2
Overall Presidential Rankings — Base Case

President	Performance Quotient	Alternative 100 Scale
1. Truman	0.654	100.0
2. Kennedy	0.465	71.2
3. Ford	0.346	53.0
4. Eisenhower	0.039	5.9
5. Reagan	0.038	5.8
6. Johnson	−0.019	−2.9
7. Nixon	−0.319	−48.8
8. Bush	−0.396	−60.6
9. Carter	−0.808	−123.5

Critique of the Ranking

In addition to the many caveats, in previous chapters, about direct comparison of presidents, some specific points regarding this analysis deserve emphasis. Accounting for some of these considerations could materially affect the rankings. The treatment of Truman, for example, is problematic, because of the post-war adjustments in the economy. Specifically, Truman benefits enormously in the ranking from the drop in inflation and the slowing of the budget growth that was merely a consequence of the military build-down after the victory in World War II.

Another critique of the ranking is that the *aggregate* weight of Part II indicators is too low compared with that of Part I indicators, especially because the federal government indicators are clearly under the control of the president and Congress. However, as already pointed out, the fact that, for some of the government indicators, it is not always clear that their changes are good or bad requires moderation of the weights assigned. There is the fear that the lower weights largely benefited Bush and Reagan because their debt and deficits grew rapidly and because they came at the end of the historical rise of the public sector as a share of GDP. However, the extent to which their records were worse than other presidents' is captured by the number of standard deviations from the mean.

The trend change variable might be improved by dividing it by the number of years that the president served. This would provide the added information of the pace at which the indicator improved or worsened. On the other hand, such an alteration might penalize two-term presidents (Truman [at least in number of years], Eisenhower, and Reagan) and reward shorter-duration presidents (Ford and Kennedy), who did not have to weather much in the way of economic cycles. On balance, however, it would probably be an improvement to use an average per year trend change. In addition, for variables that are volatile and the trend change is of little meaning, a more informative version of the trend change is the change in *average* indicator value from administration to administration, rather than the change between administration end points. In a couple of cases, this version of the trend change was used.

No Lag

A completely simplistic approach would run the presidential averages and trends exactly concurrently with the administration, not use a one-year lag. For reasons already given, it is clear that the no lag scenario is an inferior approach. Worse yet, because calendar year data end on December 31 and the president does not leave office until January 20, the president is actually still in office almost three weeks *after* his economic record ceases under the no lag scenario. For indicators based on fiscal year data, without at least a partial year lag, the last budget approved by the president *would not even be part of his record*. For example, the last budget approved by Carter was for fiscal year 1981, and halting his record in 1980 would omit that budget from his record. The last budget that the president approves is in effect for over eight months of the next administration. He also remains president for almost four months after his last budget becomes effective. Because it makes no sense to delete a president's last budget, for both the one-year and no lag scenarios, all Part II federal government indicators include the last budget that the president approved before leaving office — that is, Part II indicators have the same values for both the one-year lag and no lag scenarios.

Table 15.3 shows that, although the margins between presidents are affected, there is only one major change and one minor change in the ranking of the presidents between the lagged and unlagged cases. The large change is that Johnson vaults from sixth place in the lagged case to first place in the unlagged case. The reason for the large change for Johnson is that 1964 (the year he gained in the no lag case) was a much better year economically than was 1969 (the year he forfeits in the no lag case). Johnson's trend changes, in particular, improve substantially. The minor change is that Reagan moves ahead of Eisenhower. Nixon does not improve in ranking, but his score improves significantly, indicating that 1969 was a better economic year than 1975. As in Table 15.2, the first place finisher receives a 100 ranking, and the other presidents have positions relative to the 100 score.

TABLE 15.3
Overall Presidential Rankings — No Lag

President		Performance Quotient	Alternative 100 Scale
1.	Johnson	0.442	100.0
2.	Truman	0.410	92.6
3.	Kennedy	0.240	54.2
4.	Ford	0.134	30.4
5.	Reagan	−0.002	−0.4
6.	Eisenhower	−0.004	−1.0
7.	Nixon	−0.051	−11.6
8.	Bush	−0.472	−106.6
9.	Carter	−0.612	−138.3

Kennedy and Nixon Finish Their Terms, with One-Year Lag

It has been mentioned that, with respect to a number of economic indicators, Nixon was particularly unfortunate and Ford was fortunate that Nixon resigned during the recession in 1974 and could not preside over the strong 1976 recovery. However, although Ford was the clear beneficiary of Nixon's premature departure, good economic events did not get him reelected. Even though the economy had grown strongly four of the previous six quarters before the election, including 4.9 percent average real growth during the election year itself, Carter still secured a comfortable, if close, victory. Likewise, it would be interesting to see what would have been Kennedy's record if he had finished his term.

To resolve these questions, an overall ranking has been calculated under the assumption that they both finished their terms (Table 15.4). The strength of this scenario rests on the assumption that Nixon and Kennedy would have pursued the same policies as their successors, which may or may not be a realistic assumption — although if budget composition (which is, to some extent, a presidential choice variable) is any indicator, they likely would have followed the same policies. The result of adding the last two years onto Nixon's administration is that he improves from eighth to fourth in the overall ranks. Adding the last year to Kennedy leaves him in second place, but he moves significantly closer to Truman in overall score. Of course, Ford is not part of this ranking, so only eight presidents are included. In addition, with the one-year lag, Kennedy is now responsible for 1965 and Johnson becomes a four-year president.

TABLE 15.4
Overall Presidential Rankings — Base Case, with
Kennedy and Nixon Completing Their Terms

President	Performance Quotient	Alternative 100 Scale
1. Truman	0.679	100.0
2. Kennedy	0.642	94.5
3. Reagan	0.031	4.6
4. Nixon	0.030	4.4
5. Eisenhower	−0.018	−2.6
6. Johnson	−0.180	−26.4
7. Bush	−0.472	−63.7
8. Carter	−0.612	−121.1

Omission of Ford, Kennedy, and Truman

Finally, a ranking is presented that deletes the administrations that are problematic from a statistical point of view. Ford and Kennedy are deleted on the basis that neither served a four-year term (both served less than three years) and Truman on the basis that he immediately followed World War II and it is very difficult to separate his performance from the radical post-war transformation of the U.S. economy that played havoc with some of the indicators. Presented in Table 15.5 is the base case scenario minus these three administrations. The omission of the three presidents drastically changes the rankings, because they are the top three ranking presidents in the base case. Moreover, there is a distortion in the 100-base scale. With the top three ranking presidents dropping out, Eisenhower's fourth place finish becomes first place. Because Eisenhower's score is not strongly positive and Carter, Bush, and Nixon's records are many times worse than Eisenhower's is good, they record extremely negative scores. When Truman, Kennedy, and Ford are included in the ranking, the good performances are of a comparable magnitude to the weak performances.

TABLE 15.5
Overall Presidential Rankings — Base Case, with
Omission of Truman, Kennedy, and Ford

President		Performance Quotient	Alternative 100 Scale
1.	Eisenhower	0.032	100.0
2.	Reagan	0.029	90.6
3.	Johnson	−0.027	−84.4
4.	Nixon	−0.328	−1025.0
5.	Bush	−0.405	−1265.6
6.	Carter	−0.816	−2550.0

If the additional assumption of Nixon completing his term is included, then the rankings are further altered, because Nixon would climb to second place with a 0.03 performance quotient, just ahead of Reagan and just behind Eisenhower. This point demonstrates that under restrictive, but not outlandish, assumptions, a president who scored third from last (seventh place) in the base case can achieve nearly a first place finish. Then again, it does seriously weaken the value of a ranking when it is assumed that the years represented by Truman and Kennedy did not happen.[4]

Other Scenarios

The possible changes to the base case are endless. For example, in addition to a no lag case, a two-year lag could be used (that, incidentally, tends to improve the scores of Republican presidents strongly). Customizing the lags for each indicator or even for each indicator for each president would also be interesting cases. The selection of indicators could also be changed and/or broadened. Changing the weighting structure to reflect different levels of relative importance of the indicators, for example, doubling the weight on federal government indicators or increasing the weight on inflation, is an additional possibility against which the sensitivity of the presidential ranking might be tested. Here, only four of the more basic scenarios have been presented, using the most standard statistical methods to combine the indicators. As the scenarios become more complex, however, the path to the end results is harder to follow. In any case, unless all of the steps in developing the scenario are clearly spelled out, the results become suspect and open to charges of data manipulation.

CONCLUSIONS

The conclusions presented in this chapter are based on averages and trends of a broad range of economic and budget indicators during presidential administrations since World War II. Based on the cases presented here, it is clear that the best economic times prevailed after the war, that is, under Truman — not the highest living standard, but the strongest economic improvement. After World War II, the conditions were right for an economic takeoff. Although not yet directed toward the consumer, U.S. industry was already in high gear, the United States had no international competition but did face strong demand for its exports, and the U.S. consumer was ready to unleash 17 years of pent-up demand for consumer goods. Because Truman was president for over seven years after the war ended, the economy had time to settle down before the Eisenhower administration. The economic boost from Korean War spending also improved Truman's trend change indicators.

In most cases, Kennedy and Ford follow in second and third place, respectively. It may be significant that Truman, in first place, and Kennedy, in second place, came immediately before and after Eisenhower, who usually achieved only a distant fourth. Thus, economic performance was strong through Truman, moderated under Eisenhower, and picked up again under Kennedy, continuing through the early Johnson years. The larger point is that pure time dependency of economic performance (i.e., that much better performance occurred in the earlier years of the period and then gradually slowed down) is somewhat contradicted by the performance ranking of the first three presidents of the 1946–93 period. That is not to say that economic performance under Eisenhower was bad, but it was not at the same level as it was under Truman and Kennedy.

Ford, as has frequently been noted, is associated only with the two recovery years of 1976 and 1977, which was made possible by Nixon's early departure. Thus, Ford has a strong performance and, in the two scenarios in which he is included, there is a sharp drop to the next president's score.

In the middle of the base case ranking are Reagan, Eisenhower, and Johnson. Economic performance under Eisenhower has already been discussed and his score is comparable to that of Reagan. Economic performance under Reagan was relatively good when considering the performances of his immediate successor and predecessor. His rankings outside of the base case are third place when it is assumed that Kennedy and Nixon finished their terms and Ford drops out and second place when Truman, Ford, and Kennedy are excluded. Although Johnson, surprisingly, jumps to first place in the no lag case, the no lag case is probably the least likely to reflect real presidential performance. Johnson is somewhat of an enigma in that his overall economic performance is average, but he became president at one of the best times for the U.S. economy. Although the economy was not nearly as strong when he left office, it was not in recession, either.

At the bottom of the overall ranking for most of the test cases, as well as most of the individual indicator rankings, are Nixon, Bush, and Carter, in that order. Nixon's low ranking clearly was the result of his leaving office during a recession and just prior to a strong recovery. Had he finished his term, he would have likely ranked in the middle. General economic sluggishness during the Bush administration, with a recovery occurring only late in his administration and into the lag period, resulted in his second to last ranking. The low GDP growth of 1990–91 and high deficits particularly hurt his score. Carter consistently ranks last. His score is especially lowered by the high inflation he recorded and the adverse trend changes resulting from his taking office in the midst of a strong recovery and ending his record with a weak recovery in the lag year (1981) after an economic downturn (1980).

The main goal of this book, however, has not been to determine which president did best and which did worst in economic performance. Rather, it has been, as stated in the Introduction, to provide historical perspective, in a straightforward and reliable way, on the economic and budget indicators commonly reported in the news. Another goal has been to show what happened on each president's watch, allowing some time for the delayed effect of policies. A timeline of events has been provided to give context to the behavior of the indicators. The overall ranking of the presidents shows how the indicators can be consolidated and presents the results of one method of ranking the presidents according to a range of economic indicators. The conclusive nature of this chapter is a departure from the more neutral nature of the previous chapters. The strengths and weaknesses of the statistical method used in this chapter do not affect the value of the presentation of indicators in previous chapters or their value in other analyses or as a basis for further inquiry about the U.S. economy.

The approach taken here has been more of a sourcebook or primer than a thesis, in which data are presented with commentary but essentially are meant as a reference for further analysis. It is clear that an investigation not only into *what* happened but also into *why* it happened is needed for a true measure of performance. This book takes a necessary first step toward such an investigation. Pedagogically, it is better to lay out a body of facts, to understand the basics of the message, and, then, to gradually deepen the analysis with additional considerations. Exposure to a complex and dense analysis of economic issues before the basics are understood is almost as unproductive as the diffuse and scattered reporting of economic news in the popular media. Moreover, the less responsible media often appear more interested in evoking sensations than delivering a conscientious and balanced economic report that uses the best information available. The public is then driven to rely on pundits, politicians, and spin doctors, who supposedly have a better understanding of economic issues. Unfortunately, this dependency often results more in cynicism and misunderstanding than in enlightenment.

NOTES

1.   For each indicator, the sum of the standard deviations equals zero.

2.   In statistics, this correlation is called "multicollinearity."

3.   Actually, interest payments share of the budget would be a good performance measure, but debt and deficits already capture that aspect of performance.

4.   These years, as represented by Truman, Kennedy, and Ford, in fact, *are* used in calculating the mean and standard deviation with which the other presidents are ranked. Another way to calculate the ranking under this scenario is to recalculate the mean and standard deviation *after* deleting the records of Truman, Kennedy, and Ford.

Postscript:
The Economy after Bush:
Clinton's Early Returns

During the compilation of this book, the Clinton administration began. A brief review of early returns serves as both an epilogue to the Bush administration and a snapshot of the current status of the U.S. economy within the context of the post-war period. The statistical framework that has been applied to the nine post–World War II presidents whose records are complete can be applied also to an administration in progress, even though the record is partial.

Although President Clinton is nearing the midpoint in his presidency (or first administration, as the case may be), the lag effect of economic policies means that the first year of results for his administration is available only at the end of 1994 (i.e., the fiscal year for budget figures and calendar year for general indicators). According to the statistical framework developed here, the measurement of economic performance of the incoming president begins with his second year in office. Thus, the economic events of the first year of the Clinton administration are part of Bush's record. As previously stated, a president does exert some influence on the economy during the first year of his presidency as people look to that president for new leadership and signs as to what kind of president he will make. These observations by the public are a determinant of the level of confidence in the economy. In this respect, the president has "lead" effects on the economy in which economic effects are felt even before implementation of policy. However, the policies and budget from the outgoing president are still in place during most of the new president's first year and clearly are more influential on economic indicators than mere signals from a new president.

KEY INDICATORS

The earliest performance results that could reasonably be associated with the Clinton administration include the fiscal year 1994 budget figures and the calendar year 1994 general economic indicators, a sample of which are presented in Table P.1. Figures from 1993 are also provided, because it is important not only to look at average performance but also to compare this performance with what was inherited from the president's predecessor. As observed in the text, the Bush record, although relatively weak overall, had a fairly good second half, with two successive years (1992 and 1993) of improvement. Gross domestic product (GDP) growth accelerated, and inflation and interest rates remained low, which encouraged further investment and economic growth. In fiscal 1993, under a Bush budget, a substantial decrease in the federal deficit was achieved, in which the deficit fell from 21.0 percent of the budget to 18.1 percent. This deficit reduction was accompanied by a real *decline* of 0.8 percent in federal outlays.

TABLE P.1
Performance of Key Indicators during Bush's Last Year and Clinton's First Year — One-year Lag
(in percent)

	Inherited from Bush (end of 1993)	1994[a]	Change (percentage points)
GDP growth rate	3.1	4.0	0.9
Unemployment rate	6.8	6.1	−0.7
Employment growth	2.1[b]	2.2	0.1
Inflation rate	3.0	2.6	−0.4
Real prime interest rate	2.9	4.5	1.6
Federal outlays share of GDP	22.5	22.0	−0.5
Growth in federal outlays	−0.8	0.6	1.4
Deficits share of outlays	18.1	13.9	−4.2
National debt share of GDP	69.5	70.0	0.5
Net interest as share of outlays	14.1	13.9	−0.2

[a]Computed from data provided by the Departments of Commerce and Labor, Federal Reserve, Office of Management and Budget, and *Economic Report of the President, 1995*.
[b]A more accurate method of estimating employment data was adopted by the Bureau of Labor Statistics in 1994. Because prior years have not been calculated using the new method and, therefore, are not strictly comparable, the employment growth rates were calculated from January to December for both 1993 and 1994 rather than from annual average to following year annual average. Uemployment rates are the usual annual averages.

From these key indicators, it is apparent that the good performance of 1993 was largely sustained in 1994 and, in some cases, improved. On the up side, GDP growth improved from 3.1 to 4.0 percent, unemployment dropped from 6.8 to a more acceptable 6.1 level, and the decline in the deficit continued as its share of the budget dropped from 18.1 to 13.9 percent. In addition, employment growth continued and inflation decreased slightly from 3.0 to 2.6 percent. On the down side, although not yet particularly alarming, the real interest rate rose significantly from 2.9 to 4.5 percent, the national debt as a percent of GDP continued to grow (although only half a percentage point), and real federal outlays also began to grow again.

The initial 1994 results are also interesting because they reveal another stage of the U.S. economic recovery. The last recession ended in early 1991, but the recovery initially was so weak that there was little enthusiasm to call it a recovery, especially because President Bush had previously prematurely announced an end to the recession. In terms of GDP growth, the recovery started looking stronger by the third quarter of 1992, but significant and sustained job creation did not take place until the fourth quarter of 1993 (although there were good employment gains in February and May 1993). Unemployment also continued to fall.[1] Thus, the recovery has taken place in three stages: slow but positive growth of 1 to 2 percent until mid-1992; faster growth of 2.5 to 3 percent, with mostly modest employment gains through mid-1993; and significant employment gains and continued growth of 3 to 4 percent through the third quarter of 1994. Because the "recovery" is now four years underway and this third stage displays all-around good indicators, it is probably more appropriate to refer to the economy as in an expansion phase.

Because the numbers for 1994 are preliminary, revisions to these numbers may take place for several months, with smaller changes possibly occurring over years. Sometimes revisions can be significant. An example in the text showed that the GDP growth rates under Bush for 1990–92 were revised upward over time from 0.8 to 1.2 percent for 1990, −1.2 to −0.7 percent for 1991, and 2.3 percent to 2.8 percent for 1992. Another example is that just before the 1992 election, the estimated third quarter 1992 GDP growth rate was initially reported at 2.7 percent, but, by the time revisions were essentially complete, the estimate reached 3.4 percent. The higher growth rate might have convinced more people that the recovery was genuine. Because the initial indicator estimates can change appreciably from their initial values, care should be taken not to draw hasty conclusions from preliminary data. In any case, such conclusions are unnecessary unless they are required input into important decisions, such as voting. Fortunately, by election time, economic measurements will be more firm and complete and give a better picture of performance.

RESPONSIBILITY FOR ECONOMIC PERFORMANCE

The same question arises with Clinton as with the other presidents: to what extent is he responsible for the economic performance coinciding with his presidency? A true performance record must delve into the complexities of whether the president pursued the right course of action under the circumstances. In other words, performance depends on not just what happened on the president's watch but how this record compares with what was possible for the president to achieve. The purpose of this book has been to take the first step — to show what happened through averages and trends based on readily available indicators. The shorthand comparison of key indicators made above provides a starting point for evaluating Clinton's record. Three quarters of Clinton's record is still unknown. By the next general election, about two-thirds of his record will be available for public scrutiny and will provide a much stronger basis for evaluating economic performance under his administration. Once a reliable record of economic results is available, a link between the actions that the president took and these economic results against a background of major events that affect economic indicators can be made.

Thus far in the Clinton administration, there has been one event that could warrant inclusion in a timeline of major events. The North American Free Trade Agreement (NAFTA) might be included, although only some initial and, to date, fairly small effects are evident. Also, in terms of credit for the NAFTA policy, it is important to recognize that the NAFTA took over seven years to achieve, starting with Reagan and continuing through Bush and Clinton.

Unlike the case of Ronald Reagan, who instituted the well-known tax cut of 1981–83, which was followed by a surge in growth, and deficits, during 1983–88, it is difficult to point to a major Clinton economic policy that could be traced to economic events of 1994. The 1994 budget plan was not really a major economic event, especially considering that, every year, a federal budget must be approved, although the accompanying tax increase likely contributed to the deficit reduction in fiscal 1994. Other events that might ultimately appear on the timeline under Clinton include the General Agreement on Tariffs and Trade and health care reform, depending on its scope. Both have a chance of passing; however, although agreement on the goals of health care reform (i.e., portability of coverage, cost management, and a path toward universal coverage) appears sufficiently broad to pass the Congress, agreement on the means is not. Some of the more sweeping approaches to health reform ran into difficulty in Congress because of the anticipated budgetary impact and efficiency considerations of a larger government role.

With the Republicans gaining control of both the House and Senate in the 1994 mid-term election, there may well be timeline events that are initiatives of the new Republican majorities rather than the president. These initiatives include such longstanding components of the Republican agenda as a balanced budget amendment to the Constitution and the presidential line-item veto. Obviously, these two reforms could have profound effects on the federal budget. Tax cuts and welfare reform with a stronger Republican flavor may also be sufficiently far-reaching to be included in the timeline.

THE NEAR FUTURE

The short-term economic prospects for the United States are for continued expansion, because the major indicators have remained more or less in the "good" range. Real GDP growth is over 3 percent and steady, inflation remains low, and unemployment has been falling. The only significant negative trend is rising interest rates, although the current rise appears to be a policy choice of the Federal Reserve deemed necessary to keep inflation low. Another potential threat is shown in the president's outyear budget estimates, which project a return to increasing budget deficits by fiscal 1996. Deficit reduction undoubtedly has been a source of confidence in the economy that could be jeopardized if the projections hold true. The confidence level also has to be tempered with the fact that, although the budget deficit reductions of 1993 and 1994 have been substantial and encouraging, the deficit of 1994 in real terms is still higher than that as recently as 1990. Therefore, this basis for economic confidence may be a fragile one. Moreover, although the peace dividend from the cold war victory is still being realized, the additional yearly budgetary savings from defense are declining as defense shares near pre–World War II levels and the potential for further deficit reduction from defense cuts will be small. In the longer run, a funding crisis in the Social Security and medicare programs appears inevitable as the Clinton administration continues the practice of previous administrations of spending these programs' surpluses for general government purposes. When outlays begin to exceed receipts by the year 2010, there will be no trust fund to draw down; rather, outlays will have to be financed from general tax revenues.

How should the voter ultimately regard Clinton's performance? It has been shown that, although still very early, the Clinton record so far is a continuation and general strengthening of the economic recovery that began in early 1991 and gained steam in 1992 and 1993 under Bush. Some in the press suggest that the recovery has been furthered by a combination of Clinton's success in reducing the deficit, for which his degree of responsibility also must be assessed, and Alan Greenspan's tight lid on inflation. Others point to the declining real interest rates during the Bush administration, whose stimulative effect is now being more fully realized. Still others believe that it is part of a business cycle that has a momentum of its own and is only incidentally affected by the president, if at all. Each of these positions has varying degrees of merit, but all are, nevertheless, conjectural.

One way to evaluate, or at least track, Clinton's performance has been demonstrated. What happened is established using a set of key economic indicators. Because only a small portion of Clinton's record is known to date, only a subset of the more important indicators has been used. Over time, the indicator base should be broadened and updated. By election time, when indicators pertaining to Clinton will have been observed for two and one-half years, an analysis of the full set of indicators used in this book (and perhaps other indicators) should be carried out. Chapter 15 has offered one method for combining the indicators. The conclusions drawn should take into account, of course, that the available record is partial and should consider the likely effect of policies pursued by Clinton whose effects may not yet be evident at election time. Ultimate presidential evaluation should make a conscientious effort to relate policies pursued by the president to the actual effects on the economy.

NOTE

1.   In Chapter 3 we determined that if employment is created, then unemployment automatically falls.

APPENDIXES

Appendix A:
Technical Notes

The base year for all indicators, expressed in real terms, is 1987, unless otherwise stated.

PART I INDICATORS

Gross Domestic Product, 1946–93

Data Series

Data source: Bureau of Economic Analysis, Department of Commerce, Survey of Current Business.

The current gross domestic product (GDP) series is deflated by annual implicit GDP deflators also provided by the Bureau of Economic Analysis. Implicit deflators are different from the consumer price index (CPI) in that the quantity weights change according to actual quantities produced. GDP figures are calendar year, year-end data.

Indicators Illustrated

Real Annual GDP Growth Rate.

Indicators Ranked

1. Real average annual GDP growth rate during each administration;

2. Trend change, that is, GDP growth rate in the first year of the *next* administration minus the GDP growth rate in the first year of the administration being ranked. This variable is, thus, lagged one year.

Civilian Employment Growth and
Unemployment Rate, 1946–93

Data Series

Data source: Bureau of Labor Statistics, U.S. Department of Labor, Employment and Earnings Monthly.

Series spliced for 1946. During pre-1947, noninstitutional population was for persons 14 years old and older. Thus, series had to be made consistent with later series. Because 1947 was the first year during which labor force data are available for persons 16 years old and older, it is chosen as the overlap year from which scalar is computed. Scalar is computed by dividing figure from 16 and over series by figure from 14 and over series. Scalar is multiplied by figure for 1946.

The unemployment rate is computed by dividing the number of unemployed persons (civilians) by the size of the civilian workforce. Employment growth is the annual change in the number of total civilians employed. Employment and unemployment figures are calendar year, yearly average data.

Indicators Illustrated

1. Average annual unemployment rate;
2. Growth rate in employment.

Indicators Ranked

1. Average annual unemployment rate and employment growth rate during each administration;

2. Trend change in unemployment rate and employment growth rate.

Consumer Price Index (U Series), Inflation, 1946–93

Data Series

Data source: Bureau of Labor Statistics, U.S. Department of Labor. CPI-U Series (hereafter CPI) for all urban consumers converted from 1982–84 = 100 to 1987 = 100. Annual changes, that is, inflation rate, computed from this CPI series. Inflation figures are calendar year, yearly average data, that is, average to average.

Indicators Illustrated

Annual percent change in the CPI (inflation rate).

Indicators Ranked

1. Average annual inflation rate during each administration;
2. Trend change in inflation rate.

Money Supply (M2), 1948–92

Data Series

Data sources: 1948–58, Robert H. Rasche, "Demand Functions for Measures of U.S. Money and Debt," in *Financial Sectors in Open Economies: Empirical Analysis and Policy Issues*, edited by Peter Hooper, Karen H. Johnson, Donald L. Kohn, David E. Lindsey, Richard D. Porter, and Ralph Tryon, pp. 113–61 (Washington, D.C.: Board of Governors of the Federal Reserve, 1990). Construction of the M2 series is described in the appendix, "Estimation of Current Concepts of M2 and M3, 1948–58," p. 159. 1959–92, "Money Stock Revisions," Board of Governors of the Federal Reserve (internal publication), February 1994.

Money supply figures are seasonally adjusted calendar year, year-end data.

Definitions of M1, M2, and M3:

M1 = Currency + Travelers' Checks + Demand Deposits + Other Checkable Deposits
M2 = *M1* + Overnight Repurchases and Eurodollars + *G/P* and *B/D MMMF MMDA* + Savings and Small Time Deposits
M3 = *M2* + Large Time Deposits + Term Repurchases and Eurodollars + Institution Only *MMMF*

where:
  G/P stands for General Purpose;
  B/D, Broker/Dealer;
  MMMF, Money Market Mutual Funds; and
  MMDA, Money Market Deposit Accounts.

Indicators Illustrated

Annual growth rate in nominal M2.

Indicators Ranked

1. Average annual growth rate of M2 during each administration;
2. Trend change in M2 growth rate.

Real Prime Interest Rate, 1946–93

Data Series

Data source: Board of Governors of the Federal Reserve for the prime rate. Real interest rate calculated by deflating prime rate with CPI.

Indicators Illustrated

Annual average real prime interest rate.

Indicators Ranked

1. Average annual real prime interest rate during each administration;
2. Trend change in real prime interest rate.

Personal and Gross Private Saving Rate, 1946–93

Data Series

Data source: Department of Commerce, Bureau of Economic Analysis.

Personal saving rate is computed by dividing national income and product accounts (NIPA) personal saving by disposable income. NIPA was chosen over the flow of funds because the former is a more conservative measure of saving. It excludes consumer durables, government pensions, and so on. The gross private saving rate is calculated by adding personal to corporate saving and dividing by the GDP. Data for both saving rates are year-end, calendar year.

Indicators Illustrated

1. Gross private saving rate;
2. Personal saving (NIPA) Rate.

Indicators Ranked

1. Average annual personal and gross private saving rates during each administration;
2. Trend change in personal and gross private saving rates.

Gross Private Investment Rate, 1946–93

Data Series

Data source: Bureau of Economic Analysis, Department of Commerce.

Total investment is broken down into residential, nonresidential, and change in business inventories. Investment figures are calendar year, year-end data.

Indicators Illustrated

1. Annual gross private investment rate (share of GDP);

Indicators Ranked

1. Average annual gross private investment rate during each administration;
2. Trend change in gross private investment rate.

Productivity and Compensation,
All Business, 1947–93

Data Series

Data source: Bureau of Labor Statistics, Productivity Research Division.

The productivity index for the business sector, as described in the *Handbook of Labor Statistics* (1989, p. 346), refers to "the ratio of constant-dollar gross domestic product originating in a sector to the corresponding hours of persons engaged in the sector. The output measures are based on series prepared by the Bureau of Economic Analysis of the U.S. Department of Commerce as part of the national income and product accounts (NIPA)." The productivity measures show the changes from year to year in the amount of goods and services produced per hour. Productivity figures are calendar year, year end data.

The *Handbook of Labor Statistics* (1989, p. 346), describes compensation as follows: "Compensation includes wages and salaries, and supplemental payments such as contribution of employers to Social Security and private health and pension funds. The all persons compensation data include measures of proprietors' salaries and contributions for supplementary benefits. Real compensation per hour is derived by adjusting the compensation data by the Consumer Price Index for all Urban Consumers to reflect changes in purchasing power." Compensation figures are calendar year, year end data.

Indicators Illustrated — Productivity

Annual value of the productivity index.

Indicators Ranked — Productivity

1. Average annual growth rate of the productivity index during each administration;
2. Trend change in the growth rate of the productivity index.

Indicators Illustrated — Compensation

Annual value of the compensation index.

Indicators Ranked — Compensation

1. Average annual growth of the compensation index during each administration;
2. Trend change in the growth of the compensation index.

Percent of the Population below Poverty Line, 1959–93

Data Series

Data source: All poverty line data are from the Bureau of the Census, *Poverty in the United States: 1992* (Washington, D.C.: U.S. Department of Commerce, 1993). Updates for 1992 and 1993 are based on the 1990 census. Although this statistic was first calculated in 1965, estimates were made back to 1959. The poverty definition is based on an index developed at the Social Security Administration in 1964 and revised by federal interagency committees in 1969 and 1981. A directive from the Office of Management and Budget in 1969 established the Census Bureau's statistics on poverty as the standard data series to be used by all federal agencies.

Percent of population below the poverty line is the number of people in the poverty category, that is, who fall below the threshold income level or who belong to a family that falls below the corresponding threshold income level for that family size, divided by the population. In this case, the population is adjusted and is equal to the total U.S. population less persons living in military quarters and in dormitories, persons under 15 not related to head of household, and so on. The total U.S. population and this adjusted population differ only slightly. The threshold income for both measures is indexed by the CPI-U, and the weights for different expenditure categories that determine the threshold income are adjusted annually. Some analysts believe that the CPI-U overstated the cost of living increases in the late 1970s (which would overestimate the percentage below the poverty line), and the Bureau of Labor Statistics has constructed alternative inflation series, CPI-U-X1, and calculated new poverty figures for 1967–82 based on the alternative inflation series.[1] Poverty figures are year end, calendar year data.

Indicators Illustrated

Annual percent of population below the poverty line.

Indicators Ranked

1. Average annual percent below the poverty line during each administration;
2. Trend change in percent below the poverty line.

Dow Jones Industrials Averages, 1946–93

Data Series

Data sources: 1945–90 from Phyllis Pierce, ed., *Dow Jones Averages — 1885–1990*. 1991–93 from *Wall Street Journal*.

Dow Jones Industrials figures are year end closing values for the calendar year.

Indicators Illustrated

1. Real year end value of Dow Jones Industrials;
2. Nominal year end value of Dow Jones Industrials.

Indicators Ranked

1. Average real growth rates of Dow Jones Industrials for each administration;
2. Trend change in annual real growth rate.

PART II INDICATORS

The source of all Part II indicators is the U.S. Office of Management and Budget, Budget of the United States Government, Historical Tables, Fiscal Year 1995, and data pertain to the government fiscal year, unless otherwise noted.

Total Budget Growth and Share of GDP, 1946–93

Indicators Illustrated

1. Total federal budget as a share of GDP-current shares;
2. Real growth rate of the federal budget.

Indicators Ranked

1. Average total federal budget as a share of GDP during each administration;
2. Average annual growth rate of the federal budget;
3. Trend change of federal budget share of GDP;
4. Trend change of growth rate of federal budget.

Federal Budget Deficits and National Federal Debt, 1946–93

The national debt was converted to real terms using the government budget deflator.

Indicators Illustrated

1. Deficits as a share of the federal budget;
2. Real level of the national debt;
3. National debt as a percent of GDP.

Indicators Ranked

1. Average deficit share of the budget during each administration;

2. Average annual real growth of the national debt;

3. Average national debt as a percent of GDP during each administration;

4. Trend change in deficit share;

5. Trend change in real debt growth;

6. Trend change in national debt as a percent of GDP.

Major Categories Shares of the Federal Budget, 1946–93

Indicators Illustrated

Shares of five budget categories (including "other functions" category that is not part of the rankings) of the federal budget — current shares summing to 100 percent.

Indicators Ranked

1.–4. Average shares of the budget for human resources, defense, physical resources, and interest payments on the debt during each administration;

5.–8. Trend changes in the shares of these categories.

Social Security, 1946–93

Data Series

Data source: Social Security Administration and Office of Management and Budget.

Social Security outlays and trust fund figures are converted to real terms using the CPI. Because most of these resources are used to purchase consumer items, the real values are from the consumers' or beneficiaries' standpoint.

Indicators Illustrated

1. Real annual Social Security outlays;

2. Social Security outlays (in current dollars) as a share of total federal outlays;

3. Real level of Social Security and Disability Insurance trust fund.

Indicators Ranked

1. Average annual Social Security share of the budget for each administration;

2. Average annual real growth of Social Security for each administration;

3. Average annual real growth of Social Security trust fund for each administration;

4. Trend change in average Social Security share;
5. Trend change in real Social Security growth;
6. Trend change in Trust Fund growth.

Taxation, 1946–93

In order to calculate real growth rates, total tax receipts and major categories are converted to real series using government budget deflators. These deflators are presented in Appendix B.

Indicators Illustrated

1. Real annual tax receipts as a share of GDP;
2. Composition of tax receipts from the three major sources and other.

Indicators Ranked

1. Average annual tax receipts share of the budget for each administration;
2. Average shares of tax receipts by source for each administration;
3. Trend change in average tax receipts' share;
4. Trend change in shares of tax receipts by source.

NOTE

1. These poverty estimates are published in *Measuring the Effect of Benefits and Taxes on Income and Poverty: 1979–91* (Current Population Reports, Series P-60, No. 182-RD). Washington, D.C.: Bureau of the Census, 1991.

Appendix B:
Statistics

TABLE B.1
General Economic Indicators

| Year | Gross Domestic Product | | | Inflation | |
	GDP Current $ (billions)	Constant 1987 $ (billions)	Real GDP Growth Rate (%)	CPI (1987 = 100)	Annual Rate (%)
1946	211.9	1,272.1	−20.6	17.2	8.3
1947	234.3	1,252.8	−1.5	19.6	14.4
1948	260.3	1,300.0	3.8	21.2	8.1
1949	259.3	1,305.5	0.4	21.0	−1.2
1950	287.0	1,418.5	8.7	21.2	1.3
1951	331.6	1,558.4	9.9	22.9	7.9
1952	349.7	1,624.9	4.3	23.4	1.9
1953	370.0	1,685.5	3.7	23.5	0.8
1954	370.9	1,673.8	−0.7	23.7	0.7
1955	404.3	1,768.3	5.6	23.6	−0.4
1956	426.2	1,803.6	2.0	24.0	1.5
1957	448.6	1,838.2	1.9	24.8	3.3
1958	454.7	1,829.1	−0.5	25.4	2.8
1959	494.2	1,928.8	5.5	25.6	0.7
1960	513.3	1,970.8	2.2	26.1	1.7
1961	531.8	2,023.8	2.7	26.3	1.0
1962	571.6	2,128.1	5.2	26.6	1.0
1963	603.1	2,215.6	4.1	26.9	1.3
1964	648.0	2,340.6	5.6	27.3	1.3
1965	702.7	2,470.5	5.5	27.7	1.6
1966	769.8	2,616.2	5.9	28.5	2.9
1967	814.3	2,685.2	2.6	29.4	3.1
1968	889.3	2,796.9	4.2	30.6	4.2
1969	959.5	2,873.0	2.7	32.3	5.5
1970	1,010.7	2,873.9	0.0	34.2	5.7
1971	1,097.2	2,955.9	2.9	35.7	4.4
1972	1,207.0	3,107.1	5.1	36.8	3.2
1973	1,349.6	3,268.6	5.2	39.1	6.2
1974	1,458.6	3,248.1	−0.6	43.4	11.0
1975	1,585.9	3,221.7	−0.8	47.3	9.1
1976	1,768.4	3,380.8	4.9	50.1	5.8
1977	1,974.1	3,533.3	4.5	53.4	6.5
1978	2,232.7	3,703.5	4.8	57.4	7.6
1979	2,488.6	3,796.8	2.5	63.9	11.3
1980	2,708.0	3,776.3	−0.5	72.5	13.5
1981	3,030.6	3,843.1	1.8	80.0	10.3
1982	3,149.6	3,760.3	−2.2	84.9	6.2
1983	3,405.0	3,906.6	3.9	87.7	3.2
1984	3,777.2	4,148.5	6.2	91.4	4.3
1985	4,038.7	4,279.8	3.2	94.7	3.6
1986	4,268.6	4,404.5	2.9	96.5	1.9
1987	4,539.9	4,539.9	3.1	100.0	3.6
1988	4,900.4	4,718.6	3.9	104.1	4.1
1989	5,250.8	4,838.0	2.5	109.1	4.8
1990	5,546.1	4,897.3	1.2	115.0	5.4
1991	5,722.9	4,861.4	−0.7	119.8	4.2
1992	6,038.5	4,986.3	2.6	123.4	3.0
1993	6,377.9	5,136.0	3.0	127.1	3.0

Table B.1, continued

					Employment		
	Civilian Noninst. Population (millions)	Civilian Labor Force (millions)	Particip. Rate (%)	Number Employed (millions)	Annual Employment Growth (%)	Number Unemployed (millions)	Unemployment Rate (%)
1946	99.0	56.7	57.3	54.5	4.6	2.2	3.9
1947	101.8	59.4	58.3	57.0	4.6	2.3	3.9
1948	103.1	60.6	58.8	58.3	2.3	2.3	3.8
1949	104.0	61.3	58.9	57.6	−1.2	3.6	5.9
1950	105.0	62.2	59.2	58.9	2.2	3.3	5.3
1951	104.8	62.0	59.2	60.0	1.8	2.1	3.3
1952	105.3	62.1	59.0	60.3	0.5	1.9	3.0
1953	107.1	63.0	58.9	61.2	1.5	1.8	2.9
1954	108.3	63.6	58.8	60.1	−1.7	3.5	5.5
1955	109.7	65.0	59.3	62.2	3.4	2.9	4.4
1956	111.0	66.6	60.0	63.8	2.6	2.8	4.1
1957	112.3	66.9	59.6	64.1	0.4	2.9	4.3
1958	113.7	67.6	59.5	63.0	−1.6	4.6	6.8
1959	115.3	68.4	59.3	64.6	2.5	3.7	5.5
1960	117.2	69.6	59.4	65.8	1.8	3.9	5.5
1961	118.8	70.5	59.3	65.7	0.0	4.7	6.7
1962	120.2	70.6	58.8	66.7	1.5	3.9	5.5
1963	122.4	71.8	58.7	67.8	1.6	4.1	5.7
1964	124.5	73.1	58.7	69.3	2.3	3.8	5.2
1965	126.5	74.5	58.9	71.1	2.6	3.4	4.5
1966	128.1	75.8	59.2	72.9	2.5	2.9	3.8
1967	129.9	77.3	59.6	74.4	2.0	3.0	3.8
1968	132.0	78.7	59.6	75.9	2.1	2.8	3.6
1969	134.3	80.7	60.1	77.9	2.6	2.8	3.5
1970	137.1	82.8	60.4	78.7	1.0	4.1	4.9
1971	140.2	84.4	60.2	79.4	0.9	5.0	5.9
1972	144.1	87.0	60.4	82.2	3.5	4.9	5.6
1973	147.1	89.4	60.8	85.1	3.5	4.4	4.9
1974	150.1	91.9	61.3	86.8	2.0	5.2	5.6
1975	153.2	93.8	61.2	85.8	−1.1	7.9	8.5
1976	156.2	96.2	61.6	88.8	3.4	7.4	7.7
1977	159.0	99.0	62.3	92.0	3.7	7.0	7.1
1978	161.9	102.3	63.2	96.0	4.4	6.2	6.1
1979	164.9	105.0	63.7	98.8	2.9	6.1	5.8
1980	167.7	106.9	63.8	99.3	0.5	7.6	7.1
1981	170.1	108.7	63.9	100.4	1.1	8.3	7.6
1982	172.3	110.2	64.0	99.5	−0.9	10.7	9.7
1983	174.2	111.6	64.0	100.8	1.3	10.7	9.6
1984	176.4	113.5	64.4	105.0	4.1	8.5	7.5
1985	178.2	115.5	64.8	107.1	2.0	8.3	7.2
1986	180.6	117.8	65.3	109.6	2.3	8.2	7.0
1987	182.8	119.9	65.6	112.4	2.6	7.4	6.2
1988	184.6	121.7	65.9	115.0	2.2	6.7	5.5
1989	186.4	123.9	66.5	117.3	2.1	6.5	5.3
1990	188.0	124.8	66.4	117.9	0.5	6.9	5.5
1991	189.8	125.3	66.0	116.9	−0.9	8.4	6.7
1992	191.6	127.0	66.3	117.6	0.6	9.4	7.4
1993	193.6	128.0	66.2	119.3	1.5	8.7	6.8

Table B.1, continued

	Money Supply		Real Interest Rates		Investment
	Nominal M2 Seasonally Adjusted (billion $)	*Nominal M2 Annual Growth Rate (%)*	*Nominal Prime Rate (%)*	*Real Prime Rate (%)*	*Investment Rate (%)*
1946			1.5	−6.3	14.8
1947			1.5	−11.3	14.9
1948	174.9		1.8	−5.8	18.5
1949	177.0	1.2	2.0	3.2	14.2
1950	184.7	4.4	2.2	0.9	18.9
1951	195.7	5.9	2.5	−5.0	18.2
1952	208.3	6.5	3.0	1.1	15.4
1953	218.7	5.0	3.2	2.4	15.2
1954	232.4	6.2	3.1	2.3	14.5
1955	243.9	5.0	3.2	3.6	17.0
1956	254.6	4.4	3.8	2.2	16.9
1957	265.8	4.4	4.2	0.9	15.7
1958	287.1	8.0	3.8	1.0	14.2
1959	297.8	3.7	4.5	3.8	15.9
1960	312.3	4.9	4.8	3.1	15.3
1961	335.5	7.4	4.5	3.5	14.6
1962	362.7	8.1	4.5	3.5	15.4
1963	393.2	8.4	4.5	3.2	15.5
1964	424.8	8.0	4.5	3.2	15.7
1965	459.3	8.1	4.5	2.9	16.8
1966	480.0	4.5	5.6	2.7	17.0
1967	524.3	9.2	5.6	2.5	15.7
1968	566.3	8.0	6.3	2.0	15.7
1969	589.5	4.1	8.0	2.3	16.2
1970	628.1	6.5	7.9	2.1	14.9
1971	712.7	13.5	5.7	1.3	16.0
1972	805.2	13.0	5.3	2.0	17.0
1973	861.0	6.9	8.0	1.7	18.0
1974	908.5	5.5	10.8	−0.2	16.9
1975	1,023.2	12.6	7.9	−1.1	14.3
1976	1,163.6	13.7	6.8	1.0	16.2
1977	1,286.5	10.6	6.8	0.3	18.1
1978	1,388.6	7.9	9.1	1.4	19.4
1979	1,497.0	7.8	12.7	1.2	19.3
1980	1,629.3	8.8	15.3	1.6	17.3
1981	1,793.3	10.1	18.9	7.8	18.4
1982	1,953.2	8.9	14.9	8.1	16.0
1983	2,187.6	12.0	10.8	7.4	16.1
1984	2,377.8	8.7	12.0	7.4	19.0
1985	2,575.0	8.3	9.9	6.1	17.7
1986	2,818.2	9.4	8.3	6.3	16.8
1987	2,920.1	3.6	8.2	4.4	16.5
1988	3,081.4	5.5	9.3	5.0	16.2
1989	3,239.8	5.1	10.9	5.8	15.9
1990	3,353.0	3.5	10.0	4.4	14.6
1991	3,455.3	3.1	8.5	4.1	12.9
1992	3,509.0	1.6	6.3	3.2	13.2
1993	3,564.5	1.6	6.0	2.9	14.0

Table B.1, continued

	Savings		Productivity and Compensation, All Business Sector			
Year	Personal Saving Rate NIPA (%)	Gross Private Saving Rate NIPA (%)	Productivity Index 1987 = 100	Growth Rate (%)	Compensation Index 1987 = 100	Growth Rate (%)
1946	8.5	14.3				
1947	3.0	12.0	39.4	—	43.0	—
1948	5.7	16.3	41.2	4.5	43.2	0.5
1949	3.7	15.3	41.9	1.6	44.5	3.0
1950	5.9	15.5	45.4	8.5	47.2	6.1
1951	7.2	15.9	47.1	3.6	48.1	1.8
1952	7.3	16.1	48.8	3.7	50.1	4.3
1953	7.2	15.6	50.4	3.2	53.1	6.0
1954	6.3	15.9	51.6	2.5	54.5	2.5
1955	5.7	16.2	53.4	3.4	56.1	3.0
1956	7.2	17.0	54.1	1.3	59.0	5.1
1957	7.2	17.0	55.6	2.8	60.8	3.1
1958	7.5	17.0	57.4	3.2	61.8	1.7
1959	6.3	16.7	58.8	2.5	64.1	3.6
1960	5.7	15.9	59.8	1.6	65.7	2.6
1961	6.6	16.4	62.0	3.8	67.6	2.9
1962	6.5	16.8	64.2	3.5	70.1	3.6
1963	5.9	16.4	66.8	4.1	71.7	2.4
1964	6.9	17.2	69.7	4.3	74.5	3.9
1965	7.0	17.6	71.6	2.7	76.2	2.2
1966	6.8	17.2	73.6	2.8	79.3	4.1
1967	8.1	17.7	75.5	2.6	81.4	2.6
1968	7.1	16.5	77.8	3.0	84.5	3.8
1969	6.5	15.6	78.2	0.6	85.9	1.7
1970	8.0	16.4	79.3	1.4	87.3	1.7
1971	8.3	17.5	82.0	3.3	89.0	1.9
1972	7.0	17.0	84.6	3.2	91.8	3.1
1973	9.0	18.2	86.7	2.5	93.9	2.3
1974	8.9	17.6	85.0	−1.9	92.8	−1.1
1975	8.7	19.3	87.1	2.4	93.6	0.8
1976	7.4	18.3	89.7	3.0	96.6	3.2
1977	6.3	18.0	91.2	1.7	97.9	1.4
1978	6.9	18.5	91.8	0.6	99.1	1.2
1979	7.0	18.4	90.8	−1.1	97.6	−1.5
1980	7.9	18.4	90.0	−0.8	95.2	−2.5
1981	8.8	19.3	91.2	1.3	94.4	−0.8
1982	8.6	19.6	91.3	0.1	95.7	1.3
1983	6.8	18.8	93.4	2.3	96.2	0.6
1984	8.0	19.7	95.6	2.4	96.2	0.0
1985	6.4	18.2	97.0	1.4	97.1	0.9
1986	6.0	16.9	99.0	2.1	100.0	3.1
1987	4.3	16.1	100.0	1.0	100.0	−0.1
1988	4.4	16.4	101.0	1.0	100.2	0.2
1989	4.0	15.8	100.3	−0.7	98.9	−1.3
1990	4.2	15.4	101.0	0.7	99.2	0.3
1991	4.8	16.2	102.0	1.0	99.8	0.6
1992	5.3	16.3	105.4	3.3	101.8	2.0
1993	5.0	15.8	107.3	1.8	102.6	0.8

Table B.1, continued

	Poverty Line		Stock Market		
Year	Number below Poverty Line (thousands)	Percent below Poverty Line	DJIA Year-end Values, Nominal	DJIA Year-end Values, Real	Growth in Real DJIA (%)
1946			177.2	1,032.5	−15.2
1947			181.2	922.7	−10.6
1948			177.3	835.4	−9.5
1949			200.1	954.4	14.2
1950			235.4	1,108.3	16.1
1951			269.2	1,174.7	6.0
1952			291.9	1,249.9	6.4
1953			280.9	1,193.2	−4.5
1954			404.4	1,705.9	43.0
1955			488.4	2,068.5	21.3
1956			499.5	2,084.1	0.8
1957			435.7	1,759.9	−15.6
1958			583.7	2,293.4	30.3
1959	39,490	22.4	679.4	2,650.9	15.6
1960	39,851	22.2	615.9	2,363.1	−10.9
1961	39,628	21.9	731.1	2,777.5	17.5
1962	38,625	21.0	609.2	2,291.3	−17.5
1963	36,436	19.5	767.2	2,848.6	24.3
1964	36,055	19.0	874.1	3,204.0	12.5
1965	33,185	17.3	969.3	3,496.7	9.1
1966	28,510	14.7	785.7	2,754.6	−21.2
1967	27,769	14.2	905.1	3,077.8	11.7
1968	25,389	12.8	943.8	3,079.9	0.1
1969	24,147	12.1	800.4	2,475.8	−19.6
1970	25,420	12.6	838.9	2,455.1	−0.8
1971	25,559	12.5	890.2	2,495.4	1.6
1972	24,460	11.9	1,020.0	2,770.6	11.0
1973	22,973	11.1	850.9	2,176.2	−21.5
1974	23,370	11.2	616.2	1,419.9	−34.8
1975	25,877	12.3	852.4	1,800.3	26.8
1976	24,975	11.8	1,004.7	2,005.5	11.4
1977	24,720	11.6	831.2	1,557.9	−22.3
1978	24,497	11.4	805.0	1,402.3	−10.0
1979	26,072	11.7	838.7	1,312.7	−6.4
1980	29,272	13.0	964.0	1,329.3	1.3
1981	31,822	14.0	875.0	1,093.9	−17.7
1982	34,398	15.0	1,046.5	1,232.0	12.6
1983	35,303	15.2	1,258.6	1,435.8	16.5
1984	33,700	14.4	1,211.6	1,325.1	−7.7
1985	33,064	14.0	1,546.7	1,632.8	23.2
1986	32,370	13.6	1,896.0	1,964.2	20.3
1987	32,221	13.4	1,938.8	1,938.8	−1.3
1988	31,745	13.0	2,168.6	2,083.2	7.4
1989	31,528	12.8	2,753.2	2,523.6	21.1
1990	33,585	13.5	2,633.7	2,290.4	−9.2
1991	35,708	14.2	3,168.8	2,644.7	15.5
1992	38,014	14.8	3,301.1	2,674.9	1.1
1993	39,265	15.1	3,754.1	2,953.3	10.4

TABLE B.2
Federal Budget Indicators

Year	Total Federal Budget				Federal Budget Deficits		
	Total Current $ (billions)	Total Constant 1987 $ (billions)	Budget Percent of GDP	Real Budget Growth Rate (%)	Total Current Deficit (billions)	Deficit Percent of GDP	Deficit Percent of Budget
1946	55	463	26.0	−43.0	−15.9	−7.5	−28.9
1947	34	231	15.5	−50.2	4.0	1.7	11.6
1948	30	193	12.1	−16.3	11.8	4.5	39.6
1949	39	246	14.8	27.3	0.6	0.2	1.5
1950	43	261	16.0	6.1	−3.1	−1.1	−7.3
1951	46	286	14.5	9.8	6.1	1.8	13.4
1952	68	416	19.9	45.5	−1.5	−0.4	−2.2
1953	76	445	20.9	6.9	−6.5	−1.8	−8.5
1954	71	401	19.3	−9.7	−1.2	−0.3	−1.6
1955	68	380	17.8	−5.3	−3.0	−0.7	−4.4
1956	71	370	17.0	−2.5	3.9	0.9	5.6
1957	77	380	17.5	2.5	3.4	0.8	4.5
1958	82	388	18.4	2.2	−2.8	−0.6	−3.4
1959	92	410	19.2	5.5	−12.8	−2.6	−14.0
1960	92	392	18.3	−4.2	0.3	0.1	0.3
1961	98	406	18.9	3.5	−3.3	−0.6	−3.4
1962	107	436	19.2	7.4	−7.1	−1.3	−6.7
1963	111	438	19.0	0.4	−4.8	−0.8	−4.3
1964	119	457	19.0	4.3	−5.9	−0.9	−5.0
1965	118	446	17.6	−2.3	−1.4	−0.2	−1.2
1966	135	492	18.3	10.4	−3.7	−0.5	−2.7
1967	157	560	19.8	13.7	−8.6	−1.1	−5.5
1968	178	609	21.0	8.7	−25.2	−2.8	−14.1
1969	184	594	19.8	−2.4	3.2	0.3	1.8
1970	196	596	19.9	0.4	−2.8	−0.3	−1.5
1971	210	599	20.0	0.5	−23.0	−2.1	−11.0
1972	231	618	20.1	3.1	−23.4	−1.9	−10.1
1973	246	620	19.3	0.5	−14.9	−1.1	−6.1
1974	269	625	19.2	0.8	−6.1	−0.4	−2.3
1975	332	699	22.0	11.7	−53.2	−3.4	−16.0
1976	372	729	22.1	4.4	−73.7	−4.2	−19.8
1977	409	741	21.3	1.6	−53.7	−2.7	−13.1
1978	459	774	21.3	4.5	−59.2	−2.7	−12.9
1979	503	782	20.7	1.0	−40.2	−1.6	−8.0
1980	591	832	22.3	6.4	−73.8	−2.7	−12.5
1981	678	868	22.9	4.3	−79.0	−2.6	−11.6
1982	746	891	23.9	2.7	−128.0	−4.1	−17.2
1983	808	921	24.4	3.4	−207.8	−6.1	−25.7
1984	852	934	23.1	1.3	−185.4	−4.9	−21.8
1985	946	1,001	23.9	7.3	−212.3	−5.3	−22.4
1986	990	1,017	23.5	1.6	−221.2	−5.2	−22.3
1987	1,004	1,004	22.5	−1.3	−149.8	−3.3	−14.9
1988	1,064	1,027	22.1	2.3	−155.2	−3.2	−14.6
1989	1,143	1,057	22.1	2.9	−152.5	−2.9	−13.3
1990	1,253	1,110	22.9	5.0	−221.4	−4.0	−17.7
1991	1,324	1,122	23.3	1.1	−269.5	−4.7	−20.4
1992	1,381	1,137	23.3	1.3	−290.4	−4.8	−21.0
1993	1,408	1,127	22.4	−0.9	−254.7	−4.0	−18.1

Table B.2, continued

Year	Total Current Debt (billions)	Total Constant Debt — 1987 $ (billions)	Real Debt Growth Rate (%)	Current Debt Percent of GDP
1946	271.0	2,271.7	−0.3	127.5
1947	257.1	1,718.7	−24.3	115.3
1948	252.0	1,633.2	−5.0	102.1
1949	252.6	1,596.8	−2.2	96.2
1950	256.9	1,572.4	−1.5	96.7
1951	255.3	1,603.7	2.0	81.4
1952	259.1	1,592.4	−0.7	76.1
1953	266.0	1,553.7	−2.4	73.1
1954	270.8	1,534.1	−1.3	73.6
1955	274.4	1,523.5	−0.7	71.3
1956	272.7	1,429.9	−6.1	65.5
1957	272.3	1,350.2	−5.6	62.1
1958	279.7	1,317.0	−2.5	62.4
1959	287.5	1,278.3	−2.9	59.9
1960	290.5	1,235.5	−3.3	57.6
1961	292.6	1,215.6	−1.6	56.6
1962	302.9	1,236.3	1.7	54.6
1963	310.3	1,219.8	−1.3	53.1
1964	316.1	1,217.7	−0.2	50.6
1965	322.3	1,216.1	−0.1	48.0
1966	328.5	1,202.3	−1.1	44.7
1967	340.4	1,210.6	0.7	42.9
1968	368.7	1,259.7	4.1	43.5
1969	365.8	1,183.0	−6.1	39.5
1970	380.9	1,160.5	−1.9	38.7
1971	408.2	1,163.6	0.3	38.8
1972	435.2	1,165.0	0.1	37.9
1973	466.3	1,177.2	1.0	36.6
1974	483.9	1,123.5	−4.6	34.5
1975	541.9	1,139.0	1.4	35.9
1976	629.0	1,233.8	8.3	37.3
1977	706.4	1,279.0	3.7	36.8
1978	776.6	1,310.1	2.4	36.0
1979	828.9	1,286.9	−1.8	34.1
1980	908.5	1,279.2	−0.6	34.4
1981	994.3	1,272.0	−0.6	33.5
1982	1,136.8	1,358.4	6.8	36.4
1983	1,371.2	1,562.4	15.0	41.3
1984	1,564.1	1,714.0	9.7	42.3
1985	1,817.0	1,922.4	12.2	45.8
1986	2,120.0	2,177.7	13.3	50.2
1987	2,345.6	2,345.6	7.7	52.7
1988	2,600.8	2,510.3	7.0	54.1
1989	2,867.5	2,651.9	5.6	55.4
1990	3,206.2	2,841.2	7.1	58.5
1991	3,598.3	3,049.8	7.3	63.4
1992	4,001.9	3,294.5	8.0	67.6
1993	4,351.2	3,481.4	5.7	69.5

Table B.2, continued

	Composition of Federal Budget — Outlays				
Year	Defense %	Human Resources %	Physical Resources %	Interest on Debt %	Other %
1946	77.3	9.9	1.5	7.4	6.5
1947	37.1	28.7	3.6	12.2	22.9
1948	30.6	33.2	7.5	14.6	19.7
1949	33.9	27.8	8.0	11.6	23.3
1950	32.2	33.4	8.6	11.3	18.7
1951	51.8	24.2	8.6	10.2	10.3
1952	68.1	17.4	6.2	6.9	6.4
1953	69.4	15.6	5.3	6.8	7.7
1954	69.5	18.5	3.6	6.8	6.4
1955	62.4	21.8	4.0	7.1	9.8
1956	60.2	22.7	4.4	7.2	10.6
1957	59.3	23.7	6.0	7.0	9.4
1958	56.8	27.0	6.3	6.8	8.4
1959	53.2	27.0	8.5	6.3	10.0
1960	52.2	28.4	8.7	7.5	8.4
1961	50.8	30.5	7.9	6.9	8.8
1962	49.0	29.6	8.3	6.4	11.6
1963	48.0	30.1	7.2	7.0	13.0
1964	46.2	29.8	8.0	6.9	13.9
1965	42.8	30.9	9.5	7.3	14.5
1966	43.2	32.2	10.0	7.0	12.6
1957	45.4	32.6	9.3	6.5	10.9
1968	46.0	33.3	9.0	6.2	10.0
1969	44.9	36.2	6.5	6.9	9.9
1970	41.8	38.5	8.0	7.3	8.8
1971	37.5	43.7	8.7	7.1	7.8
1972	34.3	46.5	8.5	6.7	8.2
1973	31.2	48.6	8.4	7.1	10.2
1974	29.5	50.4	9.3	8.0	9.1
1975	26.0	52.1	10.7	7.0	8.3
1976	24.1	54.8	10.5	7.2	7.3
1977	23.8	54.2	10.0	7.3	8.4
1978	22.8	52.8	11.5	7.7	8.6
1979	23.1	53.1	10.7	8.5	8.0
1980	22.7	53.0	11.2	8.9	7.6
1981	23.2	53.4	10.5	10.1	6.9
1982	24.8	52.1	8.3	11.4	6.8
1983	26.0	52.7	7.1	11.1	7.3
1984	26.7	50.7	6.8	13.0	6.5
1985	26.7	49.9	6.0	13.7	7.2
1986	27.6	48.6	5.9	13.7	7.4
1987	28.1	50.0	5.5	13.8	6.2
1988	27.3	50.1	6.4	14.3	5.4
1989	26.6	49.7	7.1	14.8	5.1
1990	23.9	49.4	10.0	14.7	4.9
1991	20.6	52.1	10.2	14.7	5.4
1992	21.6	55.9	5.4	14.4	5.4
1993	20.7	58.8	3.3	14.1	5.8

Table B.2, continued

Year	Deflator Indexes		
	Government Budget	GDP	CPI
1946	11.9	16.7	17.2
1947	15.0	18.7	19.6
1948	15.4	20.0	21.2
1949	15.8	19.9	21.0
1950	16.3	20.2	21.2
1951	15.9	21.3	22.9
1952	16.3	21.5	23.4
1953	17.1	22.0	23.5
1954	17.7	22.2	23.7
1955	18.0	22.9	23.6
1956	19.1	23.6	24.0
1957	20.2	24.4	24.8
1958	21.2	24.9	25.4
1959	22.5	25.6	25.6
1960	23.5	26.0	26.1
1961	24.1	26.3	26.3
1962	24.5	26.9	26.6
1963	25.4	27.2	26.9
1964	26.0	27.7	27.3
1965	26.5	28.4	27.7
1966	27.3	29.4	28.5
1967	28.1	30.3	29.4
1968	29.3	31.8	30.6
1969	30.9	33.4	32.3
1970	32.8	35.2	34.2
1971	35.1	37.1	35.7
1972	37.4	38.8	36.8
1973	39.6	41.3	39.1
1974	43.1	44.9	43.4
1975	47.6	49.2	47.3
1976	51.0	52.3	50.1
1977	55.2	55.9	53.4
1978	59.3	60.3	57.4
1979	64.4	65.5	63.9
1980	71.0	71.7	72.5
1981	78.2	78.9	80.0
1982	83.7	83.8	84.9
1983	87.8	87.2	87.7
1984	91.3	91.0	91.4
1985	94.5	94.4	94.7
1986	97.3	96.9	96.5
1987	100.0	100.0	100.0
1988	103.6	103.9	104.1
1989	108.1	108.5	109.1
1990	112.8	113.2	115.0
1991	118.0	117.7	119.8
1992	121.5	121.1	123.4
1993	125.0	124.2	127.1

Table B.2, continued

| | Tax Receipts — Major Categories | | | | | | | |
| | Individual | | Corporate | | Social Insurance | | Other Receipts | |
Year	Growth Rate (%)	% of Total	Growth Rate (%)	% of Total	Growth Rate (%)	% of Total	Growth Rate (%)	% of Total
1946	−16.2	41.0	−28.9	30.2	−13.7	7.9	11.6	20.9
1947	−11.2	46.6	−42.2	22.4	−12.4	8.9	4.2	22.2
1948	4.4	46.5	8.9	23.3	6.3	9.0	3.2	21.2
1949	−21.5	39.5	12.8	28.4	−1.7	9.6	0.8	22.6
1950	−1.9	39.9	−9.6	26.5	11.1	11.0	0.1	22.6
1951	40.8	41.9	38.5	27.3	34.2	11.0	14.9	19.8
1952	26.4	42.2	47.3	32.1	11.1	9.7	3.3	16.0
1953	1.4	42.8	−4.9	30.5	0.6	9.8	11.1	16.9
1954	−3.9	42.4	−3.6	30.3	2.5	10.3	1.0	17.0
1955	−4.6	43.9	−17.0	27.3	6.9	12.0	−7.3	16.8
1956	5.7	43.2	10.4	28.0	12.0	12.5	11.1	16.4
1957	4.6	44.5	−4.1	26.5	1.4	12.5	8.3	16.5
1958	−7.4	43.6	−9.9	25.2	6.8	14.1	3.0	17.1
1959	−0.1	46.3	−18.6	21.8	−1.5	14.8	−0.7	17.0
1960	6.1	44.0	18.8	23.2	19.8	15.9	15.6	16.9
1961	−0.8	43.8	−4.8	22.2	9.4	17.4	0.4	16.6
1962	8.3	45.7	−3.8	20.6	1.9	17.1	5.6	16.6
1963	0.6	44.7	1.3	20.3	11.9	18.6	6.4	16.5
1964	0.3	43.2	6.7	20.9	8.7	19.5	5.0	16.4
1965	−1.9	41.8	6.2	21.8	−0.8	19.0	10.1	17.4
1966	10.2	42.4	14.6	23.0	11.4	19.5	−2.7	15.1
1967	7.8	41.3	9.8	22.8	24.1	21.9	4.7	13.9
1968	7.3	44.9	−18.9	18.7	−0.1	22.2	4.6	14.2
1969	20.2	46.7	21.1	19.6	8.9	20.9	10.5	12.8
1970	−2.4	46.9	−15.7	17.0	7.1	23.0	5.3	13.1
1971	−10.8	46.1	−23.7	14.3	−0.2	25.3	6.3	14.3
1972	3.2	45.7	12.8	15.5	4.3	25.4	3.9	13.4
1973	2.8	44.7	6.0	15.7	13.2	27.3	1.6	12.3
1974	6.0	45.2	−1.8	14.7	9.4	28.5	8.1	11.6
1975	−6.9	43.9	−4.8	14.6	1.9	30.3	3.2	11.3
1976	0.4	44.2	−4.9	13.9	0.2	30.5	8.7	11.5
1977	10.6	44.3	22.4	15.4	8.3	29.9	6.6	10.3
1978	7.0	45.3	1.8	15.0	5.8	30.3	3.0	9.4
1979	10.8	47.0	0.8	14.2	5.7	30.0	8.5	8.8
1980	1.6	47.2	−10.8	12.5	3.0	30.5	24.0	9.8
1981	6.4	47.7	−14.0	10.2	5.2	30.5	37.2	11.6
1982	−2.7	48.2	−24.8	8.0	3.0	32.6	−0.3	11.2
1983	−7.5	48.1	−28.3	6.2	−1.1	34.8	−5.4	10.9
1984	−0.7	44.8	47.8	8.5	10.2	35.9	9.4	10.8
1985	8.2	45.6	4.1	8.4	6.9	36.1	1.8	9.9
1986	1.3	45.4	0.0	8.2	4.0	36.9	0.1	9.5
1987	9.5	46.0	29.4	9.8	4.0	35.5	1.7	8.7
1988	−1.4	44.1	8.7	10.4	6.4	36.8	6.2	8.7
1989	6.4	45.0	4.7	10.4	3.0	36.3	4.3	8.3
1990	0.4	45.3	−13.3	9.1	1.3	36.9	10.4	8.8
1991	−4.2	44.4	0.3	9.3	−0.3	37.6	1.6	8.8
1992	−1.1	43.7	−0.7	9.2	1.5	37.9	8.9	9.2
1993	4.0	44.2	13.9	10.2	0.6	37.1	−2.5	8.5

Table B.2, continued

Year	Total Federal Taxes ($ million)	Federal Taxes % of GDP	State & Local Government Outlays % of GDP	Total State, Local & Federal Government Outlays % of GDP
1946	39,296	18.5		
1947	38,514	17.3	4.9	20.4
1948	41,560	16.8	5.6	17.7
1949	39,415	15.0	6.2	21.0
1950	39,443	14.8	7.1	23.1
1951	51,616	16.5	6.4	20.9
1952	66,167	19.4	6.4	26.3
1953	69,608	19.1	6.3	27.2
1954	69,701	18.9	6.8	26.1
1955	65,451	17.0	7.3	25.1
1956	74,587	17.9	7.2	24.2
1957	79,990	18.3	7.5	25.0
1958	79,636	17.8	8.0	26.4
1959	79,249	16.5	8.0	27.2
1960	92,492	18.3	7.8	26.1
1961	94,388	18.3	8.4	27.3
1962	99,676	18.0	8.4	27.6
1963	106,560	18.2	8.5	27.5
1964	112,613	18.0	8.6	27.6
1965	116,817	17.4	8.6	26.2
1966	130,835	17.8	8.7	27.0
1967	148,822	18.8	9.0	28.8
1968	152,973	18.1	9.3	30.3
1969	186,882	20.2	9.6	29.4
1970	192,807	19.6	9.8	29.7
1971	187,139	17.8	10.4	30.4
1972	207,309	18.1	10.2	30.3
1973	230,799	18.1	9.7	29.0
1974	263,224	18.8	10.0	29.2
1975	279,090	18.5	10.4	32.4
1976	298,060	17.7	10.4	32.5
1977	355,559	18.5	9.7	31.0
1978	399,561	18.5	9.1	30.4
1979	463,302	19.1	9.0	29.7
1980	517,112	19.6	9.2	31.5
1981	599,272	20.2	9.0	31.9
1982	617,766	19.8	9.4	33.3
1983	600,562	18.1	9.4	33.8
1984	666,457	18.0	9.0	32.1
1985	734,057	18.5	9.2	33.1
1986	769,091	18.2	9.4	32.9
1987	854,143	19.2	9.9	32.4
1988	908,954	18.9	9.9	32.0
1989	990,691	19.2	9.8	31.9
1990	1,031,308	18.8	10.2	33.1
1991	1,054,264	18.6	10.7	34.0
1992	1,090,453	18.4	11.0	34.3
1993	1,153,535	18.3	11.0	33.4

TABLE B.3
Base Case Score and Ranking

	Truman 1945–53	Eisenhower 1953–61	Kennedy 1961–63	Johnson 1963–69	Nixon 1969–74	Ford 1974–77	Carter 1977–81	Reagan 1981–89	Bush 1989–93
Performance Quotient	0.654	0.039	0.465	−0.019	−0.319	0.346	−0.808	0.038	−0.396
Presidential Rank	1	4	2	6	7	3	9	5	8
Relative Scale	100.0	5.9	71.2	−2.9	−48.8	53.0	−123.5	5.8	−60.6

TABLE B.4
Calculation of Overall Ranking, Base Case, One-year Lag — Summary of Presidential Averages and Trends
(in percent)

		Truman 1945–53	Eisenhower 1953–61	Kennedy 1961–63	Johnson 1963–69	Nixon 1969–74	Ford 1974–77	Carter 1977–81	Reagan 1981–89	Bush 1989–93
General Economic Indicators										
Real GDP Growth Rate	Average	4.0	2.3	4.8	4.1	1.9	4.6	2.1	2.9	1.5
	Trend Change	5.2	-1.0	3.0	-2.9	-3.5	5.3	-2.7	0.8	0.5
Inflation Rate	Average	4.5	1.4	1.2	3.4	6.4	6.0	10.1	3.9	3.8
	Trend Change	-7.5	0.2	0.3	4.2	3.6	-2.6	3.8	-5.5	-1.8
M2 Growth Rate (lag = 0 yr.)	Average	4.4	5.1	7.7	7.3	7.9	12.4	8.4	8.0	3.2
	Trend Change	5.2	-1.6	3.5	-0.4	-2.5	8.2	-4.9	-3.3	-4.0
Real Interest Rate	Average	-2.6	2.5	3.3	2.5	1.0	0.6	3.0	6.3	3.6
	Trend Change	8.6	1.1	-0.3	-0.8	-3.5	1.4	7.5	-2.0	-2.9
Personal Saving Rate	Average	6.1	6.6	6.4	7.1	8.3	6.8	7.7	6.1	4.8
	Trend Change	-1.3	-0.6	0.3	-0.4	2.2	-2.4	2.5	-4.8	1.0
Gross Private Saving Rate	Average	15.1	16.5	16.8	16.9	17.7	18.1	18.7	17.7	15.9
	Trend Change	1.3	0.8	0.8	-1.6	3.7	-1.3	1.3	-3.6	0.0
Gross Private Investment Growth Rate	Average	3.2	2.4	5.5	5.0	3.5	5.0	1.2	2.7	1.1
	Trend Change	2.1	-5.7	8.8	-1.7	-13.4	23.6	-9.2	-4.8	10.6
Gross Private Investment Rate	Average	16.3	15.5	15.3	16.2	16.2	16.2	18.5	16.9	13.7
	Trend Change	0.4	-0.6	1.1	0.5	-1.9	3.9	0.3	-2.6	-1.9
Dow Jones Growth Rate	Average	2.1	10.6	4.8	-5.2	-5.3	-7.2	-8.8	10.4	3.9
	Trend Change	10.7	22.1	-5.1	-32.1	46.4	-49.1	4.6	38.9	-10.7
Employment Growth Rate	Average	1.6	0.9	1.8	2.3	1.6	3.5	2.2	1.9	0.4
	Trend Change	-3.1	-1.6	2.3	0.3	-3.7	4.8	-2.6	1.0	-0.6

Unemployment Rate	Average	4.0	5.4	5.5	3.8	5.9	7.4	6.7	7.2	6.6
	Trend Change	-1.0	3.8	-1.5	-1.7	4.9	-1.4	0.6	-2.3	1.6
Percent below Poverty Line	Average	25.0	22.1	19.8	14.2	11.9	11.7	12.3	13.9	14.1
	Trend Change	-0.5	-0.5	-2.9	-6.9	0.2	-0.7	2.5	-1.2	1.7
All Business Productivity Growth Rate	Average	4.1	2.6	3.9	2.3	1.8	2.3	0.0	1.2	1.7
	Trend Change	-1.3	0.6	0.5	-3.7	1.8	-0.7	-0.4	-2.0	2.5
All Business Compensation Growth Rate	Average	3.5	3.0	3.2	2.8	1.4	2.3	-0.9	0.6	0.9
	Trend Change	5.5	-3.1	1.0	-2.2	-0.9	0.6	-2.2	-0.5	2.1
Federal Government Indicators										
Budget Share of GDP	Average	17.5	18.3	19.1	19.3	20.1	21.7	21.8	23.2	23.0
	Trend Change	-5.1	-2.0	0.1	0.8	2.2	-0.7	1.6	-0.8	0.3
Budget Growth Rate	Average	-0.6	-1.1	3.9	5.3	2.7	2.9	3.9	2.5	1.6
	Trend Change	49.9	-3.3	0.8	-6.8	14.1	-10.1	2.7	-1.3	-3.8
Debt Share of GDP	Average	93.0	62.1	51.1	42.0	35.5	35.7	33.6	46.5	63.8
	Trend Change	-56.0	-16.9	-6.2	-10.7	-4.0	1.6	-3.0	21.8	13.6
Deficit Share of Budget	Average	-2.4	2.0	5.3	4.4	7.8	16.5	11.3	19.0	19.3
	Trend Change	-20.3	-5.1	1.6	-6.8	17.8	-2.9	-1.5	1.7	4.7
Taxes Share of GDP	Average	17.2	17.9	18.1	18.5	18.5	18.1	19.4	18.7	18.5
	Trend Change	0.6	-0.8	-0.3	2.2	-1.7	0.0	1.7	-1.0	-0.9
Social Security Trust Fund Growth Rate:	Average	8.0	1.7	-3.3	4.0	0.5	-13.9	-19.1	17.4	17.2
	Trend Change	3.1	-6.3	-5.0	7.3	-3.5	-14.4	-5.2	36.5	-2.0

TABLE B.5
Calculation of Overall Ranking, Base Case, One-year Lag — Normalized Values of the Indicators
(in standard deviations from the mean)

		Truman 1945–53	Eisenhower 1953–61	Kennedy 1961–63	Johnson 1963–69	Nixon 1969–74	Ford 1974–77	Carter 1977–81	Reagan 1981–89	Bush 1989–93
General Economic Indicators										
Real GDP Growth Rate	Average	0.7	-0.7	1.4	0.8	-1.0	1.2	-0.9	-0.2	-1.4
	Trend Change	1.5	-0.5	0.8	-1.1	-1.3	1.5	-1.0	0.1	0.0
Inflation Rate	Average	0.0	-1.2	-1.3	-0.4	0.7	0.6	2.2	-0.2	-0.3
	Trend Change	-1.8	0.2	0.2	1.2	1.1	-0.5	1.1	-1.3	-0.3
M2 Growth Rate (lag = 0 yr.)	Average	-1.1	-0.8	0.2	0.1	0.3	2.1	0.5	0.3	-1.5
	Trend Change	1.2	-0.4	0.8	-0.1	-0.6	1.9	-1.1	-0.8	-0.9
Real Interest Rate	Average	-2.1	0.1	0.4	0.1	-0.6	-0.7	0.3	1.8	0.6
	Trend Change	1.9	0.0	-0.3	-0.5	-1.1	0.1	1.6	-0.7	-1.0
Personal Saving Rate	Average	-0.6	-0.1	-0.3	0.5	1.7	0.2	1.1	-0.6	-2.0
	Trend Change	-0.4	-0.1	0.3	0.0	1.2	-0.9	1.3	-2.1	0.6
Gross Private Saving Rate	Average	-1.8	-0.5	-0.2	-0.1	0.6	1.0	1.6	0.6	-1.1
	Trend Change	0.6	0.3	0.3	-0.9	1.8	-0.7	0.6	-1.9	-0.1
Gross Private Investment Growth Rate	Average	-0.1	-0.6	1.4	1.1	0.1	1.1	-1.4	-0.4	-1.4
	Trend Change	0.1	-0.6	0.7	-0.3	-1.3	2.1	-0.9	-0.5	0.9
Gross Private Investment Rate	Average	0.1	-0.5	-0.6	0.1	0.1	0.1	2.0	0.7	-2.0
	Trend Change	0.3	-0.3	0.6	0.3	-1.0	2.2	0.2	-1.3	-1.0
Dow Jones Growth Rate	Average	0.2	1.4	0.6	-0.8	-0.8	-1.1	-1.3	1.4	0.5
	Trend Change	0.3	0.7	-0.3	-1.2	1.5	-1.8	0.1	1.2	-0.5
Employment Growth Rate	Average	-0.2	-1.1	-0.1	0.6	-0.2	2.0	0.5	0.2	-1.7
	Trend Change	-1.0	-0.5	1.0	0.3	-1.3	2.0	-0.9	0.5	-0.1

Unemployment Rate	Average	-1.5	-0.4	-0.3	-1.6	0.1	1.3	0.7	1.2	0.6
	Trend Change	-0.5	1.4	-0.7	-0.8	1.9	-0.7	0.1	-1.1	0.5
Percent below Poverty Line	Average	1.9	1.3	0.8	-0.4	-0.9	-1.0	-0.8	-0.5	-0.4
	Trend Change	0.2	0.2	-0.8	-2.3	0.4	0.1	1.3	-0.1	1.0
All Business Productivity Growth Rate	Average	1.6	0.3	1.4	0.1	-0.3	0.1	-1.8	-0.8	-0.4
	Trend Change	-0.6	0.5	0.4	-1.9	1.2	-0.2	-0.1	-0.9	1.6
All Business Compensation Growth Rate	Average	1.2	0.8	1.0	0.7	-0.3	0.3	-2.0	-0.9	-0.7
	Trend Change	2.2	-1.3	0.4	-0.9	-0.4	0.2	-0.9	-0.2	0.8
Federal Government Indicators										
Budget Share of GDP	Average	-1.5	-1.1	-0.7	-0.6	-0.2	0.6	0.7	1.4	1.3
	Trend Change	-2.3	-0.8	0.2	0.6	1.3	-0.1	1.0	-0.2	0.3
Budget Growth Rate	Average	-1.5	-1.7	0.8	1.5	0.2	0.3	0.8	0.1	-0.4
	Trend Change	2.6	-0.5	-0.2	-0.7	0.5	-0.9	-0.1	-0.3	-0.5
Debt Share of GDP	Average	2.3	0.6	0.0	-0.5	-0.9	-0.9	-1.0	-0.3	0.7
	Trend Change	-2.4	-0.5	0.0	-0.2	0.1	0.4	0.2	1.4	1.0
Deficit Share of Budget	Average	-1.6	-1.0	-0.5	-0.7	-0.2	1.0	0.3	1.3	1.4
	Trend Change	-2.0	-0.4	0.3	-0.6	2.0	-0.2	0.0	0.3	0.6
Taxes Share of GDP	Average	-2.0	-0.7	-0.4	0.3	0.3	-0.4	1.9	0.7	0.3
	Trend Change	0.5	-0.6	-0.2	1.8	-1.4	0.0	1.4	-0.8	-0.7
Social Security Trust Fund Growth Rate:	Average	0.6	0.0	-0.4	0.2	-0.1	-1.3	-1.8	1.4	1.4
	Trend Change	0.1	-0.5	-0.4	0.4	-0.3	-1.1	-0.5	2.6	-0.2

Note: Normalized values of indicators are derived by, first, calculating the mean and standard deviation of each indicator. Second, the difference between each president's indicator value and the indicator mean is divided by the standard deviation for the indicator. The result is a series of normalized indicators with a mean of 0 and a standard deviation of 1.

TABLE B.6
Calculation of Overall Ranking, Base Case, One-year Lag — Weighted Normalized Values of the Indicators
(in weighted standard deviations)

		Truman 1945–53	Eisenhower 1953–61	Kennedy 1961–63	Johnson 1963–69	Nixon 1969–74	Ford 1974–77	Carter 1977–81	Reagan 1981–89	Bush 1989–93
General Economic Indicators										
Real GDP Growth Rate	Average	0.066	−0.064	0.128	0.073	−0.093	0.111	−0.078	−0.020	−0.123
	Trend Change	0.163	−0.053	0.084	−0.117	−0.138	0.165	−0.111	0.009	−0.001
Inflation Rate	Average	0.001	0.109	0.116	0.039	−0.066	−0.052	−0.195	0.022	0.025
	Trend Change	0.194	−0.022	−0.025	−0.134	−0.117	0.056	−0.123	0.138	0.034
M2 Growth Rate (lag = 0 yr.)	Average	0.000	0.000	0.000	0.000	0.000	0.000	0.000	0.000	0.000
	Trend Change	0.000	0.000	0.000	0.000	0.000	0.000	0.000	0.000	0.000
Real Interest Rate	Average	0.126	−0.008	−0.026	−0.006	0.033	0.042	−0.019	−0.106	−0.036
	Trend Change	−0.131	−0.002	0.023	0.032	0.077	−0.007	−0.111	0.052	0.067
Personal Saving Rate	Average	−0.023	−0.002	−0.011	0.018	0.069	0.006	0.044	−0.023	−0.078
	Trend Change	−0.008	−0.002	0.006	0.000	0.024	−0.019	0.027	−0.041	0.013
Gross Private Saving Rate	Average	−0.037	−0.010	−0.005	−0.003	0.012	0.020	0.031	0.012	−0.022
	Trend Change	0.012	0.007	0.007	−0.018	0.036	−0.015	0.012	−0.038	−0.002
Gross Private Investment Growth Rate	Average	0.000	0.000	0.000	0.000	0.000	0.000	0.000	0.000	0.000
	Trend Change	0.000	0.000	0.000	0.000	0.000	0.000	0.000	0.000	0.000
Gross Private Investment Rate	Average	0.006	−0.019	−0.026	0.003	0.003	0.004	0.080	0.027	−0.078
	Trend Change	0.005	−0.005	0.013	0.006	−0.020	0.043	0.004	−0.027	−0.019
Dow Jones Growth Rate	Average	0.015	0.100	0.042	−0.058	−0.059	−0.078	−0.094	0.098	0.033
	Trend Change	0.003	0.007	−0.003	−0.012	0.015	−0.018	0.001	0.012	−0.005
Employment Growth Rate	Average	−0.008	−0.044	−0.002	0.026	−0.009	0.081	0.018	0.007	−0.068
	Trend Change	−0.010	−0.005	0.010	0.003	−0.013	0.020	−0.009	0.005	−0.001

Unemployment Rate	Average	-0.045	-0.012	-0.009	0.049	-0.002	0.038	-0.021	0.035	-0.019
	Trend Change	0.022	-0.056	0.030	0.033	-0.075	0.028	-0.004	0.043	-0.020
Percent below Poverty Line	Average	-0.067	-0.046	-0.028	0.015	0.032	0.033	0.029	0.017	0.015
	Trend Change	-0.006	-0.006	0.026	0.081	-0.015	-0.003	-0.046	0.004	-0.036
All Business Productivity Growth Rate	Average	0.079	0.016	0.070	0.004	-0.017	0.004	-0.092	-0.042	-0.021
	Trend Change	-0.011	0.010	0.009	-0.038	0.023	-0.004	-0.001	-0.019	0.031
All Business Compensation Growth Rate	Average	0.011	0.007	0.009	0.006	-0.003	0.003	-0.018	-0.008	-0.006
	Trend Change	0.002	-0.001	0.000	-0.001	0.000	0.000	-0.001	0.000	0.001
Federal Government Indicators										
Budget Share of GDP	Average	0.030	0.022	0.014	0.012	0.004	-0.013	-0.014	-0.028	-0.026
	Trend Change	0.046	0.016	-0.005	-0.012	-0.025	0.003	-0.020	0.004	-0.007
Budget Growth Rate	Average	0.030	0.035	-0.016	-0.030	-0.004	-0.006	-0.016	-0.002	0.008
	Trend Change	-0.003	0.000	0.000	0.001	-0.001	0.001	0.000	0.000	0.000
Debt Share of GDP	Average	-0.046	-0.012	0.000	0.011	0.018	0.017	0.020	0.006	-0.014
	Trend Change	0.048	0.010	0.000	0.004	-0.003	-0.008	-0.004	-0.027	-0.020
Deficit Share of Budget	Average	0.032	0.020	0.011	0.013	0.004	-0.020	-0.006	-0.027	-0.027
	Trend Change	0.010	0.002	-0.001	0.003	-0.010	0.001	0.000	-0.002	-0.003
Taxes Share of GDP	Average	0.059	0.022	0.012	-0.009	-0.009	0.012	-0.057	-0.020	-0.009
	Trend Change	-0.005	0.006	0.002	-0.018	0.014	0.000	-0.014	0.008	0.007
Social Security Trust Fund Growth Rate	Average	0.006	0.000	-0.004	0.002	-0.001	-0.013	-0.018	0.014	0.014
	Trend Change	0.001	-0.005	-0.004	0.004	-0.003	-0.011	-0.005	0.026	-0.002

Notes:

Normalized indicator values are weighted using weights shown in Table B.6. Zero values reflect a zero weight assigned to the indicator in the overall ranking.

The performance quotient (Table B.7) is the sum of all weighted normalized indicators for each president and represents his overall score.

TABLE B.7
Parameters Derived for Calculation of Overall Ranking

		Mean (%)	Standard Deviation (%)	Converter	Weight	Converted Weight	Percent of Total Weight
General Economic Indicators							
Real GDP Growth Rate	Average	3.1	1.2	1	0.09	0.09	16.3
	Trend Change	0.5	3.2	1	0.11	0.11	
Inflation Rate	Average	4.5	2.6	-1	0.09	-0.09	16.3
	Trend Change	-0.6	3.9	-1	0.11	-0.11	
M2 Growth Rate (lag = 0 yr.)	Average	7.2	2.5	—	0	0	0.0
	Trend Change	0.0	4.3	—	0	0	
Real Interest Rate	Average	2.2	2.3	-1	0.06	-0.06	10.6
	Trend Change	1.0	4.1	-1	0.07	-0.07	
Personal Saving Rate	Average	6.7	1.0	1	0.04	0.04	4.9
	Trend Change	-0.4	2.2	1	0.02	0.02	
Gross Private Saving Rate	Average	17.0	1.1	1	0.02	0.02	3.3
	Trend Change	0.2	2.0	1	0.02	0.02	
Gross Private Investment Growth Rate	Average	3.3	1.5	1	0	0	0.0
	Trend Change	1.1	10.8	1	0	0	
Gross Private Investment Rate	Average	16.1	1.2	1	0.04	0.04	4.9
	Trend Change	-0.1	1.8	1	0.02	0.02	
Dow Jones Growth Rate:	Average	0.6	7.0	1	0.07	0.07	6.5
	Trend Change	2.8	29.4	1	0.01	0.01	
Employment Growth Rate:	Average	1.8	0.8	1	0.04	0.04	4.1
	Trend Change	-0.4	2.6	1	0.01	0.01	
Unemployment Rate:	Average	5.8	1.2	-1	0.03	-0.03	5.7
	Trend Change	0.3	2.5	-1	0.04	-0.04	

Percent below Poverty Line	Average	16.1	4.6	−1	0.035	−0.035	5.7
	Trend Change	−0.9	2.6	−1	0.035	−0.035	5.7
All Business Productivity Growth Rate	Average	2.2	1.2	1	0.05	0.05	5.7
	Trend Change	−0.3	1.8	1	0.02	0.02	5.7
All Business Compensation Growth Rate	Average	1.9	1.4	1	0.009	0.009	0.8
	Trend Change	0.0	2.5	1	0.001	0.001	0.8
General Economic Indicators Total Weight = 84.8							
Federal Government Indicators							
Budget Share of GDP	Average	20.4	1.9	−1	0.02	−0.02	3.3
	Trend Change	−0.4	2.1	−1	0.02	−0.02	3.3
Budget Growth Rate	Average	2.3	2.0	−1	0.02	−0.02	1.7
	Trend Change	4.7	17.2	−1	0.001	−0.001	1.7
Debt Share of GDP	Average	51.5	18.0	−1	0.02	−0.02	3.3
	Trend Change	−6.6	20.7	−1	0.02	−0.02	3.3
Deficit Share of Budget	Average	9.2	7.3	−1	0.02	−0.02	2.0
	Trend Change	−1.2	9.6	−1	0.005	−0.005	2.0
Taxes Share of GDP	Average	18.3	0.6	−1	0.03	−0.03	3.3
	Trend Change	0.0	1.2	−1	0.01	−0.01	3.3
Social Security Trust Fund Growth Rate	Average	1.4	11.7	1	0.01	0.01	1.6
	Trend Change	1.2	13.7	1	0.01	0.01	1.6
Federal Budget Indicators Total Weight = 15.2							

Note: Converter reflects whether indicator's impact on performance is positive or negative. For example, a minus sign in the case of inflation means that inflation is inversely related to performance.

TABLE B.8
Money Supply Ratios

(nominal values)

Year	M2/M1	M2/GDP	M1/GDP
1948	1.60	0.67	0.42
1949	1.63	0.68	0.42
1950	1.62	0.64	0.40
1951	1.63	0.59	0.36
1952	1.66	0.60	0.36
1953	1.73	0.59	0.34
1954	1.79	0.63	0.35
1955	1.83	0.60	0.33
1956	1.89	0.60	0.32
1957	1.99	0.59	0.30
1958	2.07	0.63	0.31
1959	2.13	0.60	0.28
1960	2.22	0.61	0.27
1961	2.31	0.63	0.27
1962	2.45	0.63	0.26
1963	2.56	0.65	0.25
1964	2.65	0.66	0.25
1965	2.74	0.65	0.24
1966	2.79	0.62	0.22
1967	2.86	0.64	0.23
1968	2.87	0.64	0.22
1969	2.89	0.61	0.21
1970	2.93	0.62	0.21
1971	3.12	0.65	0.21
1972	3.23	0.67	0.21
1973	3.28	0.64	0.19
1974	3.31	0.62	0.19
1975	3.56	0.65	0.18
1976	3.80	0.66	0.17
1977	3.89	0.65	0.17
1978	3.88	0.62	0.16
1979	3.91	0.60	0.15
1980	3.99	0.60	0.15
1981	4.11	0.59	0.14
1982	4.12	0.62	0.15
1983	4.20	0.64	0.15
1984	4.31	0.63	0.15
1985	4.15	0.64	0.15
1986	3.89	0.66	0.17
1987	3.89	0.64	0.17
1988	3.91	0.63	0.16
1989	4.08	0.62	0.15
1990	4.06	0.60	0.15
1991	3.85	0.60	0.16
1992	3.42	0.58	0.17
1993	3.16	0.56	0.18

Bibliography

Adams, F. Gerard, and Wachter, Susan M. *Savings and Capital Formation*. Lexington, Mass.: Lexington Books, 1986.

Anderson, Richard, and Kavajecz, Kenneth. "A Historical Perspective on the Federal Reserve's Monetary Aggregates: Definition, Construction, and Targeting." *Review* 76 (1994): 1–31.

Bannock, Graham, Baxter, R. E., and Davis, Evan. *The Penguin Dictionary of Economics*. London: Penguin Books, 1992.

Bass, Harold F., Jr., Bonafede, Dom, and Euchner, Charles C. *The Presidents and the Public*. Washington, D.C.: Congressional Quarterly, 1990.

Baumol, William J., Blackman, Sue Anne Batey, and Wolf, Edward N. *Productivity and American Leadership: The Long View*. Cambridge, Mass.: MIT Press, 1989.

Baumol, William J., and McLennan, Kenneth, eds. *Productivity Growth and U.S. Competitiveness*. New York: Oxford University Press, 1985.

Bernstein, Michael A. *The Great Depression*. New York: Cambridge University Press, 1987.

Bernstein, Merton C. *Social Security: The System that Works*. New York: Basic Books, 1988.

Black, Stanley W., ed. *Productivity Growth and the Competitiveness of the U.S. Economy*. Boston: Kluwer Academic Publishers, 1989.

Brody, Richard A. *Assessing the President*. Stanford, Calif.: Stanford University Press, 1991.

Brown, E. Cary. "Fiscal Policy in the Thirties: A Reappraisal." *American Economic Review* 46 (December 1956): 857–79.

Brown, T. Louise. *War and Aftermath in Vietnam*. New York: Routledge, 1991.

Budget of the United States Government Fiscal Year 1995 — Analytical Perspectives. Washington, D.C.: U.S. Government Printing Office, 1994

Budget of the United States Government — Historical Tables. Washington, D.C.: U.S. Government Printing Office, 1994.

Burton, C. Emory. *The Poverty Debate — Politics and the Poor in America*. Westport, Conn.: Greenwood, 1992.

Campbell, Colin, and Rockman, Bert A. *The Bush Presidency: First Appraisals*. Chatham, N.J.: Chatham House, 1991.

Carson, Carol S., and Jaszi, George. "The National Income and Product Accounts: An Overview." *Survey of Current Business* 61 (February 1981): 22–34.

Clayton, Gary E., and Giesbrecht, Martin Gehard. *A Guide to Everyday Economics*. New York: McGraw Hill, 1990.

Collender, Stanley E. *The Guide to the Federal Budget — Fiscal 1994.* Washington, D.C.: Urban Institute Press, 1993.

Compagna, Anthony G. *U.S. National Economic Policy 1917–1985.* New York: Praeger, 1987.

Conlan, Timothy J., Beam, David R., and Wrightson, Margaret T. *Taxing Choices.* Washington, D.C.: Congressional Quarterly, 1990.

Davies, David G. *United States Taxes and Tax Policy.* New York: Cambridge University Press, 1986.

Denison, Edward F. *Accounting for Slower Economic Growth: The United States in the 1970s.* Washington, D.C.: The Brookings Institution, 1979.

Economic Report of the President. Washington, D.C.: U.S. Government Printing Office, numerous years between 1948 and 1995.

Eisner, Robert. *The Misunderstood Economy.* Boston, Mass.: Harvard Business School Press, 1994.

Federal Reserve Bulletin. A monthly publication of the Federal Reserve, numerous issues.

The Federal Reserve System — Purposes and Functions. Washington, D.C.: Board of Governors of the Federal Reserve System, 1984.

Fender, John. *Inflation — Welfare Costs, Positive Theory and Policy Options.* Ann Arbor: University of Michigan Press, 1990.

Fink, Richard H., and High, Jack C. *A Nation in Debt.* Frederick, Md.: University Publication of America, 1987.

Fisher, Kenneth L. *The Wall Street Waltz — 90 Visual Perspectives — Illustrated Lessons from Financial Cycles and Trends.* New York: Contemporary Books, 1987.

Fixler, Dennis. "The Consumer Price Index: Underlying Concepts and Caveats." *Monthly Labor Review* December 1993, pp. 3–46.

Flow of Funds Accounts 1970–1987. Washington, D.C.: Board of Governors of the Federal Reserve System, 1988.

Friedman, Milton, and Schwartz, Anna. *A Monetary History of the United States — 1867–1960.* Princeton, N.J.: Princeton University Press, 1963.

Frumkin, Norman. *Tracking America's Economy.* Armonk, N.Y.: M.E. Sharpe, 1987.

Graham, Andrew, and Seldon, Anthony, eds. *Government and Economies in the Postwar World — Economic Policies and Comparative Performance, 1945–85.* New York: Routledge, 1990.

Hacker, Louis M. *The Course of American Economic Growth and Development.* New York: John Wiley, 1970.

Hall, Robert E., ed. *Inflation, Its Causes and Effects,* National Bureau of Economic Research Project Report. Chicago: University of Chicago Press, 1982.

Hughes, Jonathan, R.T. *American Economic History.* Glenview, Ill.: Scott, Foresman, 1983.

"Integrated Economic and Environmental Satellite Accounts." *Survey of Current Business* 74 (April 1994): 33–49..

Kamphuis, Robert W., Jr., Kormendi, Roger C., and Watson, J. W. Henry, eds. *Black Monday and the Future of Financial Markets.* Homewood, Ill.: Dow-Jones Irwin, 1989.

Kelly, Brian. *Adventures in Porkland.* New York: Times Books, 1993.

Kendrick, John. *International Comparisons of Productivity and Causes of the Slowdown.* Cambridge, Mass.: Ballinger, 1984.

Keynes, John Maynard. *The General Theory of Employment, Interest and Money.* London: Macmillan, 1936.

Kingson, Eric R., and Berkowitz, Edward D. *Social Security and Medicare — A Policy Primer.* Westport, Conn.: Auburn House, 1993.

Lanoue, David J. *From Camelot to the Teflon President — Economics and Presidential Popularity since 1960*. Westport, Conn.: Greenwood Press, 1988.

Lipsey, Richard G., Steiner, Peter O., and Purvis, Douglas D. *Economics*, Chapter 13. New York: Harper & Row, 1984.

Mervin, David. *Ronald Reagan and the American Presidency*. New York: Longman, 1990.

Meyer, Annette E. *Evolution of United States Budgeting — Changing Fiscal and Financial Concepts*. Westport, Conn.: Greenwood Press, 1989.

Meyer, Charles W., and Wolf, Nancy. *Social Security and Individual Equity*. Westport, Conn.: Greenwood Press, 1993.

Millet, Allan R., ed. *A Short History of the Vietnam War*. Bloomington: Indiana University Press, 1978.

Money Stock Revisions (M1, M2, M3). Washington, D.C.: Board of Governors of the Federal Reserve, 1994 .

Moore, Geoffrey H. *Business Cycles, Inflation, and Forecasting*. Cambridge, Mass.: Ballinger, 1983.

Nash, Gerald, Pugash, Noel H., and Thomasson, Richard F., eds. *Social Security — The First Half-Century*. Albuquerque: University of New Mexico Press, 1988.

Niemi, Albert W., Jr. *U.S. Economic History: A Survey of the Major Issues*. Chicago: Rand McNally, 1975.

Paarlberg, Don. *An Analysis and History of Inflation*. Westport, Conn.: Praeger, 1993.

Pechman, Joseph A., ed., *Setting National Priorities*. Washington, D.C.: The Brookings Institution. (An annual publication by Brookings, approximately 24 editions beginning in 1971.)

Pierce, Phyllis, ed. *Dow Jones Averages — 1885–1990*. Homewood, Ill.: Irwin, 1991.

Price, Harry Bayard. *The Marshall Plan and Its Meaning*. Ithaca, N.Y.: Cornell University Press, 1955.

Rasche, Robert H. "Demand Functions for Measures of U.S. Money and Debt." In *Financial Sectors in Open Economies: Empirical Analysis and Policy Issues*, edited by Peter Hooper, Karen H. Johnson, Donald L. Kohn, David E. Lindsey, Richard D. Porter, and Ralph Tryon, p. 159. Washington, D.C.: Board of Governors of the Federal Reserve, 1990.

Sahu, Anandi P., and Tracy, Ronald L. *The Economic Legacy of the Reagan Years: Euphoria or Chaos?* Westport, Conn.: Praeger, 1991.

Scammon, Richard M., and McGillivray, Alice V. *America Votes 19: A Handbook of Contemporary American Election Statistics*. Washington, D.C.: Congressional Quarterly, 1991.

Schier, Steven E. *A Decade of Deficits — Congressional Thought and Fiscal Action*. Albany, N.Y.: State University of New York Press, 1992.

Social Security Administration. *Annual Statistical Supplement to the Social Security Bulletin*. Washington, D.C.: U.S. Government Printing Office, 1993.

Sommers, Albert T. *The U.S. Economy Demystified — What the Major Economic Statistics Mean and Their Significance for Business*. Lexington, Mass.: D. C. Heath, 1985.

Stein, Herbert. *Presidential Economics*. New York: Simon and Schuster, 1984.

____. *The Fiscal Revolution in America*. Washington, D.C.: AEI Press, 1990.

Steinmo, Sven. *Taxation and Democracy*. New Haven, Conn.: Yale University Press, 1993.

Stillman, Richard J. *Dow Jones Industrial Average*. Homewood, Ill.: Dow Jones-Irwin, 1984.

Strassels, Paul N. *The 1986 Tax Reform Act*. Homewood, Ill.: Dow Jones-Irwin, 1987.

Teweles, Richard J., and Bradley, Edward S. *The Stock Market*. New York: John Wiley, 1987.

"Understanding the Consumer Price Index: Answers to Some Questions." Washington, D.C.: U.S. Department of Labor, Bureau of Labor Statistics, April 1993.

U.S. Department of Commerce. *Survey of Current Business*. Washington, D.C.: U.S. Government Printing Office, numerous issues.

U.S. Department of Commerce, Economics and Statistics Administration, Bureau of the Census. *Poverty in the United States: 1992*, (also for 1991), Current Population Reports, Consumer Income, Series P-60, No. 185. Washington, D.C.: U.S. Government Printing Office, 1993.

U.S. Department of Commerce, Economics and Statistics Administration, Bureau of Economic Analysis. *National Income and Product Accounts of the United States*, Vols. 1 (1929–58) and 2 (1959–88). Washington, D.C.: U.S. Government Printing Office, 1992.

U.S. Department of Commerce, Bureau of the Census. *Measuring the Effect of Benefits and Taxes on Income and Poverty: 1979–91*, Current Population Reports, Series P-60, No. 182–RD. Washington, D.C.: U.S. Government Printing Office, 1991.

____. *Historical Statistics of the United States: Colonial Times to 1970*, parts 1 and 2. Washington, D.C.: U.S. Government Printing Office, 1975.

____. *Statistical Abstract of the United States: 1990*. Washington, D.C.: U.S. Government Printing Office, numerous issues.

U.S. Department of Labor. *Employment and Earnings, Monthly*. Washington, D.C.: U.S. Government Printing Office, numerous issues.

____. *The BLS Handbook of Methods*, Chapter 19. Washington, D.C.: U.S. Government Printing Office, 1992.

____. *Handbook of Labor Statistics*. Washington, D.C.: U.S. Government Printing Office, 1989

____. *Labor Force Statistics Derived From the Current Population Survey 1948–87*. Washington, D.C.: U.S. Government Printing Office, 1988.

U.S. Office of Management and Budget. *Budget of the United States Government — Historical Tables*. Washington, D.C.: U.S. Government Printing Office, 1994.

Walker, Charls E., Bloomfield, Mark A., and Thorning, Margo, eds. *The U.S. Savings Challenge — Policy Options for Productivity and Growth*. Boulder, Colo.: Westview, 1990.

Young, Alan H., and Tice, Helen Stone. "Introduction to National Economic Accounting." *Survey of Current Business* 65 (March 1985): 59–76.

Index

ABOUT THE AUTHOR

RICHARD J. CARROLL is an economist and financial analyst in Washington, D.C. He holds a BA and an MA in economics from Georgetown University and an MBA from the Wharton School. He also analyzes the economies of countries in Asia and Africa.

ISBN 0-275-94836-6